Not in Our Time

for tenor and baritone soloists,
SATB chorus, children's chorus and orchestra

by

Richard Blackford

VOCAL SCORE

NOVELLO

Not in Our Time was commissioned by the Bournemouth Symphony Chorus for its Centenary and first performed in The Town Hall, Cheltenham on September 11th, 2011. It was performed by the Bournemouth Symphony Chorus, the Bournemouth Symphony Youth Chorus and the Bournemouth Symphony Orchestra, conducted by Gavin Carr. The soloists were Paul Nilon and Stephen Gadd.

NOTE ON THE TEXT

Not in Our Time is about the universal theme of how religion is used as a pretext or justification for war. The piece opens with an orchestral cataclysm - the reverberation of the collapse of the Twin Towers and the shock waves it sent around the world. From it emerge the soft, measured tones of George W. Bush, whose references to "crusade" and "God is not neutral" also sent, in their turn, shockwaves around the Arab world.

Not in Our Time takes extracts from speeches of the last two American presidents as bookends. Obama's Cairo University speech about reconciliation is the antithesis of Bush's evangelical call to arms and to demonise the "evildoers".

The primary texts deliberately juxtapose speeches and poems on holy war and divinely sanctioned violence a thousand years apart, from the first Crusade, to 9/11. I reprise four times, however, Hilda Doolittle's poem "Not in our time, O Lord, the ploughshare for the sword": first in sorrowful response to the militant Arab reaction to President Bush, by the Childrens' Chorus in response to Pope Urban II's call for the first Crusade, in commentary on Abul-Muzzafar Al-Abyurdi's poignant vision of the aftermath of war and, finally, in passionate response to the terrifying call for Holy War in the sermon given in Jerusalem after Saladin's victory in 1187AD. The universality of H.D.'s poem is reminiscent of the Passion Chorale in which the text is repeated but its context and musical setting is different.

The result of Pope Urban II's launch of the first Crusade at Clermont in 1095AD was the unification of the warring knights of Europe in a common purpose; namely to slaughter Muslims, sanctioned in the name of God. The cry of the two thousand present, "God wills it", is well documented, and mirrors the cry for Holy War in the Sermon at Jerusalem by Mohammed Ben Zeky ninety-two years later. In my work, Urban's cry launches a musical/military setting of the Crusader hymn *O Crux ave spes unica*, with percussion and blazing trumpets setting the scene for the immense throng that journeyed to the Holy Land under the banner of the Cross. By contrast, the poet Abul-Muzzafar's fragile song of the ravaging effects of war is overwhelmed by the Crusader juggernaut hymn.

Parts III and IV are also mirrors - Part III describes the Fall of Jerusalem by Fulcher of Chartres at which, almost incredibly, the blood-spattered Crusaders, fresh from slaughter, pile into the Church of the Holy Sepulchre to worship Jesus. In choosing the resplendent Latin hymn *Lucis largitor splendide*, I try to evoke the magnificence and power of Christian devotion in a sustained choral sequence. At the centre of the work is the contemporary reporter Tom Junod's description of the nameless man falling from the World Trade Centre, a man who seemed to embody humanity's fall that day.

Aftermath explores the experience of the individual affected by warfare. The Chorus, as if tormented by the unbreakable cycle of violence asks, in a passage from the Old Testament Book of Habakkuk, "How long, O Lord? I cry for help - but you do not listen!" In a contrasting section, the Children's Chorus sings a fragment of the poet from the town of Ma'arra, completely destroyed by the Crusaders. The question of God's will, so confidently attested by the warmongers, is unanswered by the Chorus.

In Part VI the call for holy war that begun with Pope Urban II in Part II, is now taken up by Mohammed Ben Zeky following Saladin's capture of Jerusalem in 1187AD. His cry to "Purify the rest of the earth of those nations with whom God and his messenger are angry" prompts the Chorus' final, desperate plea of "Not in our time, O Lord". Both the tenor and baritone protagonists unite for the first time to sing words from Barack Obama's Cairo address in 2009, in which he challenges young people of all faiths to "re-imagine the world". In citing the peaceful messages of the Quran, the Torah and the Bible he is effectively pleading for an end of the crusader mentality in the hope that "The Holy land of the three great faiths is the land of peace God intended it to be".

Richard Blackford 21/12/10

Duration: 55 minutes

Not in Our Time

PART I - INFERNO

(Orchestral Prelude - cataclysm. September 2001 - following the attack on the World Trade Centre, New York. The reverberation of the collapse of the Twin Towers sends shock waves around the world.)

1.   **GEORGE W. BUSH**

TENOR :   *This is a new kind of evil. The American people are beginning to understand this crusade. This war on terror is going to take a while.*

CHORUS :   *...a new kind of evil...this...crusade....*

TENOR :   *But I can assure the American people it is time for us to win the first war of the twenty-first century. Freedom and fear, justice and cruelty have always been at war, and we know that God is not neutral between them.*

CHORUS :   *God is not neutral....*

(President George Bush, September 16th 2001 and an Address to Congress, September 20th 2001)

2.   **ADAM GADAHN AND AYMAN AL-ZAWAHIRI**

BARITONE :   *Bush, you thought you would be remembered by history as the president who waged a crusade against the Muslims. Instead you will go down in history as the president who sent the United States on its death march towards destruction. The crusades against us have never stopped. They have only differed by their form and magnitude through the ages.*

CHORUS :   *The crusades against us have never stopped. Continuing through the ages....*

BARITONE :   *By the grace of Allah, we shall strike back hard. This year, next year, the year after that, till the last crusader goes home, waving a white flag or in a flag-covered casket. We will target you at home and abroad, just as you target us at home and abroad, until and unless you heed our demands.*
Stop the crusade and leave the Muslims alone.

(Adam Gadahn and Ayman al-Zawahiri, *al-Jazeera.* 2001)

3.   **POEM: "H.D"**

CHORUS :   *Not in our time, O lord,*
                           The ploughshare for the sword.

                           Not in our time, the knife,
                           Sated wth blood and life,

                           To trim the barren vine;
                           No grape-leaf for the thorn,

                           No vine-flower for the crown;
                           Not in our time, O King,

                           The voice to quell the re-gathering
                                   Thundering storm.

            (Hilda Doolittle ("H.D.") 1912-1944)

PART II - THE FIRST CRUSADE

4.   **POPE URBAN II**

TENOR :   *A race absolutely alien to God has invaded the land of the Christians,*
                           has reduced the people with sword, rape and flame. I, or rather the Lord,
                           beseech you to persuade people of all rank to carry aid to those Christians
                           and destroy that vile race.
                           Moreover Christ commands it.

CHILDREN : (softly)   *Not in our time, O Lord.*

TENOR :   *Undertake this journey for the remission of your sins, assured of the glory*
                           of the Kingdom of Heaven.

                           God wills it!

CHORUS :   *God wills it!*

                           Undertake this journey [etc.]

TENOR :   *Let this then be your war-cry in combat, because this word is given to you by*
                           God.

CHORUS :   *By God!*

TENOR :   *Let this one cry be raised by the soldiers of God.*
                           It is the will of God! God wills it!

CHORUS :   *God wills it!*
                           It is the will of God!

            (Pope Urban II 1095AD Council of Clermont)

                           (Orchestral march. Pounding war drums, blazing trumpets - the first mighty
                           Crusader army on the move.)

5.   **HYMN**

CHORUS *:*

Vexilla regis prodeunt,
Fulget crucis mysterium,
Qua vita mortem pertulit
Et morta vitam protulit.

CHILDREN :

Abroad the royal banners fly
And bear the gleaming Cross on high;
That Cross whereon Life suffered death
And gave us life with dying breath.

O Crux ave, spes unica,
Hoc Passionis tempore
Piis adauge gratiam,
Reisque dele crimina.

Hail, Cross, of hope the most sublime,
Now a mournful Passion time,
Grant to the just increase of grace
And every sinner's crime efface.

Deus vult!
God wills it!

6.   **ABUL-MUZZAFAR AL-ABYURDI**

BARITONE :

We mingle blood with flowing tears and there is no room for pity.
Shedding tears is man's worst weapon when swords stir up the embers of war.

CHORUS :

(in the distance)
Vexilla regis prodeunt [etc.]
Deus vult! Deus vult!

BARITONE :

Must the foreigners feed on our shame, while you trail behind like men whose
world is at peace? When blood has been spilt, when sweet girls must for shame
hide their lovely faces in their hands, then this is war!

This is war!

(Reprise of Orchestral March at full strength.)

CHORUS :

Vexilla regis prodeunt [etc.]

BARITONE :

The infidel's sword is naked in his hand, ready to be buried in men's skulls. We
mingle blood with flowing tears, and there is no room for pity.

(Abul-Muzzafar Al-Abyurdi, poet 1099AD)

(The Orchestral March and Latin Hymn build to a terrifying climax. Sudden,
hushed tremolo strings with flute obligato.)

CHILDREN :

Not in our time, O Lord,
The ploughshare for the sword.

PART III - THE FALL OF JERUSALEM (1099AD)

7.   **FULCHER OF CHARTRES**

TENOR :

*The defenders fought against our men with amazing courage, casting fire and
stones. Thereafter death was present and sudden for both sides. The defenders
fled along the walls and through the city. Our men went after them killing them,
cutting them down as far as Solomon's Temple. There was such massacre that
our men were wading up to their ankles in enemy blood. They dragged the dead
Saracens out in front of the gates and piled them up in mounds as big as houses.
No one had ever seen or heard of such slaughter of pagans, for they burned on
pyres like pyramids. No one save God alone knows how many there were.*

*Rejoicing from excessive gladness, our men came to worship
at the Sepulchre of our Saviour Jesus.*

Rejoicing and weeping [etc.]

(Fulcher of Chartres - 12th-century chronicler)

(A blaze of orchestral sound as sunlight and a thousand candles illuminate the
Church of the Holy Sepulchre in Jerusalem.)

8.   **HYMN**

CHORUS :

*Lucis largitor splendide,
Cuius sereno lumine
Post lapsa noctis tempora
Dies refusus panditur:*

*Tu verus mundi Lucifer,
Non is, qui parvi sideris,
Venturae lucis nuntius
Angusto fulget lumine:*

*Sed toto sole clarior,
Lux ipse totus et dies,
Interna nostri pectoris
Iluminans praecordia.*

*O Glorious Father of the Light
From whose effulgence, calm and bright
Soon as the hours of night are fled
The brilliance of the dawn is shed:*

*Thou art the dark world's truest ray:
No radiance of that lesser day
That heralds in the morn begun,
The advent of our darker sun:*

*But brighter than its noontide gleam
Thyself full daylight's fullest beam.
The inmost mansions of our breast,
Thou by Thy grace illuminest.*

PART IV: THE FALLING MAN (9/11)

(Very soft , abstract orchestral introduction. Time and motion in a state of suspension.)

9.   **TOM JUNOD**

TENOR/CHORUS :   *He departs this earth like an arrow. If he were not falling he might well be flying. He appears comfortable in the grip of unimaginable motion. He does not appear intimidated by gravity's divine suction or what awaits him.*

He is perfectly vertical, in accord with the lines of the buildings behind him. He is the essential element in the creation of a new flag, a banner composed entirely of steel bars shining in the sun.

He is fifteen seconds past 9.41am Eastern Standard Time, accelerating at thirty-two feet per second per second, as though he were a missile, a spear, bent on attaining his own end.

(Tom Junod, *Esquire*, September 7th. 2003)

PART V - AFTERMATH

10.

CHORUS :   *How long, O Lord? I cry for help - but you do not listen!*
I cry out to you, "Violence!" but you do not intervene.
Why do you let me see ruin; why must I look at misery?
Destruction and violence are before me; strife and contention around me.
How long, O Lord? [etc.]

(*Habakkuk 1:2-3*)

11.

CHILDREN :   *I do not know if my native land is a grazing land for wild beasts*
or still my home.

(Anon poet of Ma'arra 1098AD)

CHORUS :   *We are shattered by Fate as though we were glass. Never, never our shards are gathered together.*

(Abu'l Ala al Ma'ari 11th century)

How long, O Lord? [etc.]

PART VI - GOD'S WILL

12.   **MOHAMMED BEN ZEKY**

BARITONE :   *Praise God, who has raised Islam to glory; who rules worldly things by his will, who made easy for you the deliverance of this city we had lost to the infidels. The gates of Heaven have been opened for this conquest; its splendour has cast a light which has penetrated the deepest darkness: the angels who approach the Divine Majesty rejoice; the eyes of the prophets behold it with joy.*

Did you think that your swords of steel, your horses, your untiring perseverance have gained you this victory? No, it was the will of God. From him alone came your victory.

The Holy War! The Holy War!
Help God and He will help you;
Hold to God and He will hold to you;
Remember Him and he will remember you;
Purify the earth of those nations
With whom God and his messenger are angry.
God is great!
If God helps you, you have no conqueror to fear.

(Mohammed Ben Zeky; Sermon at Jerusalem, given the first Friday after Saladin's victory 1187AD)

CHORUS (urgent, pleading) :   *Not in our time, O Lord, [etc.]*

13.   **BARACK HUSSEIN OBAMA**

TENOR/BARITONE :   *Human history has often been a record of nations and tribes, and yes, religions, subjugating one another in pursuit of their own interests. Yet in this new age, such attitudes are self defeating.*

It's a story with a simple truth: violence is a dead end. TO shoot rockets at sleeping children, to blow up old women on a bus is neither a sign of courage or power. Too many tears have been shed. Too much blood has been shed. All of us have to work for the day when the Holy Land of the three great faiths is the place of peace God intended it to be.

To young people of every faith, in every country, you, more than anyone, you have the ability to re-imagine the world, to re-make the world.

The Holy Quran tells us:

CHORUS :   *"O mankind! We created you male and female; and we have made you into nations and tribes, so that you may know one another."*

TENOR/BARITONE :   *The Talmud tells us:*

CHORUS :   *"The whole of the Torah is for the purpose of promoting peace."*

TENOR/BARITONE :   *The Holy Bible tells us:*

CHORUS :   *"Blessed are the peacemakers, for they shall be called the children of God."*

TENOR/BARITONE :   *The people of the world can live in peace. We know that is God's vision.*
Now it must be our work here on Earth.

CHORUS :   *That is God's vision.*
That is God's will,
Now it must be our work here on Earth.

(President Barack Obama's speech to students from Cairo University 2009)

NOT IN OUR TIME

Richard Blackford

PART I - INFERNO

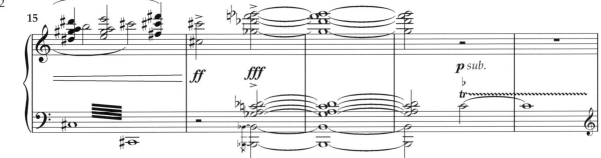

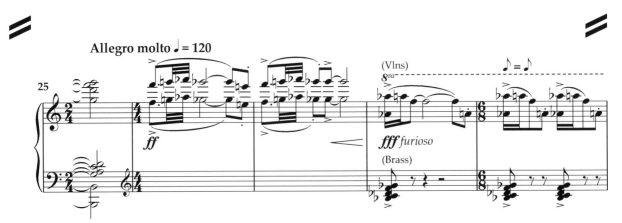

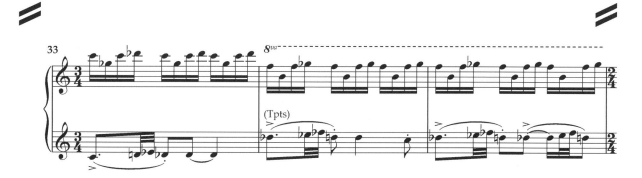

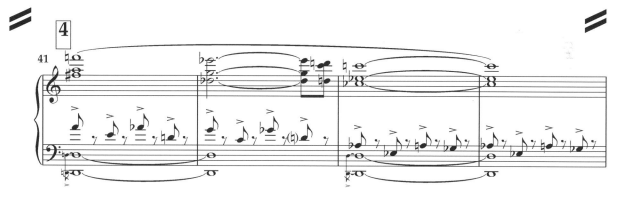

4

1. GEORGE W. BUSH

L'istesso tempo ♩ = ♩

This__ is a new kind of e - vil.__ The A -

7

It is time for us to win the first war_____ of the

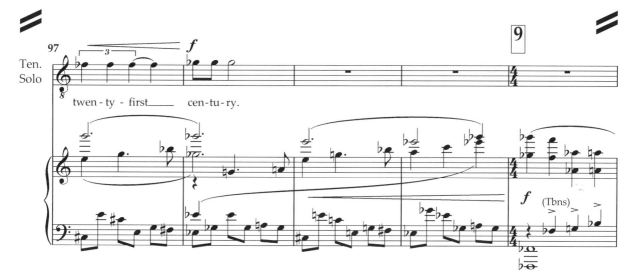

twen - ty - first_____ cen-tu-ry.

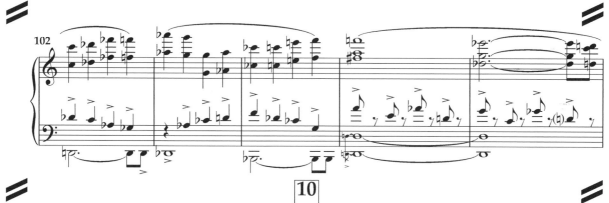

Free-dom and fear, just-ice and cru-el-ty have

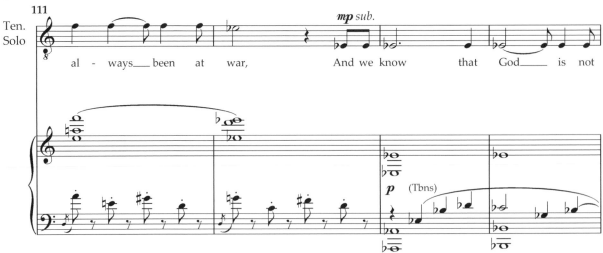

al - ways____ been at war, And we know that God____ is not

11

neu - tral____ be - tween them.

God____ is not neu - tral.

God____ is not neu - tral.

God____ is not neu - tral.

God____ is not neu - tral.

2. ADAM GADAHN and AYMAN AL-ZAWAHIRI

on its death-march to-wards de - struc-tion.

(Ob.)

16

The cru - sades a-gainst us have ne-ver stopped.

They have on-ly dif-fered by their form and mag-ni-tude, through the

3. POEM: "H.D."
Adagio ♩ = 60

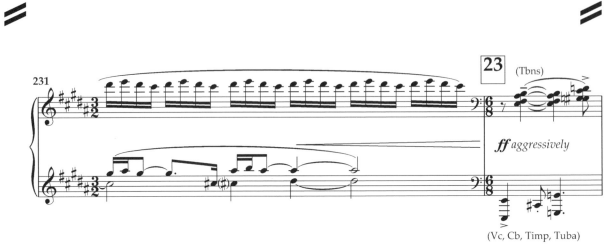

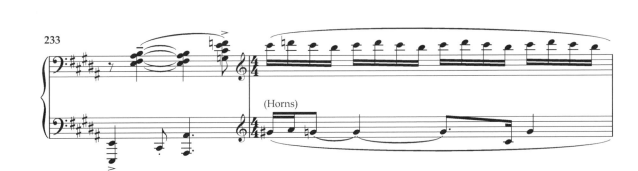

PART II - THE FIRST CRUSADE

4. POPE URBAN II

L'istesso tempo

A race_____ ab - so-lute-ly a - li-en to God

has in - vad - ed the land of the Chri - stians, has re duced the peo-ple with sword,

rape and flame._____ I,_____

5. HYMN - Vexilla Regis Prodeunt

gra-ti-am, Re-is-que, re-is-que de-le cri-mi-na.

39

Hail, Cross, of hope the most su-blime,

Now a mourn-ful Pas-sion time, Grant to the just in-crease of grace

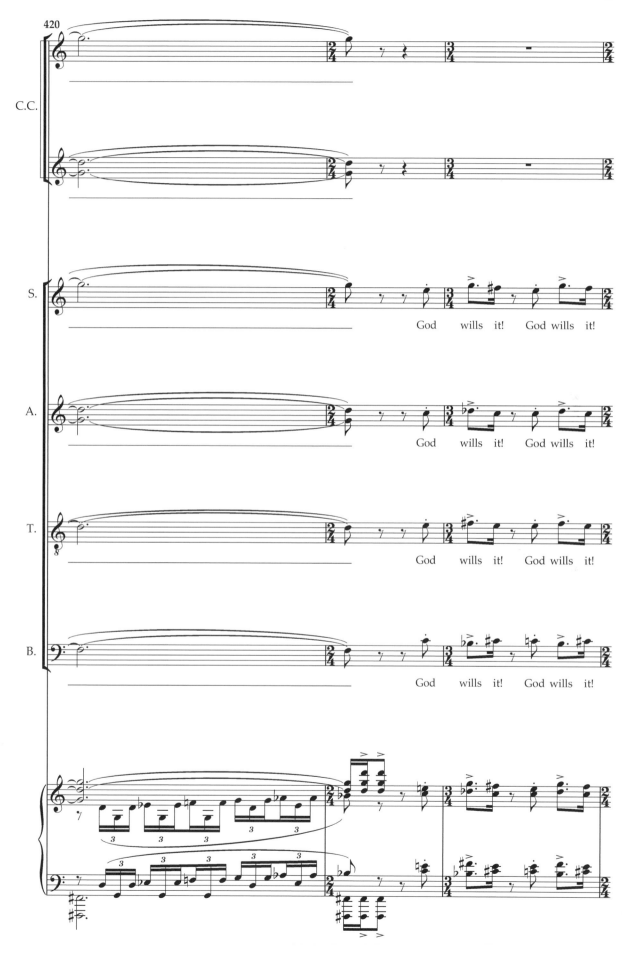

6. ABUL-MUZZAFAR AL-ABYURDI

50

52

em - bers of war.

pro-tu-lit Ah

pro-tu-lit Ah

pro-tu-lit Ah

pro-tu-lit Ah

rall. . . . . . . **50** Tempo I ♩ = 76

mp espr.

We min gle

(Fl, Ob)
_8va_-----

_p_

(Vlns con sord.)

PART III - THE FALL OF JERUSALEM (1099AD)

7. FULCHER OF CHARTRES

Allegro non troppo ♩ = 116

py-ra-mids. No - one save God___

___ a - lone knows how ma-ny there were.___

___ Re-joi-cing___ from ex-ces-sive glad - ness, our

8. HYMN - Lucis Largitor Splendide

66

74

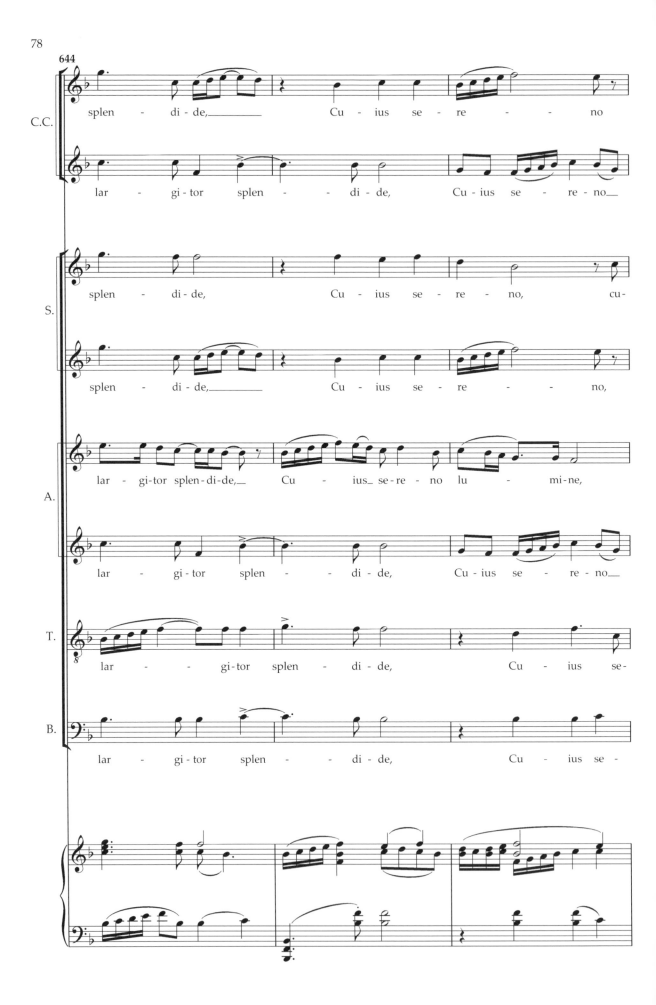

To Gavin Carr

PART IV - THE FALLING MAN (9/11)

9. TOM JUNOD

Adagio sostenuto ♩ = 66

PART V - AFTERMATH

10. HOW LONG, O LORD?

11. POET OF MA'ARRA

Andante ♩ = 66

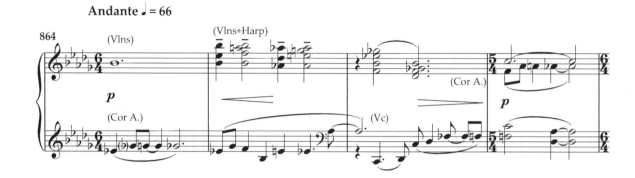

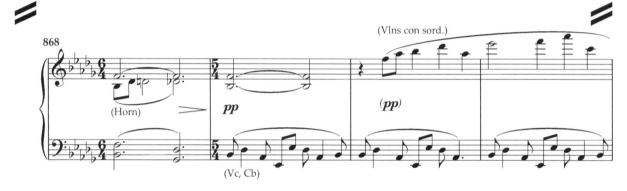

87 CHILDREN'S CHORUS
mp semplice

I do not know___ if my na-tive land_____ is a

gra-zing land for wild beasts___ or still___ my home.

88

880 SOPS.

S. *mp*
We are shat-tered by Fate as though we were glass.____

ALTOS

A. *mp*
We are shat-tered by Fate as though we were glass.____

rall. - - - - - - - -

884

S. *mf*
Ne - ver, ne - ver____ our shards are gath - ered to - ge - ther.____

A. *mf*
Ne - ver, ne - ver____ our shards are gath - ered to - ge - ther.

mf

warmly

889 **Tempo I** **89** CHILDREN'S CHORUS

C.C. *mp*
I do not know____ if my na-tive land____ is a

p

gra-zing land for wild beasts___ or still___ my home.

How long, O Lord?

How long, O Lord?

attacca

PART VI - GOD'S WILL

12. MOHAMMED BEN ZEKY

Bar. Solo: we had lost____ to the in - fi - dels.

The gates of Heav'n_____have been o - pened__ for this con - quest;

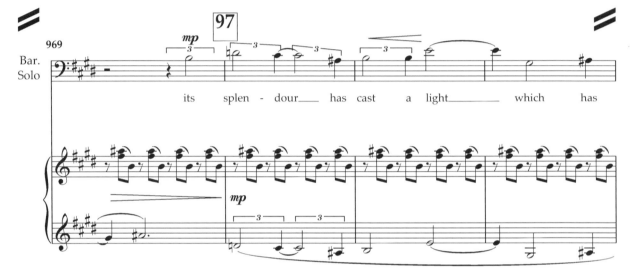

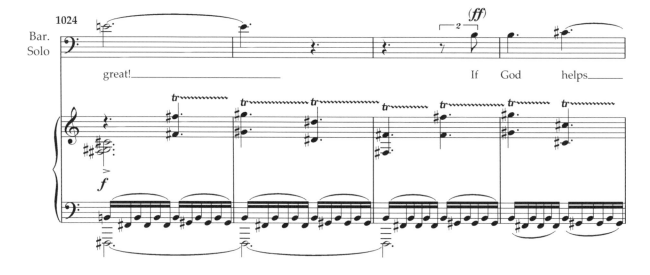

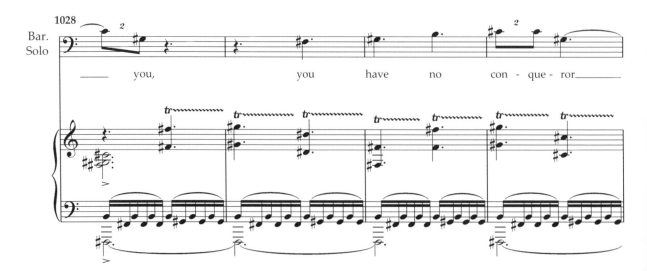

13. BARACK HUSSEIN OBAMA

109

Ten. Solo: It's a sto-ry with a sim-ple truth: Vio - lence is a

Bar. Solo: It's a sto-ry with a sim-ple truth: Vio - lence is a

Ten. Solo: dead end. To shoot ro-ckets at sleep-ing chil - dren, to

Bar. Solo: dead end. To shoot ro-ckets at sleep-ing chil - dren, to

Ten. Solo: blow up old wo-men___ on a bus is nei - ther a sign of

Bar. Solo: blow up old wo-men___ on a bus is nei - ther a sign of

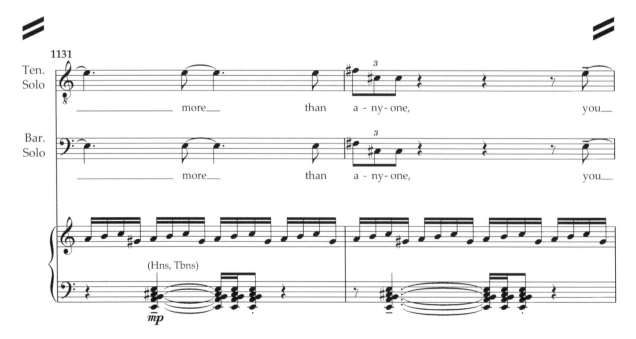

have the a - bi - li - ty _____ to re - i - ma - gine

To re - make the world. _____

S.
"The whole of the To - rah is for the pur - pose of pro - mo - ting peace."

A.
"The whole of the To - rah is for the pur - pose of pro - mo - ting peace."

T.
"The whole of the To - rah is for the pur - pose of pro - mo - ting peace."

B.
"The whole of the To - rah is for the pur - pose of pro - mo - ting peace."

Ten. Solo
The Ho - ly Bi - ble tells____ us:

Bar. Solo
The Ho - ly Bi - ble tells____ us:

136

142

MAHABHARATA

Mahabharata I

The Kuru Princes

Editor: Anant Pai
Illustrations: Dilip Kadam

This volume of Mahabharata contains the following titles:

	TITLE	SCRIPT
1.	Veda Vyasa	Kamala Chandrakant & TMP Nedungadi
2.	Bheeshma's Vow	Kamala Chandrakant & Subba Rao
3.	The Advent of the Kuru Princes	Kamala Chandrakant, Subba Rao & TMP Nedungadi
4.	The Pandavas at Hastinapura	Kamala Chandrakant & Subba Rao
5.	Enter Drona	Kamala Chandrakant & TMP Nedungadi
6.	Enter Karna	Kamala Chandrakant & TMP Nedungadi
7.	The Conspiracy	Kamala Chandrakant, Subba Rao & Yagya Sharma
8.	The Escape	Kamala Chandrakant & TMP Nedungadi
9.	The Birth of Ghatotkacha	Kamala Chandrakant & TMP Nedungadi
10.	The Pandavas at Ekachakrapura	Kamala Chandrakant & TMP Nedungadi
11.	Enter Draupadi	Kamala Chandrakant & TMP Nedungadi
12.	Draupadi's Swayamvara	Kamala Chandrakant & TMP Nedungadi
13.	The Pandavas Recalled to Hastinapura	Kamala Chandrakant & TMP Nedungadi
14.	Arjuna's 12-year Exile	Lopamudra

Amar Chitra Katha Pvt Ltd

© Amar Chitra Katha Pvt Ltd, 1998, Reprinted July 2012, ISBN 978-81-905990-2-3
Published & Printed by Amar Chitra Katha Pvt. Ltd., Krishna House, 3rd Floor,
Raghuvanshi Mill Compound, S.B.Marg, Lower Parel (W), Mumbai- 400 013. India
For Consumer Complaints Contact Tel : +91-22 40497436
Email: customerservice@ack-media.com

MAHABHARATA-1
VEDA VYASA

RISHI KRISHNA-DWAIPAYANA WAS KNOWN AS VEDA VYASA BECAUSE HE HAD BY PENANCE AND MEDITATION, ANALYSED, DIVIDED AND INTERPRETED THE VEDAS.

AND THEN THAT TIMELESS SEER, FOR THREE LONG YEARS, CONTEMPLATED ON THE LIVES AND PHILOSOPHIES OF HIS ANCIENTS AND HIS DESCENDANTS.

AND HE DWELT LONG ON THE CIRCUMSTANCES THAT LED TO THE GREAT WAR AMONGST HIS GRANDSONS, THE KAURAVAS AND THE PANDAVAS; ON THE WAR ITSELF; AND ON ITS AFTERMATH.

AND IN HIS WISDOM HE SAW THEM AND THEIR ACTS AS NEITHER WHITE NOR BLACK BUT GREY. HE SAW IN THEIR LIVES THE HUMAN CONDITION WITH AN INSIGHT, A UNIVERSALITY THAT IS GIVEN ONLY TO THE GREATEST OF POETS.

FOR PRONUNCIATION AND MEANING OF SANSKRIT WORDS AND PROPER NAMES, PLEASE SEE PAGE 32.

AND THEN AS HE BEGAN TO PONDER ON HOW HE SHOULD RECORD WHAT HE SAW FOR THE BENEFIT OF MANKIND, BRAHMA, THE CREATOR, CAME TO HIM.

O DIVINE BRAHMA, I HAVE COMPOSED A POEM BUT I CANNOT THINK OF ANY SCRIBE WHO WILL BE ABLE TO TAKE IT DOWN.

YOU CALL THE WORK A POEM, O MUNI. SO IT SHALL BE A POEM.

THERE SHALL HOWEVER BE NO POET WHOSE WORK WILL SURPASS THIS ONE.

THEREFORE, O MUNI, LET GANESHA BE THE SCRIBE.

AND BRAHMA RETIRED TO HIS ABODE.

VYASA CLOSED HIS EYES AND CALLED GANESHA TO MIND.

2

NO SOONER WAS THAT REMOVER OF OBSTACLES THOUGHT OF THAN HE WAS THERE.

VYASA PAID OBEISANCE TO HIM AND WAITED TILL HE WAS SEATED. THEN—

O GANESHA, BE THE SCRIBE OF THE BHARATA WHICH I HAVE CONCEIVED.

I WILL BE THE SCRIBE OF YOUR WORK IF YOU CAN RECITE IT WITHOUT A PAUSE.

AND YOU WILL NOT INSCRIBE ANYTHING IF THE MEANING IS NOT CLEAR TO YOU.

GANESHA HAVING NODDED HIS ASSENT, VYASA BEGAN WITH THE INVOCATION.

OM! HAVING INVOKED THE GRACE OF NARAYANA AND NARA AND SARASWATI, MUST THE WORD JAYA*BE UTTERED.

* LITERALLY 'VICTORY.' MAHABHARATA WAS ALSO REFERRED TO AS JAYA.

3

AND VYASA CONTINUED TO RECITE IN ACCORDANCE WITH THE PACT BY TURNING OUT PORTIONS THAT WERE COMPLEX AND PROFOUND.

EVEN THE OMNISCIENT GANESHA HAD TO STOP OCCASIONALLY TO GRASP THOSE PORTIONS WHILE VYASA WENT ON WITH OTHER VERSES IN THEIR HUNDREDS.

TO THIS DAY NO ONE IS ABLE TO PENETRATE THE MEANING OF THOSE CLOSELY KNIT VERSES, SO MYSTERIOUS IS THEIR IMPORT.

WHEN AT LAST THE WORK WAS COMPLETED, VYASA TAUGHT HIS DISCIPLES — SUMANTA, JAIMINI, PAILA, VAISHAMPAYANA AND HIS OWN SON SHUKA — THE FOUR VEDAS AND THE MAHABHARATA AS THE FIFTH.

BUT ONLY AFTER THE MAIN CHARACTERS OF HIS WORK HAD DEPARTED FROM THE EARTH, DID HE PERMIT THEIR STORY TO BE RECITED IN PUBLIC. AND THIS IS HOW IT CAME TO PASS.

LEARNING THAT JANAMEJAYA, HIS GRANDSON'S GREAT-GRANDSON, WAS INSTALLED FOR THE SARPA* SATRA† VYASA WITH HIS DISCIPLES CAME TO THE SACRIFICIAL PAVILION.

AFTER RECEIVING HIM AND WORSHIPPING HIM ACCORDING TO THE PRESCRIBED RITES, JANAMEJAYA SAID TO VYASA:

YOU HAVE BEEN A WITNESS, O SAGE, TO THE FEUD BETWEEN THE KAURAVAS AND THE PANDAVAS. I WISH TO HEAR FROM YOU OF THOSE EVENTS.

O VAISHAMPAYANA, NARRATE TO THE KING WHAT YOU HAVE HEARD FROM ME.

THE DISCIPLE FIRST PROSTRATED HIMSELF BEFORE HIS GURU...

...AND THEN ADDRESSED THE KING.

O MONARCH, I SHALL RECITE IT. BUT THIS HISTORY TOLD BY RISHI VYASA CONSISTS OF OVER A HUNDRED THOUSAND VERSES AND WILL TAKE TIME.

IT IS A DISCOURSE ON DHARMA, ON ARTHA, ON KAMA. WHAT IS CONTAINED IN THIS WORK ABOUT VIRTUE, WEALTH, PLEASURE AND SALVATION MAY BE SEEN ELSEWHERE. BUT...

...WHATEVER IS NOT CONTAINED IN THIS, IS NOT TO BE FOUND ANYWHERE. HE THAT KNOWS IT MAY BE REGARDED AS ONE WHO KNOWS THE VEDAS.

THIS HISTORY OF THE BHARATA RACE—COMMENCING FROM MANU, THE GRANDSON OF ADITI, THE MOTHER OF THE DEVAS—IS CALLED THE MAHABHARATA.

"IN THE KRITA YUGA THE POWER OF KINGS WAS UNTAINTED BY GREED, LUST AND ANGER.

"THE BRAHMANAS WHO WERE WELL-VERSED IN VEDIC LORE DID NOT TURN THE VEDAS INTO A COMMODITY OF TRADE.

"AND NO VAISHYA IN THOSE DAYS EVER EXPLOITED THE TILLER OF THE SOIL, OR SOUGHT TO DECEIVE PEOPLE BY USING FAULTY MEASURES.

"BUT AS THE TRETA AND DWAPARA YUGAS SET IN, MANY UNJUST, GREEDY, TYRANT KINGS DEVOID OF TRUTH AND VIRTUE RAVISHED THE EARTH.

AND, AS MY GURU PERCEIVED, VIRTUE DIMINISHED BY ONE QUARTER WITH EACH YUGA AND THE LIFE AND STRENGTH OF MEN DIMINISHED WITH THE YUGAS.

8

"AND THEN, O MONARCH, BHOOMI DEVI, OPPRESSED BY THE RISE OF THE WICKED, CALLED TO MIND BRAHMA, THE GRANDSIRE OF ALL CREATURES, WHO DIVINING HER PURPOSE SAID:

I SHALL APPOINT THE CELESTIALS TO EASE YOUR BURDEN. FARE YOU WELL.

"THE CREATOR THEN SAID TO THE DEVAS, APSARAS AND GANDHARVAS:

GO TAKE BIRTH IN THE RACE OF MEN, IN YOUR RESPECTIVE ROLES IN FORMS OF YOUR CHOICE, AND SEEK STRIFE WITH THE WICKED ON EARTH.

"AND THE DEVAS WENT TO NARAYANA AT VAIKUNTHA AND SAID:

BE INCARNATE!

LET IT BE SO.

AND THE CELESTIALS, ONE AFTER ANOTHER, BECAME INCARNATE ON EARTH IN THE RACES OF BRAHMARSHIS AND RAJARSHIS.

AND THIS, O MONARCH, IS AN ACCOUNT OF YOUR OWN RACE COMMENCING FROM MANU THE GRANDSON OF ADITI.

MANU'S DAUGHTER ILA BEGOT PURURAVAS WHOSE SON AYUS BEGOT NAHUSHA, THE FATHER OF YAYATI. THE YADAVAS AND THE PAURAVAS ARE THE DESCENDANTS OF YAYATI'S SONS, YADU AND PURU.

AND IN PURU'S LINE AFTER SEVEN-TEEN GENERATIONS OF KINGS, WAS BORN THE MIGHTY BHARATA THE SON OF DUSHYANTA.

"KING DUSHYANTA WANTING TO MEET SAGE KANWA, ONCE ARRIVED AT HIS ASHRAMA ALL ALONE. THE RISHI WAS NOT THERE BUT SHAKUNTALA*, HIS FOSTER-DAUGHTER, RECEIVED THE KING WITH HONOUR. ENCHANTED BY HER GRACE AND BEAUTY, THE KING SAID:

OH BEAUTIFUL ONE, BE MY WIFE.

O KING, LET MY FATHER WHO HAS GONE OUT RETURN AND BESTOW ME ON YOU.

*KALIDASA'S ADAPTATION OF THE STORY OF SHAKUNTALA DIFFERS FROM THE ORIGINAL MAHABHARATA VERSION.

"AND WHEN HE WAS BARELY SIX, THE BOY WOULD CHASE AND SEIZE TIGERS...

...AND RIDE ON THEM. AND WATCHING THESE FEATS, THE SAGE KNEW THAT THE TIME HAD COME FOR THE BOY TO TAKE HIS PLACE AS THE PRINCE AMONG MEN.

"SO HE SAID TO HIS DISCIPLES:

LEAD OUR SHAKUNTALA AND HER SON TO THE PALACE OF HER HUSBAND WITHOUT DELAY.

SO BE IT.

"AND THE RISHI'S DISCIPLES WITH SHAKUNTALA AND HER SON, WENDED THEIR WAY TO DUSHYANTA'S CAPITAL.

12

"WHEN THEY REACHED THE PRESENCE OF THE KING, THEY LEFT SHAKUNTALA WITH HIM AND WENT AWAY, PRESENTING HER SON, SHAKUNTALA SAID:

THIS IS YOUR SON, O KING. FULFIL THE PROMISE YOU GAVE ME TO INSTALL HIM AS YOUR HEIR-APPARENT.

"BUT THE KING, THOUGH HE REMEMBERED EVERYTHING, SAID:

WHO ARE YOU?

YOU HAD APPROACHED ME, O KING, WHEN I WAS UNDER THE PROTECTION OF MY FATHER, SAGE KANWA.

"THE KING REPLIED:

ARE YOU NOT ASHAMED TO SPEAK THUS TO ME, O WOMAN IN THE GARB OF AN ASCETIC?

"ON HEARING THESE WORDS, SHAKUNTALA'S EYES BLAZED AND HER LIPS QUIVERED IN ANGER. AND SHE SAID:

YOU THINK NO ONE KNOWS OF YOUR DEED. BUT NARAYANA, THE OMNISCIENT ONE, LIVES IN THE HEARTS OF ALL BEINGS. AND HE HAS SEEN YOU.

"THEN, HER VOICE TURNING DEEP WITH SORROW, SHE SAID:

O KING, THERE IS NO VIRTUE EQUAL TO TRUTH. TRUTH IS THE SELF. TRUTH IS GOD. THEREFORE DO NOT VIOLATE YOUR PLEDGE.

WOMAN, I DO NOT KNOW WHAT PLEDGE YOU SPEAK OF.

WHEN YOU DENY WHAT YOU KNOW TO BE THE TRUTH, YOU DENY YOURSELF. IT IS DEMEANING AND BEFITS ONLY A LOWLY PERSON.

WOMAN, I DON'T KNOW YOU.

BUT AFTER YOU, THIS SON OF MINE SHALL RULE THE EARTH SURROUNDED BY THE OCEAN AND ADORNED BY THE KING OF MOUNTAINS!

"AND THEN, A VOICE FROM THE REALMS ABOVE ADDRESSED DUSHYANTA:

O DUSHYANTA, SHAKUNTALA HATH SPOKEN THE TRUTH. THEREFORE CHERISH THOU, THY SON BORN OF HER.

"HEARING THESE WORDS, THE FACE OF DUSHYANTA, THE LORD OF PURU'S RACE, WAS SUFFUSED WITH JOY AND HE SAID:

DID YOU LISTEN CAREFULLY TO THAT CELESTIAL MESSAGE? I KNOW THIS BOY TO BE MY SON. BUT...

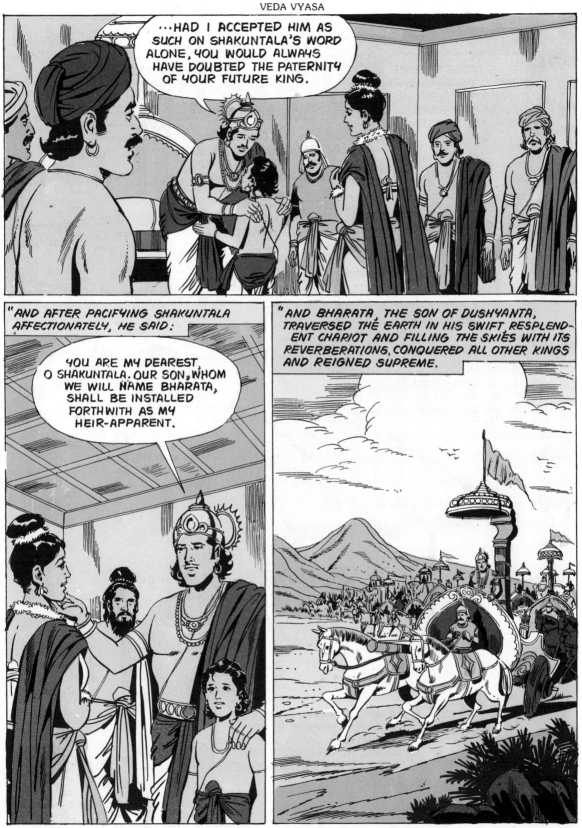

...HAD I ACCEPTED HIM AS SUCH ON SHAKUNTALA'S WORD ALONE, YOU WOULD ALWAYS HAVE DOUBTED THE PATERNITY OF YOUR FUTURE KING.

"AND AFTER PACIFYING SHAKUNTALA AFFECTIONATELY, HE SAID:

YOU ARE MY DEAREST, O SHAKUNTALA. OUR SON, WHOM WE WILL NAME BHARATA, SHALL BE INSTALLED FORTHWITH AS MY HEIR-APPARENT.

"AND BHARATA, THE SON OF DUSHYANTA, TRAVERSED THE EARTH IN HIS SWIFT RESPLENDENT CHARIOT AND FILLING THE SKIES WITH ITS REVERBERATIONS, CONQUERED ALL OTHER KINGS AND REIGNED SUPREME.

IT IS AFTER BHARATA TOO, O MONARCH, THAT THE GREAT RACE IN WHICH YOU WERE BORN IS NAMED.

AND IN THE LINE OF THIS BHARATA WERE BORN MANY GODLIKE KINGS OF WHOM **SAMVARANA**, THE SIXTH, WAS THE FATHER OF **KURU**... AND PRATIPA, THE THIRTEENTH, THE FATHER OF **SHANTANU**.

AND SHANTANU'S SON, DEVAVRATA, BORN OF GANGA, CAME TO BE KNOWN AS BHEESHMA FOR THE TERRIBLE VOW HE TOOK.

WHAT WAS THAT VOW, O SAGE? WHY DID THE SON OF GANGA TAKE IT?

IT WAS TO BENEFIT HIS FATHER, O MONARCH. HE RESEMBLED HIS FATHER IN LOOKS, IN BEHAVIOUR AND MOST OF ALL IN TRUTHFULNESS OF SPEECH.

"WHEN DEVAVRATA CAME OF AGE, SHANTANU SUMMONED ALL THE PAURAVAS TO HASTINAPURA, THE CAPITAL OF THE KURUS, AND IN THEIR PRESENCE INSTALLED HIM AS HEIR-APPARENT.

"FOUR YEARS LATER, WHEN SHANTANU WAS WALKING IN THE WOODS ON THE BANK OF THE YAMUNA, A SWEET SCENT FILLED THE AIR. AND AS HE WALKED ON WONDERING ABOUT ITS SOURCE, HE CHANCED UPON A BEAUTIFUL WOMAN WITH LARGE DARK EYES HE ASKED:

O MAIDEN, WHO ARE YOU? WHAT ARE YOU DOING HERE?

I AM SATYAVATI. AT THE BEHEST OF MY FATHER, THE CHIEF OF THE FISHERMEN, I FERRY PASSENGERS ACROSS THE RIVER.

"AND SHANTANU, DESIRING HER FOR A WIFE, WENT TO HER FATHER AND SOUGHT HIS CONSENT. THE FISHERMAN HEARD ALL AND THEN SAID:

O KING, I WOULD OF COURSE BESTOW MY DAUGHTER ON YOU. FOR TRULY I COULD NEVER GET HER A HUSBAND EQUAL TO YOU. BUT...

...THERE IS A WISH I HAVE ALWAYS CARRIED WITH ME. IF YOU WANT TO MARRY MY DAUGHTER, PROMISE TO FULFIL IT.

BEFORE MAKING A PROMISE, I SHOULD KNOW THE NATURE OF YOUR WISH.

THIS THEN, O KING, IS WHAT I ASK OF YOU.

PROMISE ME THAT NONE ELSE BUT THE SON BORN TO SATYAVATI SHALL BE YOUR SUCCESSOR.

"SHANTANU HEARD HIS REQUEST AND HE KNEW HE COULD NOT GRANT IT.

"YET HE RETURNED TO HASTINAPURA THINKING ALL THE WAY ABOUT THE FISHERMAN'S DAUGHTER.

20

"AND THERE SHANTANU SPENT HIS TIME IN HOPELESS SOLITUDE TILL THE DAY DEVAVRATA DECIDED TO FIND OUT THE REASON FOR HIS SORROW.

THE KINGDOM PROSPERS. ALL CHIEFS OBEY YOU. WHY THEN DO YOU GRIEVE SO?

MY MIND KNOWS NO PEACE. I AM SORELY TROUBLED ABOUT THE UNCERTAINTY OF HUMAN LIFE.

O SCION OF BHARATA'S RACE, YOU ARE MY ONLY SON. SHOULD ANYTHING HAPPEN TO YOU, I WOULD BE SON- LESS.

YET YOU ARE AS DEAR TO ME AS A HUNDRED SONS, SO I DO NOT WISH TO WED AGAIN FOR OTHER SONS.

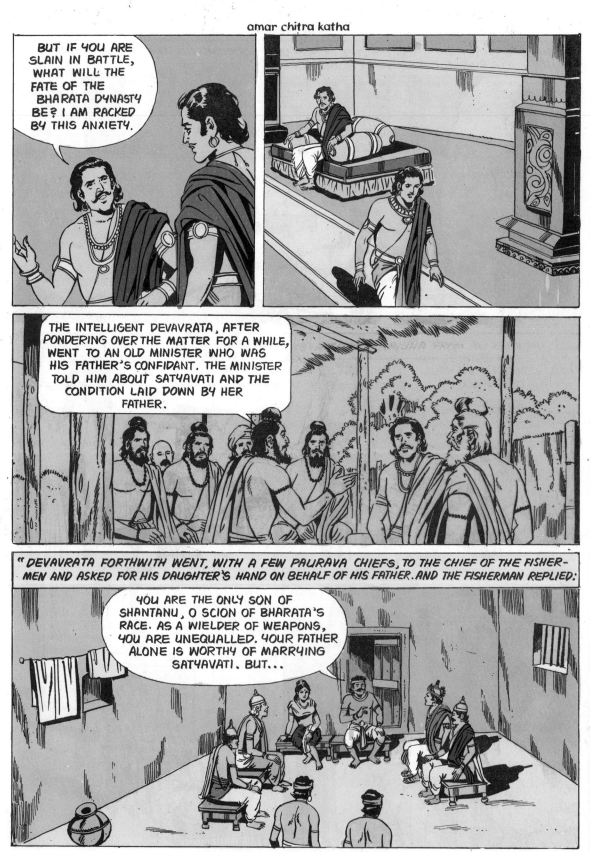

BUT IF YOU ARE SLAIN IN BATTLE, WHAT WILL THE FATE OF THE BHARATA DYNASTY BE? I AM RACKED BY THIS ANXIETY.

THE INTELLIGENT DEVAVRATA, AFTER PONDERING OVER THE MATTER FOR A WHILE, WENT TO AN OLD MINISTER WHO WAS HIS FATHER'S CONFIDANT. THE MINISTER TOLD HIM ABOUT SATYAVATI AND THE CONDITION LAID DOWN BY HER FATHER.

" DEVAVRATA FORTHWITH WENT, WITH A FEW PAURAVA CHIEFS, TO THE CHIEF OF THE FISHER-MEN AND ASKED FOR HIS DAUGHTER'S HAND ON BEHALF OF HIS FATHER. AND THE FISHERMAN REPLIED:

YOU ARE THE ONLY SON OF SHANTANU, O SCION OF BHARATA'S RACE. AS A WIELDER OF WEAPONS, YOU ARE UNEQUALLED. YOUR FATHER ALONE IS WORTHY OF MARRYING SATYAVATI. BUT...

...THERE IS ONE DRAWBACK. THE PRESENCE OF A CO-WIFE'S SON.

O DESTROYER OF FOES, ONE WHO HAS A RIVAL IN YOU HAS NO SECURITY. THIS IS ALL I HAVE TO SAY.

" URGED BY THE WISH TO SEE HIS FATHER HAPPY, DEVAVRATA SAID:

O FISHERMAN, THE PROMISE YOU DEMAND IS GRANTED. THE SON BORN OF THIS MAIDEN AND MY FATHER SHALL BE OUR KING.

" BUT, GOADED BY THE DESIRE TO MAKE THE THRONE SECURE FOR HIS DAUGHTER'S SON, THE FISHERMAN SAID:

O FOREMOST OF TRUTHFUL MEN, I AM CONFIDENT THAT YOU WOULD NEVER BREAK A PROMISE ONCE GIVEN. BUT I HAVE MY DOUBTS ABOUT WHAT THE CHILDREN YOU WILL BEGET WOULD DO.

"AND WITNESSING ALL THIS THE FISHERMAN EXCLAIMED:

I GIVE MY DAUGHTER IN MARRIAGE TO THE KING!

"BHEESHMA THEN TURNED TO SATYAVATI AND SAID:

O MOTHER, LET US GO TO HASTINAPURA WITHOUT DELAY.

"THEN BHEESHMA HELPED HER INTO HIS CHARIOT AND TOOK HER TO HASTINAPURA.

"AMAZED BY THE EXTRAORDINARY ACT OF HIS SON, SHANTANU BESTOWED ON HIM THE BOON OF DEATH AT WILL.

DEATH SHALL NEVER COME TO YOU AS LONG AS YOU WISH TO LIVE. O SINLESS ONE, ONLY AT YOUR BIDDING SHALL DEATH APPROACH YOU.

I HAVE HEARD THE LEARNED AND THE WISE SAY THAT SATYAVATI WAS IN TRUTH THE DAUGHTER OF VASU UPARICHARA AND THE MOTHER OF VEDA VYASA. ENLIGHTEN US ON THE TRUTH OF THESE MATTERS, O RISHI.

WHAT YOU HAVE HEARD IS TRUE. THIS IS THE TURN OF THOSE EVENTS. VASU, THE KING OF CHEDI, WAS ALSO CALLED UPARICHARA BECAUSE HE COURSED THROUGH THE SKY IN A CELESTIAL CHARIOT GIVEN TO HIM BY INDRA, KING OF THE DEVAS.

"ONCE THE SEED OF THIS UPARICHARA WAS SWALLOWED BY A FISH IN THE WATERS OF THE YAMUNA.

"A FEW MONTHS LATER, THE FISH WAS CAUGHT BY SOME FISHERMEN AND IN THE STOMACH OF THAT FISH THEY FOUND A MALE AND A FEMALE CHILD. THE FISHERMEN WONDERED AT THEIR FIND...

...AND GOING TO UPARICHARA SAID:

O KING, WE FOUND THESE TWO BEINGS OF HUMAN FORM IN THE BODY OF A LARGE FISH!

"UPARICHARA TOOK THE MALE CHILD WHO LATER BECAME THE KING OF MATSYA...

...AND GAVE THE FEMALE CHILD WHO SMELT STRONGLY OF FISH TO THE FISHERMAN, SAYING:

REAR HER AS YOUR DAUGHTER.

"WHEN SHE GREW UP, THAT GIRL, WHO WAS SATYAVATI, PLIED A BOAT FOR HER FOSTER-FATHER ON THE WATERS OF THE YAMUNA.

"WHILE THUS ENGAGED, SATYAVATI WAS SEEN ONE DAY BY THE VENERABLE RISHI PARASHARA.

"AND AS SOON AS HE BEHELD HER, THE RISHI WAS SMITTEN WITH DESIRE.

"HE THEREUPON CREATED A FOG WHICH SHUT OUT THE LIGHT.

"AND THE MAID BEHOLDING THE FOG WONDERED AT THE MARVEL.

"AND THAT BEST OF RISHIS SMILED AND SAID:

SWEET MAID OF FAIR SMILES, SEEK THE BOON YOU DESIRE.

LET THE ODOUR OF FISH THAT MY BODY NOW EMITS BE TRANSFORMED INTO A SWEET SCENT.

SO BE IT.

" THE RISHI GRANTED HER WISH FORTHWITH AND SATYAVATI CAME TO BE KNOWN ALSO AS GANDHAVATI, THE SWEET-SCENTED ONE.

" AND BY THE GRACE OF RISHI PARASHARA, GANDHAVATI BROUGHT FORTH, ON THAT ISLAND, A CHILD OF GREAT ENERGY WHO DEVELOPED HIS BODY BY HIS WILL ALONE AS SOON AS HE WAS BORN.

" AND THE ILLUSTRIOUS ONE SETTING HIS MIND ON ASCETICISM SAID:

THINK OF ME WHEN YOU NEED ME, MOTHER, AND I SHALL APPEAR BEFORE YOU.

"AND HE WENT AWAY.

THUS WAS MY GURU VYASA BORN TO SATYAVATI OF PARASHARA.

AS HE WAS BORN ON AN ISLAND HE WAS CALLED DWAIPAYANA AND BECAUSE OF HIS DARK COLOUR, KRISHNA.

THE LEARNED KRISHNA DWAIPAYANA ARRANGED THE VEDAS. AND FOR THIS HE CAME TO BE CALLED VEDA VYASA.

THE PRIEST HAD COME TO TELL JANAMEJAYA THAT HIS PRESENCE WAS REQUIRED FOR THE NEXT RITE.

SO ALL OF THEM ROSE, WALKED TOWARDS THE "HOMA KUNDA"...

...AND TOOK THEIR PLACES BEFORE THE SACRIFICIAL FIRE.

AND THUS ENDS THE FIRST SESSION OF OUR RENDERING OF VAISHAMPAYANA'S RECITAL (DURING THE INTERVALS IN THE RITES OF JANAMEJAYA'S SARPA SATRA) OF VYASA'S IMMORTAL ITIHASA, THE MAHABHARATA.

MAHABHARATA-2
Bheeshma's Vow

VYASA'S EPIC ON THE BHARATA RACE WAS FIRST RECITED IN PUBLIC, BY HIS DISCIPLE VAISHAMPAYANA, AT THE BEHEST OF THE AGELESS SEER VYASA HIMSELF.

THE RECITAL TOOK PLACE IN THE AUGUST PRESENCE OF KING JANAMEJAYA — GREAT-GRANDSON OF THE GRANDSON OF VYASA — AND THE MANY LEARNED SAGES WHO HAD ASSEMBLED FOR JANAMEJAYA'S SARPA* SATRA.⊛

THE FIRST SESSION OF OUR RENDERING OF VAISHAMPAYANA'S RECITAL, INCLUDED THE INCIDENTS LEADING TO BHEESHMA (THE SON OF SHANTANU) TAKING A VOW OF CELIBACY AND SHANTANU MARRYING SATYAVATI.

* SNAKE   ⊛ -12-YEAR-LONG YAGNA

O MONARCH, TWO SONS WERE BORN TO SATYAVATI AND SHANTANU OF BHARATA'S RACE. THEY WERE CALLED CHITRANGADA AND VICHITRAVEERYA.

YEARS LATER, SHANTANU PASSED AWAY AND BHEESHMA CROWNED CHITRANGADA AS THE KING OF HASTINAPURA. VANQUISHING THE DENIZENS OF THIS WORLD AND THE OTHER WORLDS HE REIGNED SUPREME.

" IRKED BY HIS SUPREMACY, A GANDHARVA OF THE SAME NAME CHALLENGED HIM TO A FIGHT ON THE FIELD OF KURUKSHETRA.

"AFTER A TERRIBLE COMBAT, WHICH LASTED THREE YEARS, CHITRANGADA WAS SLAIN, AND THE GANDHARVA RETURNED TO HIS CELESTIAL ABODE.

"VICHITRAVEERYA, WHO WAS STILL A MINOR, WAS PLACED ON THE THRONE BY BHEESHMA. THE BOY RULED THE ANCESTRAL KINGDOM, GUIDED BY BHEESHMA WHOM HE ADORED' FOR HIS VALOUR AND VIRTUE.

WHEN VICHITRAVEERYA CAME OF AGE AND WAS READY FOR MARRIAGE, BHEESHMA, THE EVER-WATCHFUL, HEARD THAT THE THREE DAUGHTERS OF THE KING OF KASHI WOULD BE CHOOSING THEIR HUSBANDS AT A SWAYAMVARA CEREMONY.

SO, WITH THE PERMISSION OF SATYAVATI, BHEESHMA, THE FIERCE WARRIOR AND THE FAITHFUL REGENT, WENT TO KASHI IN A SINGLE CHARIOT.

"THERE HE SAW THOSE THREE MAIDENS AND THE MANY KINGS WHO HAD COME FOR THE SWAYAMVARA. AND ADDRESSING THE KING OF KASHI AND THE ASSEMBLED SUITORS IN A DEEP THUNDERING VOICE, HE SAID:

A MAIDEN MAY BE GIVEN AWAY TO A SUITABLE GROOM ALONG WITH MANY VALUABLE GIFTS, OR SHE MAY BE GIVEN AWAY IN EXCHANGE FOR A FEW COWS OR FOR A FIXED SUM OF GOLD.

SOME TAKE AWAY MAIDENS BY FORCE AND SOME WED THEM WITH THEIR CONSENT. MARRIAGE WITH THE MAIDEN'S CONSENT IS SPOKEN OF HIGHLY. BUT...

...A PRECIOUS WIFE IS ONE WHO HAS BEEN SNATCHED AWAY FROM CONTENDING SUITORS.

4

"SMARTING UNDER THE SCORN OF BHEESHMA, THE ARRAY OF KINGS STOOD UP AS ONE MAN READY TO FIGHT.

"WITHOUT A MOMENT'S LOSS, THE KINGS CAST OFF THEIR WEDDING FINERY AND REACHED FOR THEIR ARMOUR. THE SPARKLE OF THEIR ORNAMENTS, THE GLEAM OF THEIR WEAPONS AND THE CLANG OF METALS, RENT THE AIR WITH THE BRILLIANCE OF A METEORIC BURST.

"THE IMPATIENT KINGS, IN THEIR MARTIAL RAGE, BRANDISHED THEIR WEAPONS AND PURSUED THE CHIEF OF THE KURUS.

AND THEN THERE FOLLOWED, O MONARCH, A TERRIBLE FIGHT. THE SWARM OF ARROWS, FROM THE MULTITUDE OF KINGS, WAS CHECKED BY BHEESHMA WITH A SHOWER OF ARROWS FROM HIS SINGLE BOW — A SHOWER AS INNUMERABLE AS THE HAIR ON ONE'S BODY.

THE BATTLE RAGED SO FIERCE, WITH CLASHING WEAPONS AND FLYING MISSILES, THAT IT STRUCK TERROR IN THE HEARTS OF EVEN THOSE WHO WERE MERE SPECTATORS.

IN NO TIME, THE GROUND WAS STREWN WITH HEADS SEVERED FROM BODIES, FLAGSTAFFS FROM CHARIOTS, AND ARMOUR FROM HEAVING CHESTS.

AND SUCH WAS THE PROWESS OF BHEESHMA THAT EVEN THE ENEMIES WHO CAME TO FIGHT HIM REMAINED TO APPLAUD.

" AS THE VICTORIOUS BHEESHMA TURNED HIS CHARIOT TOWARDS HASTINAPURA, SHALVA, THE KING OF SAUBHA, CHALLENGED HIM TO SINGLE COMBAT.

" BHEESHMA, READY TO FACE THE FRESH FOE, SAID TO HIS CHARIOTEER:

TAKE THE CHARIOT TOWARDS SHALVA. HE SHALL HAVE WHAT HE DESERVES.

" BHEESHMA SLEW SHALVA'S STEEDS AND CHARIOTEER, BUT SPARED HIS LIFE, AND PROCEEDED WITH THE MAIDENS TOWARDS HASTINAPURA.

"RUTHLESS ON THE BATTLEFIELD, BHEESHMA WAS FULL OF TENDERNESS WHEN IT CAME TO LOOKING AFTER THE MAIDENS AS HE BROUGHT THEM TO VICHITRAVEERYA.

" WHEN THE DETAILS OF THE WEDDING WERE SETTLED BY BHEESHMA AND APPROVED BY SATYAVATI, AMBA, THE ELDEST OF THE MAIDENS, SAID TO BHEESHMA:

EVEN BEFORE THE SWAYAMVARA WAS HELD, I HAD CHOSEN THE KING OF SAUBHA. HE HAD ACCEPTED AND MY FATHER HAD APPROVED.

NOW THAT YOU KNOW THIS, DO AS YOU CHOOSE.

THE WISE AND VIRTUOUS BHEESHMA, AFTER PONDERING ON THE MATTER, PERMITTED AMBA TO DO AS SHE LIKED, BUT GAVE AMBIKA AND AMBALIKA IN MARRIAGE TO HIS BROTHER, VICHITRAVEERYA.

... I CHARGE YOU WITH A RESPONSIBILITY.

I CHARGE YOU TO BEGET CHILDREN WITH THESE PRINCESSES OF KASHI AND KEEP SHANTANU'S LINE ALIVE.

INSTALL YOURSELF ON THE THRONE AND RULE OVER THE KINGDOM.

" AND TO THIS, BHEESHMA SAID:

I CANNOT BEGET CHILDREN NOR BE THE KING. MY VOW IS WELL KNOWN.

" SATYAVATI REPLIED:

I KNOW THAT YOUR VOW WAS ON MY ACCOUNT. BUT THIS CALAMITY WAS UNFORESEEN.

IF YOU ADHERE TO YOUR VOW, YOUR ANCESTORS WILL BE DENIED THEIR RIGHT TO SALVATION.

"THUS URGED BY WORDS UTTERED IN DESPERATE SORROW BY SATYAVATI, BHEESHMA SAID:

BREACH OF TRUTH IS NEVER APPROVED BY OUR SACRED TEXTS. HOWEVER, THE KSHATRIYAS DO HAVE RECOURSE TO A CUSTOM, WHICH HAS BEEN SANCTIONED BY TRADITION.

AN ACCOMPLISHED MAN COULD BE INVITED TO RAISE OFFSPRING IN THE WIVES OF VICHITRAVEERYA.

" SATYAVATI SMILING BASHFULLY THEN SAID:

O PRINCE, IN OUR RACE YOU ARE VIRTUE, YOU ARE TRUTH, YOU ARE OUR SOLE REFUGE. THEREFORE, LISTEN TO MY STORY AND DO WHAT IS PROPER.

AND SATYAVATI TOLD BHEESHMA IN PRIVATE OF HOW SHE MET PARASHARA WHEN SHE WAS A MAIDEN AND OF THE SON, KRISHNA DWAIPAYANA, BORN TO THEM. THE SON WHO IS VYASA, MY GURU.

"AND THEN SATYAVATI SAID:

IF YOU APPROVE OF IT, O BHEESHMA, MY SON THE GREAT ASCETIC KRISHNA DWAIPAYANA WILL COME AND BEGET THE OFFSPRING WE DESIRE.

"AT THE MENTION OF MY GURU'S NAME, BHEESHMA JOINED HIS PALMS AND SAID:

O QUEEN, WHAT YOU HAVE SUGGESTED IS IN KEEPING WITH PROPRIETY, AND HAS MY FULL APPROVAL. FOR...

...THE ACTS OF AN INTELLIGENT MAN, ARISING FROM DEEP AND PATIENT THOUGHT WILL ONLY LEAD VIRTUE TO GREATER VIRTUE.

"AND WHEN BHEESHMA SAID THIS, SATYAVATI THOUGHT OF SAGE DWAIPAYANA...

...WHO WAS THEN ENGAGED IN INTERPRETING THE VEDAS.

इन्द्रं मित्रं वरुणमग्निमाहु...।
एकं सद्विप्रा बहुधा वदन्ति...।

"DIVINING THAT HE WAS NEEDED BY HIS MOTHER MY GURU CAME INSTANTLY TO HER WITHOUT ANYBODY'S KNOWLEDGE.

* THEY ADDRESS HIM AS INDRA, MITRA, VARUNA AND AGNI. THE ONE REALITY IS CALLED BY VARIOUS NAMES BY THE SAGES — RIG VEDA 1-164-46

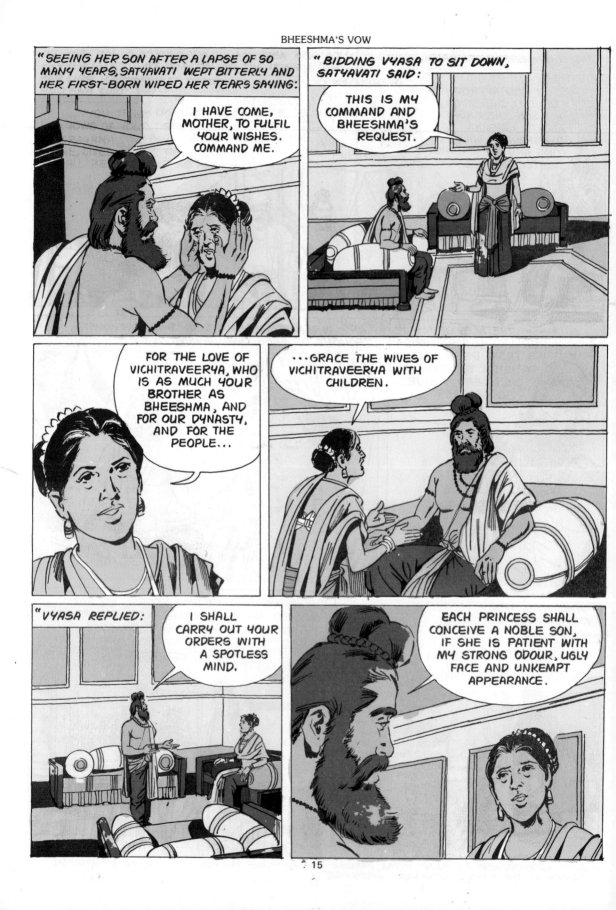

"SEEING HER SON AFTER A LAPSE OF SO MANY YEARS, SATYAVATI WEPT BITTERLY AND HER FIRST-BORN WIPED HER TEARS SAYING:

I HAVE COME, MOTHER, TO FULFIL YOUR WISHES. COMMAND ME.

"BIDDING VYASA TO SIT DOWN, SATYAVATI SAID:

THIS IS MY COMMAND AND BHEESHMA'S REQUEST.

FOR THE LOVE OF VICHITRAVEERYA, WHO IS AS MUCH YOUR BROTHER AS BHEESHMA, AND FOR OUR DYNASTY, AND FOR THE PEOPLE...

...GRACE THE WIVES OF VICHITRAVEERYA WITH CHILDREN.

"VYASA REPLIED:

I SHALL CARRY OUT YOUR ORDERS WITH A SPOTLESS MIND.

EACH PRINCESS SHALL CONCEIVE A NOBLE SON, IF SHE IS PATIENT WITH MY STRONG ODOUR, UGLY FACE AND UNKEMPT APPEARANCE.

15

"AFTER MUCH PERSUASION FROM SATYAVATI, AMBIKA RECEIVED THE RISHI IN HER CHAMBER. BUT TERRIFIED BY HIS FORBIDDING LOOKS, SHE SHUT HER EYES.

AND SHE KEPT HER EYES SHUT AS LONG AS THE RISHI REMAINED IN HER CHAMBER.

"LATER, WHEN SATYAVATI ASKED HIM:

SHALL THE PRINCESS HAVE A NOBLE SON?

"THE RISHI REPLIED:

THE SON SHALL HAVE THE STRENGTH OF TEN THOUSAND ELEPHANTS. HE SHALL, IN HIS TIME, BEGET A HUNDRED SONS BUT...

...HIS MOTHER SHUT OUT HER VISION, SO HE SHALL BE BORN BLIND.

"HEARING THESE WORDS, SATYAVATI CRIED OUT:

HOW CAN A BLIND MAN BE A KING? IN ALL PROPRIETY YOU MUST GIVE THE KURUS ANOTHER KING.

"SO, AFTER THE BIRTH OF THE BLIND SON, DHRITARASHTRA, VYASA APPROACHED AMBALIKA, THE YOUNGER PRINCESS. GRIPPED BY FEAR AT THE SIGHT OF THE RISHI, SHE TURNED PALE, AND VYASA SAID:

FEAR HAS TURNED YOU PALE, FOR WHICH YOUR SON SHALL BE PALE OF SKIN. AND HE SHALL BE NAMED PANDU.

DISAPPOINTED A SECOND TIME, SATYAVATI BEGGED OF THE RISHI FOR ANOTHER CHILD BY AMBIKA. BUT WHEN THE TIME CAME, THE SELF-WILLED AMBIKA SENT IN HER MAID, DECKED IN HER OWN ORNAMENTS, TO RECEIVE THE SAGE. THE MAID WAITED UPON HIM WITH RESPECT AND REVERENCE.

"THE SAGE WAS PLEASED AND SAID:

YOU SHALL NO LONGER BE A SLAVE. AND THE CHILD THAT YOU BEAR SHALL BE INTELLIGENT AND WISE.

AND THE SON BORN TO HER BY THE GRACE OF MY GURU VYASA WAS VIDURA, THE BROTHER OF DHRITARASHTRA AND PANDU, THE PROPAGATORS OF THE KURU RACE.

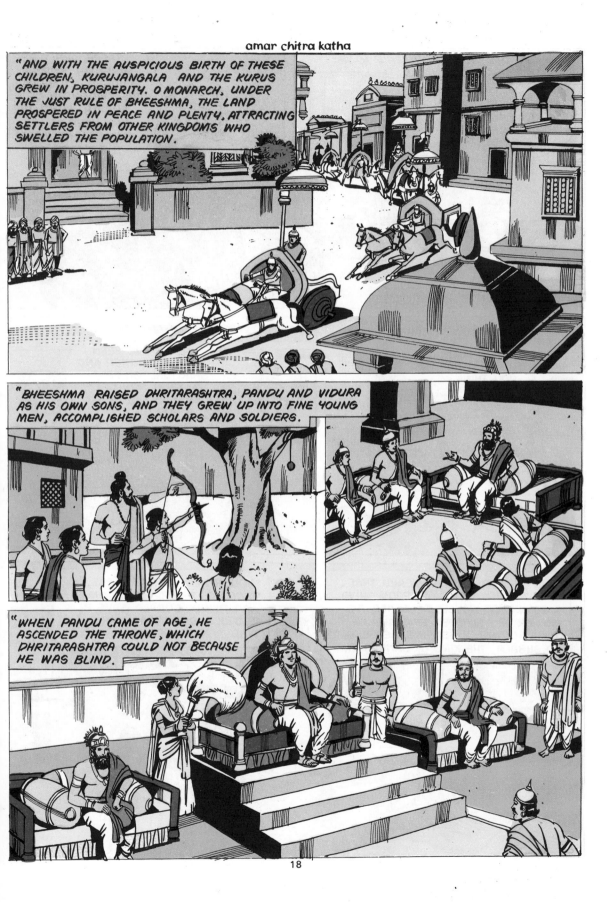

"AND WITH THE AUSPICIOUS BIRTH OF THESE CHILDREN, KURUJANGALA AND THE KURUS GREW IN PROSPERITY. O MONARCH, UNDER THE JUST RULE OF BHEESHMA, THE LAND PROSPERED IN PEACE AND PLENTY, ATTRACTING SETTLERS FROM OTHER KINGDOMS WHO SWELLED THE POPULATION.

"BHEESHMA RAISED DHRITARASHTRA, PANDU AND VIDURA AS HIS OWN SONS, AND THEY GREW UP INTO FINE YOUNG MEN, ACCOMPLISHED SCHOLARS AND SOLDIERS.

"WHEN PANDU CAME OF AGE, HE ASCENDED THE THRONE, WHICH DHRITARASHTRA COULD NOT BECAUSE HE WAS BLIND.

"THEN ONE DAY, BHEESHMA SAID TO THE WISE AND LEARNED VIDURA:

THE TIME IS RIPE FOR US TO PLAN THE FUTURE OF OUR DYNASTY.

THERE ARE THREE EMINENTLY WORTHY MAIDENS — GANDHARI, THE DAUGHTER OF SUBALA, KUNTI THE DAUGHTER OF SHOORA, AND MADRI THE SISTER OF SHALYA.

I THINK THEY WILL MAKE IDEAL WIVES FOR OUR PRINCES TO KEEP OUR RACE ALIVE. WHAT DO YOU THINK?

"TO THIS, VIDURA REPLIED:

YOU HAVE BEEN MOTHER, FATHER AND SPIRITUAL GUIDE TO US. WHAT YOU DEEM BEST, IS THE BEST FOR US.

AND THEN, BHEESHMA HEARD THAT GANDHARI HAD OBTAINED, FROM SHIVA, A BOON THAT WOULD MAKE HER THE MOTHER OF A HUNDRED SONS. AND HE LOST NO TIME IN SENDING MESSENGERS TO SUBALA, THE KING OF GANDHARA.

THOUGH HESITANT AT FIRST, BECAUSE THE BRIDEGROOM WAS BLIND, SUBALA GAVE IN BECAUSE DHRITARASHTRA WAS A KURU PRINCE.

"WHEN GANDHARI HEARD THAT SHE WAS TO BE MARRIED TO A BLIND PRINCE, SHE BLINDFOLDED HERSELF IN A GESTURE OF LOVE AND RESPECT.

"SHAKUNI, THE SON OF SUBALA, ESCORTED HIS SISTER TO THE LAND OF THE KURUS...

"...WHERE SHE WAS RESPECTFULLY RECEIVED.

"AND THERE, UNDER BHEESHMA'S DIRECTIONS, THE WEDDING OF DHRITARASHTRA AND GANDHARI WAS CELEBRATED WITH GREAT POMP.

THEN SHAKUNI, HAVING GIVEN AWAY HIS SISTER ALONG WITH MANY VALUABLE ROBES, RETURNED TO GANDHARA.

THUS DID DHRITARASHTRA OBTAIN THE DAUGHTER OF SUBALA FOR A WIFE.

"AS SOON AS DURVASA WENT AWAY, THE CURIOUS PRINCESS, TO SEE IF THE MANTRA WOULD WORK, SUMMONED SURYA THE LORD OF LIGHT.

" AND A SON WAS BORN TO HER, CLAD IN ARMOUR AND DECKED WITH EARRINGS — THE SON WHO LATER BECAME KNOWN IN THE WORLD AS KARNA.

" DISTRESSED BY THE BIRTH OF A SON IN HER MAIDENHOOD, AND AFRAID OF HER RELATIVES, KUNTI THOUGHT DEEPLY ON WHAT WAS BEST FOR HER TO DO.

AND SHE CAST THE INFANT INTO THE RIVER, WHERE THE HUSBAND OF RADHA OF THE SOOTA CASTE FOUND HIM.

"AND HE AND HIS WIFE RAISED THE INFANT AS THEIR OWN SON. AND BECAUSE HE WAS CLAD IN ARMOUR AND GOLD EARRINGS, THEY CALLED HIM VASUSHENA.

"MEANWHILE, KUNTIBHOJA INVITED SEVERAL PRINCES AND KINGS SO THAT KUNTI COULD SELECT A HUSBAND FROM AMONG THEM. AND KUNTI BEHELD PANDU, THE NOBLEST IN THE ROYAL ASSEMBLY.

" PANDU, THE SCION OF THE KURU RACE, MAGNIFICENT LIKE ANOTHER INDRA IN HIS ROYAL SPLENDOUR, ATTRACTED KUNTI. AND WITH BECOMING MODESTY, SHE ADVANCED TOWARDS HIM AND GARLANDED HIM.

"AFTER THE WEDDING, KUNTIBHOJA PRESENTED HIS SON-IN-LAW WITH MANY VALUABLE GIFTS. PANDU, ALONG WITH KUNTI, THEN RETURNED TO HASTINAPURA.

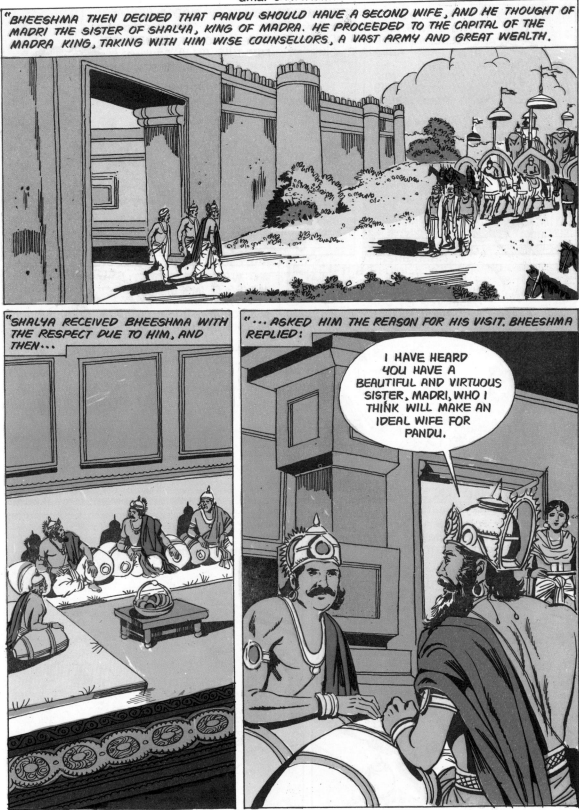

"BHEESHMA THEN DECIDED THAT PANDU SHOULD HAVE A SECOND WIFE, AND HE THOUGHT OF MADRI THE SISTER OF SHALYA, KING OF MADRA. HE PROCEEDED TO THE CAPITAL OF THE MADRA KING, TAKING WITH HIM WISE COUNSELLORS, A VAST ARMY AND GREAT WEALTH.

"SHALYA RECEIVED BHEESHMA WITH THE RESPECT DUE TO HIM, AND THEN...

"...ASKED HIM THE REASON FOR HIS VISIT. BHEESHMA REPLIED:

I HAVE HEARD YOU HAVE A BEAUTIFUL AND VIRTUOUS SISTER, MADRI, WHO I THINK WILL MAKE AN IDEAL WIFE FOR PANDU.

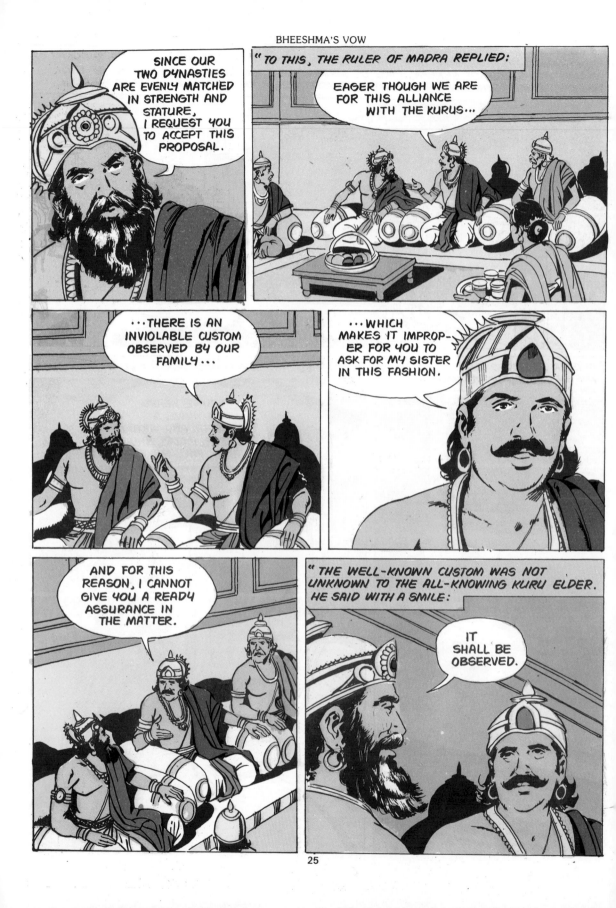

SINCE OUR TWO DYNASTIES ARE EVENLY MATCHED IN STRENGTH AND STATURE, I REQUEST YOU TO ACCEPT THIS PROPOSAL.

"TO THIS, THE RULER OF MADRA REPLIED:

EAGER THOUGH WE ARE FOR THIS ALLIANCE WITH THE KURUS...

...THERE IS AN INVIOLABLE CUSTOM OBSERVED BY OUR FAMILY...

...WHICH MAKES IT IMPROPER FOR YOU TO ASK FOR MY SISTER IN THIS FASHION.

AND FOR THIS REASON, I CANNOT GIVE YOU A READY ASSURANCE IN THE MATTER.

"THE WELL-KNOWN CUSTOM WAS NOT UNKNOWN TO THE ALL-KNOWING KURU ELDER. HE SAID WITH A SMILE:

IT SHALL BE OBSERVED.

"AND BHEESHMA, CONFORMING TO THE MADRA CUSTOM, GAVE SHALYA UNTOLD WEALTH IN GOLD, PEARLS, CORALS, PRECIOUS STONES AND CLOTH, BESIDES ELEPHANTS, HORSES AND CHARIOTS. SHALYA READILY ACCEPTED THOSE PRECIOUS GIFTS AND...

"...GAVE AWAY HIS SISTER, DECKED IN ORNAMENTS, TO THE KURUS.

"PLEASED WITH HIS MISSION, BHEESHMA RODE OUT TO HASTINAPURA WITH MADRI BY HIS SIDE

" LATER, ON AN AUSPICIOUS DAY AND MOMENT, PANDU WAS UNITED WITH MADRI.

"PANDU SPENT THE NEXT THIRTY DAYS IN THE COMPANY OF HIS TWO WIVES. THEN WITH A WELL-EQUIPPED ARMY, HE SET OUT ON A CAMPAIGN OF CONQUEST.

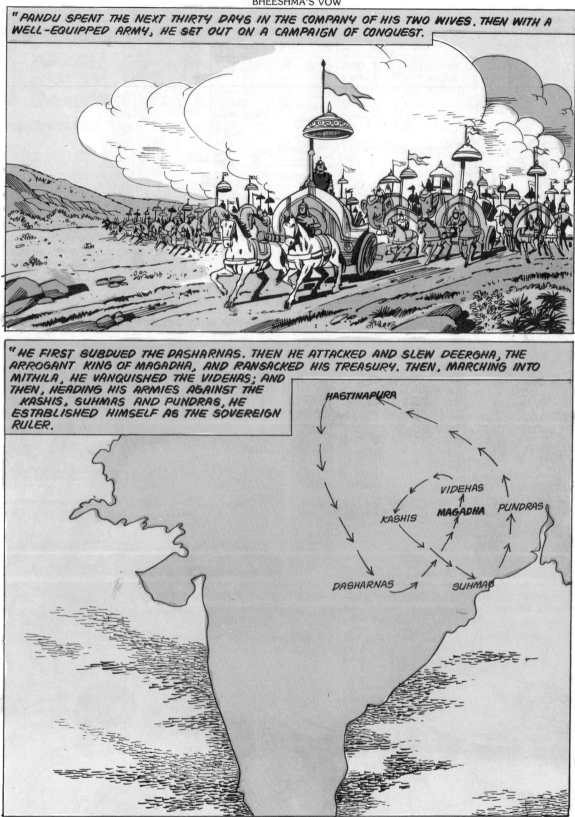

"HE FIRST SUBDUED THE DASHARNAS. THEN HE ATTACKED AND SLEW DEERGHA, THE ARROGANT KING OF MAGADHA, AND RANSACKED HIS TREASURY. THEN, MARCHING INTO MITHILA, HE VANQUISHED THE VIDEHAS; AND THEN, HEADING HIS ARMIES AGAINST THE KASHIS, SUHMAS AND PUNDRAS, HE ESTABLISHED HIMSELF AS THE SOVEREIGN RULER.

HASTINAPURA

VIDEHAS
MAGADHA
PUNDRAS
KASHIS

DASHARNAS
SUHMAS

"LIKE A MIGHTY FIRE, WHOSE FAR-REACHING FLAMES WERE HIS ARROWS, WHOSE SPLENDOUR HIS WEAPONS, PANDU VANQUISHED ALL THE OTHER KINGS ON HIS ROUTE, AND MADE THEM VASSALS OF THE KURUS.

"AND THESE VASSAL KINGS BROUGHT HIM GIFTS OF PRECIOUS STONES, PEARLS, CORALS, MUCH GOLD AND SILVER, AND COWS AND HORSES AND FINE CHARIOTS AND ELEPHANTS AND ASSES AND CAMELS AND BUFFALOES AND GOATS AND SHEEP AND BLANKETS AND BEAUTIFUL HIDES AND CLOTH WOVEN OUT OF FUR.

THE KING OF HASTINAPURA ACCEPTED THESE GIFTS AND RETURNED TO HIS CAPITAL.

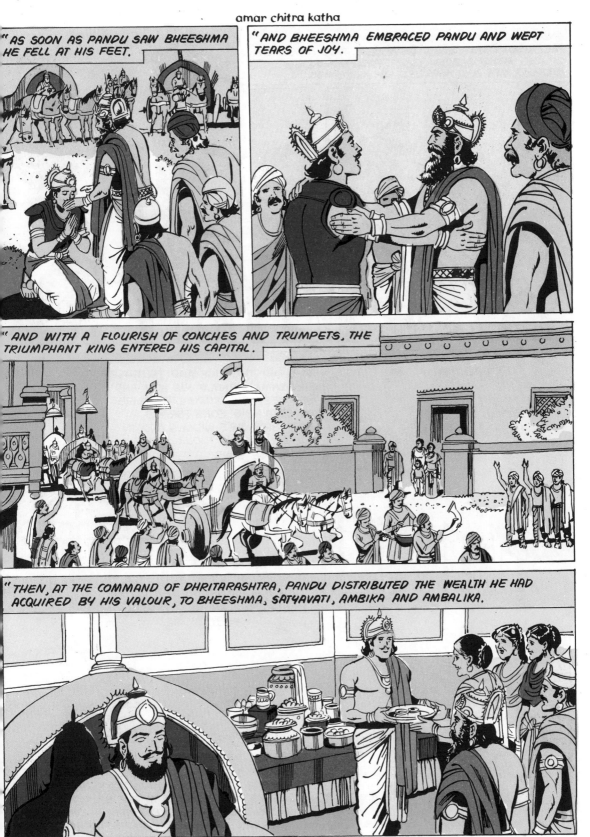

"AS SOON AS PANDU SAW BHEESHMA HE FELL AT HIS FEET.

"AND BHEESHMA EMBRACED PANDU AND WEPT TEARS OF JOY.

"AND WITH A FLOURISH OF CONCHES AND TRUMPETS, THE TRIUMPHANT KING ENTERED HIS CAPITAL.

"THEN, AT THE COMMAND OF DHRITARASHTRA, PANDU DISTRIBUTED THE WEALTH HE HAD ACQUIRED BY HIS VALOUR, TO BHEESHMA, SATYAVATI, AMBIKA AND AMBALIKA.

"AND PANDU SENT A PORTION TO VIDURA ALSO. BHEESHMA THEN HEARD OF A BEAUTIFUL DAUGHTER OF KING DEVAKA, BORN TO A SHOODRA WIFE. HE BROUGHT HER AND MARRIED HER TO VIDURA.

THUS DID THE WISE AND TRUTHFUL BHEESHMA UPHOLD HIS VOW AND YET KEEP THE KURU LINE ALIVE BY OBTAINING SONS FOR HIS STEP-BROTHER'S WIDOWS AND, IN DUE COURSE, VIRTUOUS WIVES FOR THOSE SONS.

AND THUS ENDS THE SECOND SESSION OF OUR RENDERING OF VAISHAMPAYANA'S NARRATION— DURING THE INTERVALS IN THE SACRIFICIAL RITES OF JANAMEJAYA'S SARPA SATRA — OF VYASA'S IMMORTAL ITIHASA, THE MAHABHARATA.

MAHABHARATA-3
The Advent of the Kuru Princes

VEDA VYASA'S EPIC ON THE BHARATA RACE WAS FIRST RECITED IN PUBLIC, BY HIS DISCIPLE VAISHAMPAYANA, AT THE BEHEST OF THE AGELESS SEER VYASA HIMSELF.

THE RECITAL TOOK PLACE IN THE AUGUST PRESENCE OF KING JANAMEJAYA — THE GREAT-GRANDSON OF THE GRANDSON OF VYASA — AND THE MANY LEARNED SAGES WHO HAD ASSEMBLED FOR JANAMEJAYA'S SARPA⊗ SATRA.*

THE SECOND SESSION OF OUR RENDERING OF VAISHAMPAYANA'S RECITAL DESCRIBED THE ROLES PLAYED BY BHEESHMA AND VYASA IN KEEPING THE KURU LINE ALIVE. IT ENDED WITH PANDU GIVING AWAY ALL THE WEALTH HE HAD ACQUIRED IN CONQUESTS TO BHEESHMA, SATYAVATI, AMBIKA, AMBALIKA AND VIDURA.

⊗ SNAKE ⊛ 12-YEAR-LONG-YAGNA.
FOR PRONUNCIATION AND MEANING OF SANSKRIT WORDS AND PROPER NAMES, PLEASE SEE PAGE 32.

AFTER GIVING AWAY THE WEALTH HE HAD ACQUIRED BY HIS VALOUR, YOUR GREAT-GRANDFATHER PANDU WENT TO LIVE IN THE FORESTS ALONG WITH HIS WIVES, KUNTI AND MADRI. AND THERE HE SPENT MOST OF HIS TIME HUNTING DEER.

"HE CHOSE FOR HIS STAY A SYLVAN SLOPE OF THE SOUTHERN HIMALAYAS.

"HE ROAMED THE FOREST, RESPLENDENT IN HIS ARMOUR AND FEARLESS WITH HIS SWORD, BOW AND ARROWS. AND THE FOREST DWELLERS LOOKED UPON HIM AS IF HE WERE A DEVA COME DOWN AMONG THEM.

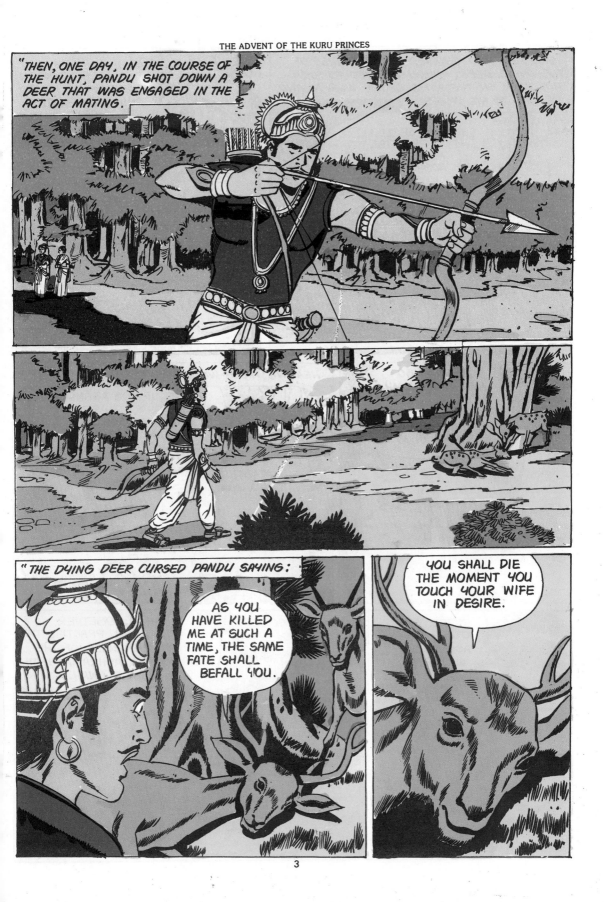

"THEN, ONE DAY, IN THE COURSE OF THE HUNT, PANDU SHOT DOWN A DEER THAT WAS ENGAGED IN THE ACT OF MATING.

"THE DYING DEER CURSED PANDU SAYING:

AS YOU HAVE KILLED ME AT SUCH A TIME, THE SAME FATE SHALL BEFALL YOU.

YOU SHALL DIE THE MOMENT YOU TOUCH YOUR WIFE IN DESIRE.

"SHOCKED AND GRIEVED AT THE CURSE OF THE DYING DEER, PANDU DECIDED TO TURN HIS BACK ON THE WAYS OF THE WORLD. AND HE SAID TO HIS WIVES:

I SHALL PRACTISE ABSTINENCE AND ADOPT AN ASCETIC MODE OF LIFE.

I SHALL FORSAKE YOU AND MY RELATIVES, AND WANDER OVER THE WORLD WITH A SHAVEN HEAD AND A BEGGING-BOWL.

YOU MAY GO AND INFORM MY MOTHER, VIDURA, BHEESHMA AND ALL AT HASTINAPURA OF THIS.

"HEARING THESE WORDS KUNTI AND MADRI SAID:

O KING, IF YOU ABANDON US, WE SHALL THIS VERY MOMENT GIVE UP OUR LIVES.

THERE ARE OTHER PATHS TO ASCETICISM WHERE WE YOUR WIVES CAN BE YOUR COMPANIONS. WE TOO SHALL RENOUNCE THE TEMPTATIONS OF THE WORLD.

"PANDU REPLIED:

THEN, TOGETHER WE SHALL PRACTISE THE AUSTERE PENANCES OF THE VANAPRASTHA ASHRAMA, UNTIL I PASS AWAY.

THE KURU KING THEN DISTRIBUTED, TO DESERVING BRAHMANAS, ALL THE VALUABLE ROBES AND ORNAMENTS BELONGING TO HIM AND HIS WIVES.

"AND HE SUMMONED HIS ATTENDANTS AND SAID:

LET IT BE KNOWN TO ALL AT HASTINAPURA THAT PANDU AND HIS WIVES HAVE RENOUNCED THE WORLD AND GONE TO THE FOREST.

"AND THE ATTENDANTS MADE THEIR WAY TO HASTINAPURA WITH HEAVY HEARTS.

"WHEN DHRITARASHTRA HEARD WHAT THEY HAD TO SAY, HE BROODED OVER HIS BROTHER'S FATE, AND WAS GRAVELY DISTURBED.

"MEANWHILE, ONE DAY, MY GURU VYASA CAME WEARY AND HUNGRY TO THE PALACE AT HASTINAPURA.

PLEASED BY GANDHARI'S HOSPITALITY, HE GRANTED HER THE BOON SHE DESIRED; A HUNDRED SONS EQUAL IN MIGHT TO DHRITARASHTRA.

"IN DUE COURSE, GANDHARI CONCEIVED. BUT TWO YEARS WENT BY, WITHOUT HER BEING DELIVERED.

"AND SHE HEARD THAT A BRILLIANT SON WAS BORN TO KUNTI. THE SON WAS YUDHISHTHIRA.

TURNING DESPERATE AND RASH WITH IMPATIENCE AND ENVY, SHE STRUCK HERSELF WITH GREAT FORCE. AND SHE WAS DELIVERED OF A LUMP OF FLESH AS HARD AS AN IRON BALL.

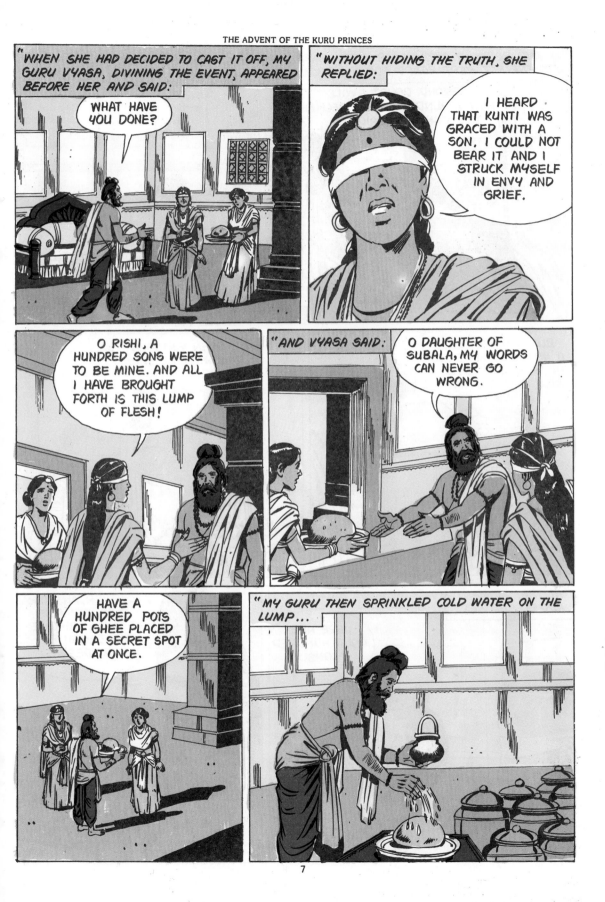

"WHEN SHE HAD DECIDED TO CAST IT OFF, MY GURU VYASA, DIVINING THE EVENT, APPEARED BEFORE HER AND SAID:

WHAT HAVE YOU DONE?

"WITHOUT HIDING THE TRUTH, SHE REPLIED:

I HEARD THAT KUNTI WAS GRACED WITH A SON. I COULD NOT BEAR IT AND I STRUCK MYSELF IN ENVY AND GRIEF.

O RISHI, A HUNDRED SONS WERE TO BE MINE. AND ALL I HAVE BROUGHT FORTH IS THIS LUMP OF FLESH!

"AND VYASA SAID:

O DAUGHTER OF SUBALA, MY WORDS CAN NEVER GO WRONG.

HAVE A HUNDRED POTS OF GHEE PLACED IN A SECRET SPOT AT ONCE.

"MY GURU THEN SPRINKLED COLD WATER ON THE LUMP...

"...AND BROKE IT INTO THUMB-SIZED PARTS. EACH PART WAS DEPOSITED BY A MIDWIFE INTO THE POT KEPT READY FOR IT. WHILE THIS WAS GOING ON, GANDHARI THOUGHT TO HERSELF:

BEYOND DOUBT I WILL HAVE A HUNDRED SONS BECAUSE THE MUNI HAS SAID SO.

BUT A DAUGHTER, A YOUNGER SISTER TO THESE HUNDRED SONS, WILL GIVE ME IMMENSE JOY.

IF I HAVE BEEN VIRTUOUS, LET A DAUGHTER BE BORN TO ME.

"AT THAT MOMENT MY PERCEPTIVE GURU ADDRESSED HER:

HERE ARE YOUR HUNDRED SONS.

HOWEVER, AN EXTRA PART REMAINS. IT SHALL BECOME THE DAUGHTER YOU DESIRE.

"GRIPPED BY FEAR, DHRITARASHTRA SUMMONED BHEESHMA, VIDURA, AND OTHER WISE MEN AND SAID:

BY VIRTUE OF HIS BIRTH, YUDHISHTHIRA THE FIRSTBORN PRINCE WILL RULE THE LAND; WHICH IS AS IT SHOULD BE.

BUT AFTER HIM, WILL THIS SON OF MINE BECOME KING? TELL ME TRULY WHAT THE FUTURE HOLDS FOR HIM.

REE-EE-K

YEO-O-O-O

"EVEN AS DHRITARASHTRA SPOKE, THE AIR WAS RENT WITH THE WIERD HOWLS OF BEASTS OF PREY. MARKING THESE ILL OMENS, VIDURA SAID:

THESE OMENS PORTEND THAT YOUR ELDEST SON SHALL BE THE RUIN OF YOUR RACE AND THIS LAND.

YEO-O-OO

GR-R-R-R

YEO-O-OO

ABANDON HIM FOR THE SAKE OF YOUR RACE.

YOU WILL STILL HAVE NINETY-NINE SONS LEFT. FOR THE SAKE OF YOUR OWN RACE AND THE LAND, DISCARD THIS CHILD.

IT IS SAID THAT AN INDIVIDUAL MAY BE GIVEN UP FOR THE GOOD OF THE CLAN; A CLAN FOR THE VILLAGE, A VILLAGE FOR THE COUNTRY, AND THUS THE EARTH ITSELF FOR THE SOUL.

BUT LOVE FOR HIS SON DID NOT LET DHRITARASHTRA HEED THE ADVICE.

SOON AFTER THE BIRTH OF DURYODHANA WAS BORN YUYUTSU, THE SON OF DHRITARASHTRA AND A WOMAN OF THE VAISHYA CASTE.

THEN CAME THE REMAINING NINETY-NINE SONS OF GANDHARI AND THE DAUGHTER DUHSHALA.

12

"PANDU SOON BECAME A FAVOURITE OF THE HOLY MEN AT SHATASHRINGA. ONCE WHEN THEY WERE ABOUT TO SET OUT FOR THE ABODE OF BRAHMAN, PANDU WITH HIS WIVES JOINED THEM. THEN THE RISHIS SAID:

THE MOUNTAINS BEYOND SHATASHRINGA ARE FORMIDABLE. HOW WILL THESE PRINCESSES CLIMB OVER THOSE HEIGHTS? DO NOT COME WITH US.

"SO PANDU SAID:

THEN YOU TELL ME, RECALLING THE EVENTS THAT LED TO MY BIRTH, MAY I OBTAIN CHILDREN IN THE SAME MANNER?

"THE RISHIS REPLIED:

SEERS THAT WE ARE, WE SEE PROGENY IN STORE FOR YOU. ACHIEVE BY YOUR EFFORTS WHAT DESTINY HOLDS FOR YOU.

DO WHAT YOU OUGHT TO DO. YOU SHALL BE REWARDED.

"AFTER LISTENING TO THE WORDS OF THE RISHIS AND EVER AWARE OF THE CURSE OF THE DEER, PANDU CALLED KUNTI ASIDE AND SAID:

MANU HAS SAID THAT MEN, FAILING TO HAVE OFFSPRING OF THEIR OWN, MAY BEGET THEM THROUGH OTHER CHOSEN ONES.

THEREFORE HEARKEN TO ME AND BRING FORTH THE CHILDREN BY THE GRACE OF ONE WHO HAS REALISED BRAHMAN.

"KUNTI REPLIED:

NOT EVEN IN MY THOUGHTS CAN I ENTERTAIN A MAN OTHER THAN YOU. BESIDES, WHO IS THERE WHO EXCELS YOU AMONG MEN?

I AM YOUR LAWFUL WIFE. YOU BEGET OUR CHILDREN AND WHEN THEY ARE BORN I SHALL FOLLOW YOU TO HEAVEN.

"PANDU, WELL VERSED IN THE WAYS OF MORALITY, TOLD HER:

IN THE DAYS OF YORE, WOMEN WERE FREE TO CONDUCT THEIR LIVES AS THEY DESIRED. THEY WERE NOT EVEN BOUND TO ONE MAN.

THE PRACTICE WAS CONSIDERED RIGHT, AND NOT IMMORAL. BESIDES IT IS ETERNALLY FAVOURABLE TO WOMEN.

IT WAS SHWETAKETU, THE SON OF RISHI UDDALAKA, WHO FORCED THE PRESENT RESTRAINTS ON WOMEN.

YOU ARE ALSO AWARE, KUNTI, HOW OUR OWN LINE OF THE KURUS WAS KEPT ALIVE BY KRISHNA DWAIPAYANA. THEREFORE DO WHAT IS RIGHT AS I HAVE STATED.

" THEN, KUNTI TOLD PANDU OF HER MANTRA FROM RISHI DURVASA AND SAID:

THE POWER OF THE MANTRA CAN SUMMON ANY DEITY TO BEGET CHILDREN FOR US. TELL ME WHICH DEITY I SHOULD SUMMON.

" PANDU REPLIED:

SUMMON DHARMA, WITHOUT DELAY. BEING THE DEITY OF RIGHTEOUSNESS, HE WILL RENDER OUR ACTION IMMACULATE, AND THE SON BORN WILL BE THE MOST RIGHTEOUS OF THE KURUS.

" KUNTI CHANTED THE MANTRA AND DRAWN BY ITS POWER...

"...DHARMA, THE PRESIDING DEITY OF RIGHTEOUSNESS, ARRIVED TO DO HER BIDDING.

" AND BY HIS GRACE KUNTI OBTAINED AN EXCELLENT SON. AND AS SOON AS HE WAS BORN, A VOICE FROM THE REALMS ABOVE SAID:

THIS FIRST CHILD OF PANDU SHALL BE NAMED YUDHISHTHIRA. HE SHALL REIGN AS A KING, FAMOUS IN ALL THE THREE WORLDS FOR HIS UNFLINCHING RIGHTEOUSNESS AND HONESTY.

"AFTER THE BIRTH OF YUDHISHTHIRA, PANDU SAID TO KUNTI:

IT IS SAID THAT PHYSICAL STRENGTH IS THE DISTINCTION OF A KSHATRIYA.

THEREFORE OBTAIN A SON OF IMMENSE MIGHT.

"ACCORDINGLY, KUNTI INVOKED VAYU AND THAT POWERFUL DEITY OF WIND ARRIVED AND SAID:

O KUNTI, TELL ME WHAT IS ON YOUR MIND.

"SMILING MODESTLY, KUNTI REPLIED:

GIVE ME A STRONG SON WHOSE MIGHT WILL HUMBLE THE PRIDE OF THE MIGHTIEST.

"AND THEN WAS BORN BHEEMA OF MATCHLESS STRENGTH AND VALOUR, AND A VOICE FROM THE REALMS ABOVE SAID:

THIS CHILD SHALL BE THE MIGHTIEST OF THE MIGHTY.

"SOON AFTER HIS BIRTH, O MONARCH, BHEEMA WAS SLEEPING IN KUNTI'S LAP...

"...WHEN, STARTLED BY THE GROWL OF A TIGER, SHE SUDDENLY ROSE AND BHEEMA WAS THROWN OFF.

"THE INFANT FELL ON A ROCK, WHICH HIS BODY, HARD AS AGATE, BROKE INTO SMITHEREENS.

AND AS IT HAPPENED, BHEEMA WAS BORN ON THE SAME DAY AS DURYODHANA.

" AFTER THE BIRTH OF BHEEMA, PANDU REFLECTED:

HOW SHALL I OBTAIN A SON WHO WILL WIN THE ADMIRATION OF THE WHOLE WORLD?

* DESTINY AND HUMAN EFFORT TOGETHER MAKE THE WORLD GO. WITHOUT TIMELY EFFORT DESTINY CAN NEVER FULFIL ITSELF.

I KNOW INDRA TO BE THE MOST POTENT AND GLORIOUS AMONG THE DEVAS.

I SHALL PLEASE HIM, BY MY UNSTINTED PENANCE, TO OBTAIN A SON WHO IS SUPERIOR TO ALL AND INVINCIBLE IN BATTLE.

THEN, TO GRATIFY INDRA, PANDU PRESCRIBED OBSERVANCE OF A YEAR— LONG VOW FOR KUNTI. AS FOR HIMSELF, HE OBSERVED DIRE PENANCES AND DEEP MEDITATION, STANDING HIMSELF UP ON ONE LEG FROM DAWN TO DUSK.

* दैवे पुरुषकारे च लोकोऽयं हि प्रतिष्ठितः ।
तत्र दैवं तु विधिना कालयुक्तेन लभ्यते ।

"WHEN MUCH TIME HAD ELAPSED, INDRA CAME TO PANDU AND SAID:

I SHALL GIVE YOU A SON WHO WILL BE A FRIEND TO THE VIRTUOUS AND A DESTROYER TO HIS FOES. HE SHALL BE FAMOUS IN ALL THE THREE WORLDS.

"PANDU THEN SAID TO KUNTI:

THE CHIEF OF DEVAS IS WELL PLEASED. YOU SHALL SOON HAVE A SON WHO IS BRILLIANT AND SUPERHUMAN IN SKILLS. NOBLE AND HANDSOME, HE WILL ALSO BE INVINCIBLE IN BATTLE.

INVOKE INDRA FOR A SON WHO WILL BE THE EMBODIMENT OF KSHATRIYA GLORY.

INVOKED BY THE POWER OF THE MANTRA, O MONARCH, INDRA APPEARED BEFORE KUNTI. AND THE SON BORN TO HER BY INDRA'S GRACE WAS ARJUNA, YOUR GREAT-GRANDFATHER.

"AND AS SOON AS THE CHILD WAS BORN, THE EARTH AND THE SKY RESOUNDED WITH A VOICE FROM THE REALMS ABOVE WHICH ADDRESSED KUNTI THUS IN LOUD, CLEAR TONES:

THIS INVINCIBLE CHILD WILL MAKE YOU FAMOUS.

IN VALOUR HE WILL EQUAL VISHNU, SHIVA AND PARASHURAMA.

HIS MIGHT WILL ONE DAY SET THE KHANDAVA FOREST ABLAZE AND GRATIFY AGNI WITH THE FAT OF THE CREATURES IN IT.

HE WILL WIN THE ADMIRATION OF SHIVA IN COMBAT AND WILL THEREBY OBTAIN THE PASHUPATA WEAPON FROM HIM.

HE WILL, AT THE BEHEST OF INDRA, ANNIHILATE THE NIVATAKAVACHAS, FOES OF THE DEVAS.

HE WILL ACQUIRE ALL THE MYSTERIOUS MISSILES AND RESTORE THE GLORY OF THE KURUS.

"THESE WORDS, LOUD AND CLEAR, GLADDENED THE HEARTS OF THE RISHIS OF SHATASHRINGA AND THE DEVAS ABOVE. OTHER CELESTIAL BEINGS OF DIVERSE ORDERS, TOO, CROWDED THE SKIES IN ADORATION OF THIS SON OF KUNTI.

THE RISHIS OF SHATASHRINGA WERE THE ONLY WITNESSES TO THE UNIQUE SCENE. AND IT MADE THEM CHERISH THE SONS OF PANDU EVEN MORE.

"WHEN PANDU, EAGER FOR MORE CHILDREN, SPOKE TO KUNTI AGAIN, SHE REPLIED:

* THE WISE HAVE DECREED AGAINST A FOURTH CHILD EVEN IN TIMES OF CALAMITY.

THOUGH YOU KNOW WHAT IS ORDAINED IN THE SHASTRAS, WHY DO YOU IN YOUR EAGERNESS FOR OFFSPRING ASK ME TO DEVIATE?

HOW THEN WERE MY ANCESTORS THE TWINS NAKULA AND SAHADEVA BORN, O SAGE?

* नातश्चतुर्थं प्रसवमापत्स्वपि वदन्त्युत।

22

THEY WERE BORN TO PANDU'S SECOND WIFE, MADRI THE SISTER OF SHALYA.

" AFTER THE BIRTH OF CHILDREN TO KUNTI AND TO GANDHARI, MADRI SAID TO PANDU:

THE PREFERENCE SHOWN BY YOU TO KUNTI LITTLE GRIEVES ME, FOR I AM HER JUNIOR.

NEITHER DOES THE BIRTH OF A HUNDRED SONS TO GANDHARI CAUSE ME ANY ANGUISH.

BUT WHAT IS MOST PAINFUL IS THAT, THOUGH I AM YOUR WIFE AS KUNTI IS, I REMAIN CHILDLESS.

IF KUNTI WERE TO LET ME BENEFIT BY THE MANTRA, IT WOULD BENEFIT YOU ALSO.

BUT AS SHE IS MY RIVAL FOR YOUR AFFECTION, I CONSIDER IT DEMEANING TO GO TO HER FOR A FAVOUR.

IF WHAT I SAY HAS YOUR APPROVAL, PLEASE SPEAK TO KUNTI ON MY BEHALF.

PANDU REPLIED: THE THOUGHT HAS ALWAYS BEEN WITH ME. I HESITATED TO REVEAL IT BECAUSE I DID NOT KNOW THE DRIFT OF YOUR MIND.

NOW THAT I AM ASSURED BY YOU, I SHALL APPROACH KUNTI WHO, I THINK, WILL AGREE.

"AND PANDU WENT TO KUNTI AND SAID: TO ENSURE THE EXPANSION OF MY RACE AND TO MAKE YOUR NAME IMMORTAL, O KUNTI, DO WHAT WILL INDEED BE HARD FOR YOU. HELP MADRI TO BECOME A MOTHER.

KUNTI ACCEDED TO PANDU'S REQUEST. AND MADRI DULY BROUGHT FORTH THE TWINS NAKULA AND SAHADEVA BY INVOKING THE TWIN DEITIES, THE ASHWINS

"AND AS SOON AS THEY WERE BORN, A VOICE FROM THE REALMS ABOVE SAID:

IN VIGOUR AND BEAUTY THE TWINS SHALL EXCEL ALL.

" AFTER THEIR BIRTH, PANDU ONCE AGAIN SPOKE TO KUNTI ON BEHALF OF MADRI. BUT KUNTI REPLIED:

USING THE MANTRA ONCE, SHE HAS BROUGHT FORTH TWO SONS.

ARTLESS THAT I WAS, I DID NOT THINK OF INVOKING THE TWINS FOR TWIN CHILDREN.

HER STEALTHY WAYS CAUSE ME ANXIETY. THEREFORE DO NOT COMMAND ME FURTHER.

PANDU LET THE MATTER REST. THEN THE RISHIS OF SHATASHRINGA CONDUCTED THE RITES OF INITIATION OF THE FIVE CHILDREN AND CEREMONIALLY NAMED THEM, YUDHISHTHIRA, BHEEMA, ARJUNA, NAKULA AND SAHADEVA.

"THE RISHIS OF SHATASHRINGA WATCHED THE SONS OF PANDU GROW INTO YOUNG BOYS OF LION-LIKE PROWESS AND THEY MARVELLED. AND PANDU HIMSELF WAS ELATED AT THE SIGHT OF HIS SONS NURTURED UNDER HIS MIGHTY ARM.

"THEN ONE DAY IN THE SEASON OF SPRING, WHICH STIRS THE SENSES OF ALL CREATED THINGS, PANDU STROLLED THROUGH THE WOODS ACCOMPANIED BY MADRI.

IN THAT SENSUOUS SCENERY, MADRI LOOKED IRRESISTIBLE TO PANDU. SEEKING A COMPULSIVE UNION WITH HER, HE FELL A VICTIM TO THE INESCAPABLE LAWS OF FATE.

AND, CLASPING THE LIFE-LESS PANDU IN DEEP GRIEF, MADRI BEGAN TO WEEP ALOUD. HER LOUD WAILS BROUGHT KUNTI AND THE CHILDREN TO THAT SPOT.

"AND MADRI CRIED OUT IN ANGUISH:

LEAVE THE CHILDREN THERE AND COME HERE ALONE.

"KUNTI LEFT THE CHILDREN WHERE THEY WERE AND RAN TOWARDS MADRI, CRYING:

I AM UNDONE!

27

"TO THIS MADRI REPLIED:

O REVERED SISTER, IF I SURVIVE YOU, IT IS CERTAIN I WILL NOT BE ABLE TO REAR YOUR CHILDREN AS IF THEY WERE MINE.

BUT YOU, O KUNTI, WILL WITHOUT DOUBT BRING UP THE CHILDREN IN EQUAL GRACE.

AS IT WAS IN THE PURSUIT OF MY BODY THAT THE KING MET WITH HIS DEATH, IT IS THIS BODY OF MINE THAT SHOULD BE BURNT WITH HIS.

WITH THESE FINAL WORDS, MADRI ASCENDED THE FUNERAL PYRE OF HER HUSBAND.

"THE RISHIS OF SHATASHRINGA, WITNESSING THE DEATH OF PANDU, CONFERRED AMONGST THEMSELVES AND SAID:

THE WORTHY KING PANDU HAD COME HERE AND HAD SOUGHT TO LIVE THE LIFE OF A RECLUSE WITH US. IT IS OUR DUTY TO LEAD HIS WIFE AND CHILDREN BACK TO HIS KINGDOM.

" THEN, TO ENTRUST THE SONS OF PANDU TO BHEESHMA AND DHRITARASHTRA, THE RISHIS SET OUT FOR HASTINAPURA WITH KUNTI, THE CHILDREN AND THE CHARRED REMAINS OF PANDU AND MADRI.

AND THUS ENDS THE THIRD SESSION OF OUR RENDERING OF VAISHAMPAYANA'S RECITAL OF VYASA'S IMORTAL ITIHASA, THE MAHABHARATA.

MAHABHARATA-4
The Pandavas at Hastinapura

VEDA VYASA'S EPIC ON THE BHARATA RACE WAS FIRST RECITED IN PUBLIC, BY HIS DISCIPLE VAISHAMPAYANA, AT THE BEHEST OF VYASA HIMSELF.

THE RECITAL TOOK PLACE IN THE AUGUST PRESENCE OF KING JANAMEJAYA—GREAT-GRANDSON OF THE GRANDSON OF VYASA—AND THE MANY LEARNED SAGES WHO HAD ASSEMBLED FOR JANAMEJAYA'S SARPA SATRA.

THE THIRD SESSION OF OUR RENDERING OF VAISHAMPAYANA'S RECITAL, OF VYASA'S MAHABHARATA, DESCRIBED THE MARVELLOUS BIRTHS OF THE PANDAVAS AND THE KAURAVAS AND THE DEATH OF PANDU AND MADRI. IT ENDED WITH THE ASCETICS OF SHATASHRINGA LEAVING WITH KUNTI AND THE PANDAVAS FOR HASTINAPURA.

FOR PRONUNCIATION AND MEANING OF SANSKRIT WORDS AND PROPER NAMES, PLEASE SEE PAGE 32.

WHEN KUNTI AND THE ENTOURAGE ARRIVED AT THE PORTALS OF THE CITY OF HASTINAPURA, THE RISHIS ASKED THE GUARDS TO INFORM THE KING OF THEIR ARRIVAL.

"THE GUARDS LOST NO TIME IN CONVEYING THE MESSAGE. THE CITIZENS OF HASTINAPURA WERE SURPRISED TO HEAR OF THE ARRIVAL OF THE LARGE GROUP OF RISHIS AND BARDS.

"MEN AND WOMEN OF ALL CASTES THRONGED THE STREETS; SOME ON FOOT, SOME IN VEHICLES, ALL EAGER TO SEE THE VISITORS.

"THE CONCOURSE, THOUGH VAST, WAS PEACEFUL BECAUSE IT WAS ORDERLY AND FREE FROM SCUFFLE.

"THEN THERE CAME BHEESHMA, DHRITARASHTRA, VIDURA, SATYAVATI, AMBIKA, AMBALIKA, GANDHARI AND OTHER LADIES OF THE ROYAL HOUSEHOLD, AND THE SONS OF DHRITARASHTRA ADORNED WITH JEWELS AND ORNAMENTS.

"THE KAURAVAS BOWED TO THE RISHIS AND THE CITIZENS PROSTRATED THEMSELVES BEFORE THE HOLY GROUP.

THEN BHEESHMA WELCOMED THEM WITH BEFITTING HONOUR AND PLACED AT THEIR DISPOSAL THE WEALTH THAT WAS THE KINGDOM.

" THEN THE OLDEST OF THE RISHIS, WITH MATTED LOCKS AND CLAD ONLY IN DEERSKIN, SPOKE THUS FOR ALL OF THEM:

PANDU, THE KING AND THE SOVEREIGN CHIEF OF THE KURUS, RENOUNCING WORLDLY PURSUITS, CAME TO THE SHATASHRINGA MOUNTAINS TO LEAD THE LIFE OF A BRAHMACHARI.

AND THE COMPANY OF ASCETICS AND BARDS VANISHED, AS IF IT NEVER WAS, LEAVING THE BEHOLDERS IN WONDER.

"DHRITARASHTRA THEN SAID TO VIDURA:

DO NOT GRIEVE FOR PANDU WHO LIVED AS A WORTHY KING AND HAS LEFT BEHIND FIVE NOBLE SONS.

O, VIDURA, I CHARGE YOU TO OVERSEE THE FUNERAL RITES OF PANDU AND MADRI CONDUCTED BEFITTING THEIR REGAL STATUS.

LET CATTLE, CLOTH AND PRECIOUS GEMS BE DISTRIBUTED FREELY IN THE NAME OF PANDU AND MADRI.

AND LET THE LAST RITES OF MADRI BE CONDUCTED AS KUNTI WOULD HAVE IT.

AFTER CONSULTING BHEESHMA, VIDURA SELECTED A SACRED SPOT FOR THE LAST RITES OF PANDU. THE COURTIERS AND THE CITIZENS THEN COVERED WITH FLOWERS, THE BIER WHICH CARRIED THE REMAINS OF THE KING AND HIS CONSORT, AND DECKED IT WITH RICH HANGINGS AND FRAGRANT GARLANDS.

"THE BIER WAS CARRIED AWAY FROM THE CITY BY MEN, AND THE CORTEGE WAS LED BY PRIESTS, TO THE ACCOMPANIMENT OF DIRGE AND DRUMS. COMMONERS FOLLOWED THE CORTEGE LAMENTING LOUDLY:

O KING, WHERE HAVE YOU GONE, LEAVING US BEREFT AND DESOLATE?

AND BHEESHMA AND VIDURA AND THE PANDAVAS TOO WEPT ALOUD.

8

"THUS THEY REACHED THE EXPANSIVE BANKS OF THE GANGA WHERE THE BIER WAS LAID DOWN.

GUIDED BY THE PRIESTS, THEY CONCLUDED THE FUNERAL RITES AND SET FIRE TO THE REMAINS OF THE BODIES.

" AS THE FLAMES LEAPT UP, AMBALIKA CRIED OUT IN ANGUISH:

O MY SON, MY SON!

"AND WITNESSING THE GRIEF-STRICKEN MOTHER FALL TO THE GROUND, THE CITIZENS WAILED IN DEEP SORROW:

ALAS! ALAS!

"THE DISTRAUGHT CRY OF KUNTI MOVED THE HEART OF EVEN THE BIRDS AND BEASTS, AND MADE THE WISE BHEESHMA AND VIDURA SAD. WITH TEAR-DIMMED EYES THEY, ALONG WITH DHRITARASHTRA, THE PANDAVAS AND THE KURU LADIES, PERFORMED THE LAST CEREMONY FOR THE DEPARTED.

"THE CITIZENS THEN CONSOLED THE DISTRESS-ED SONS OF PANDU. YOUNG AND OLD ALIKE, ENGULFED IN SORROW LIKE THE PANDAVAS, MOURNED WITH THEM FOR FULL TWELVE DAYS.

THE SHRADDHA WAS COMPLETED BY BHEESHMA AND KUNTI WITH A GRAND FEAST AND LAVISH DONATIONS. PURIFIED THUS BY RITUALS, THE BHARATAS AND THE REST THEN RETURNED TO HASTINAPURA.

"THEN MY ESTEEMED GURU VYASA CAME TO SATYAVATI, HIS MOTHER, AND SAID:

OUR DAYS OF PROSPERITY ARE ON THE WANE. DAYS OF CORRUPTION ARE CREEPING IN, ROBBING THE WORLD OF ITS GLOW.

THE WICKEDNESS OF THE KAURAVAS WILL BRING DESTRUCTION UPON THIS WORLD.

THEREFORE GO INTO THE FOREST AND SEEK PEACE THROUGH THE PRACTICE OF YOGA.

" HEEDING THE WORDS OF VYASA, AND WITH THE APPROVAL OF BHEESHMA, SATYAVATI ACCOMPANIED BY AMBIKA AND AMBALIKA, WENT TO THE FOREST.*

* AFTER LEADING THE LIFE OF A HOUSEHOLDER TILL THE AGE OF USUALLY 50 YEARS, PEOPLE LIVED IN PLACES AWAY FROM HUMAN HABITATIONS, EITHER ALONE OR IN SMALL GROUPS, GIVING UP THE COMFORTS OF LIFE IN PREPARATION FOR THE FOURTH STAGE — SANNYASA.

IN DUE COURSE, WHILE ENGAGED IN PROFOUND MEDITATION, THE GOOD WOMEN ATTAINED MUKTI.

"MEANWHILE THE PANDAVAS GREW UP IN AFFLUENCE IN THEIR FATHER'S PALACE, AND PROVED THEIR SUPERIOR STRENGTH EVEN WHILE AT PLAY WITH THE SONS OF DHRITARASHTRA.

" IN RUNNING...

"...IN CONSUMING FOOD...

"...AND IN SCATTERING DUST, BHEEMASENA BEAT THEM ALL.

"HE PULLED THEIR HAIR...

"...AND, LAUGHING ALL THE WHILE, MADE THEM FIGHT AMONG THEMSELVES.

"WHEN THE SONS OF DHRITARASHTRA CLAMBERED UP THE TREES TO PLUCK FRUIT...

...BHEEMA WOULD SET THE TREE ALL A-TREMBLE WITH A MIGHTY KICK.

"AND DOWN WOULD COME FRUIT, FRUIT-PLUCKERS AND ALL.

THE 100 SONS OF DHRITARASHTRA WERE NO MATCH FOR ONE BHEEMA. HOWEVER, HIS DISPLAY OF RUGGED STRENGTH WAS PROMPTED BY CHILDISH GLEE AND NOT BY ILL WILL.

"BUT THIS OBVIOUS STRENGTH OF BHEEMA AROUSED THE HOSTILITY OF DURYODHANA, THE ELDEST SON OF DHRITARASHTRA.

" AND HE SAID TO HIMSELF:

IN MIGHT BHEEMA EXCELS ALL OF US. HE WILL HAVE TO BE REMOVED BY CUNNING.

I SHALL THROW HIM INTO THE GANGA WHEN HE IS ASLEEP.

I SHALL THEN IMPRISON YUDHISHTHIRA AND ARJUNA AND REIGN AS THE UNDISPUTED KING.

"AND WHEN ALL WAS COMPLETED, THE CRAFTY PRINCE SAID TO THE PANDAVAS:

LET ALL OF US GO FOR SOME SPORT TO THE GANGA AND HER SYLVAN BANKS.

RESOLUTE IN HIS WICKED THOUGHT, DURYODHANA KEPT A SHARP WATCH FOR AN OPPORTUNITY. AND, O MONARCH, AT LENGTH HE SET UP AN ALLURING CAMP FOR WATER SPORTS AT PRAMANAKOTI ON THE BANKS OF THE GANGA. HE HAD IT ADORNED WITH RICH CLOTH HANGINGS AND EMBELLISHED WITH GAY FLAGS. AND THE CUISINE THERE WAS EQUIPPED TO SERVE FOOD AND DRINK OF CHOICE TASTE.

" WHEN YUDHISHTHIRA AGREED TO IT, THE PANDAVAS AND THE SONS OF DHRITARASHTRA PROCEEDED TO THAT SPOT, SOME IN CHARIOTS AND SOME ON ELEPHANTS.

" WHEN THEY REACHED PRAMANAKOTI THEY DISMISSED THEIR ATTENDANTS AND ENTERED THE RESIDENCE.

" THEY ADMIRED THE PRETTY DESIGNS DECORATING THE INTERIOR. THEN. THEY LOOKED OUT OF THE WINDOWS OPENING UPON WELL-LAID GARDENS FULL OF FRAGRANT FLOWERS AND CLEAR FOUNTAINS AND PONDS DECKED WITH LOTUS BLOOMS.

"AFTER THE KAURAVAS AND THE PANDAVAS HAD THEIR FILL OF PLEASURES...

"...THEY TOOK TURNS AT FEEDING EACH OTHER WITH CHOICE DELICACIES.

"MEANWHILE DURYODHANA HAD ALREADY PREPARED HEAVILY POISONED FOOD TO KILL BHEEMASENA.

"CONCEALING HIS EVIL DESIGNS WITH SWEET SMILES, HE WENT OVER TO BHEEMA...

"...AND FED HIM FREELY WITH THE POISONED FOOD.

"THEN ALL OF THEM MOVED OVER TO THE RIVER TO AMUSE THEMSELVES IN THE WATER.

"AFTER A WHILE THEY CAME OUT OF THE WATER AND DRESSED THEMSELVES IN FRESH CLOTHES.

"BHEEMA HAD BEEN MORE VIGOROUS THAN THE OTHERS IN THE WATER.

"SO WHEN HE CAME OUT, HE FLUNG HIMSELF ON THE GROUND IN SHEER FATIGUE.

"AND THE STRONG POISON, AND THE SOFT RIVER BREEZE, LULLED HIM INTO A DEEP SLUMBER.

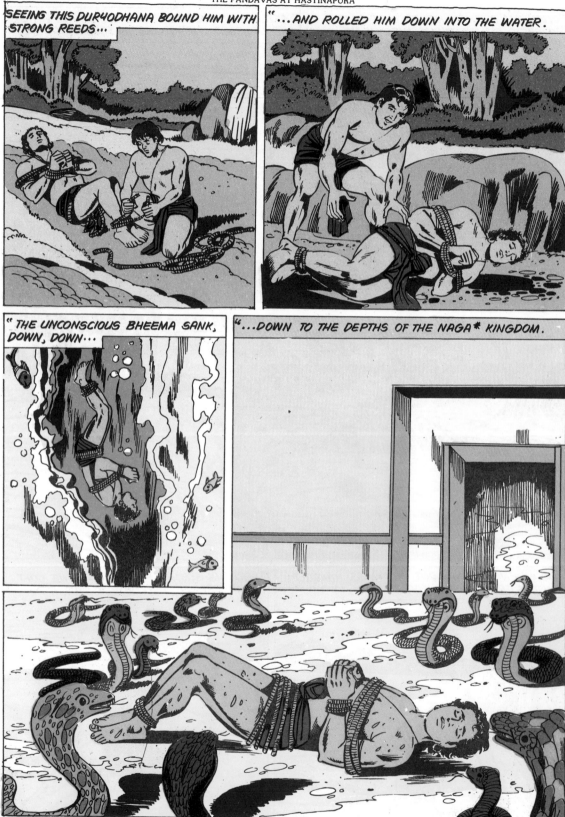

SEEING THIS DURYODHANA BOUND HIM WITH STRONG REEDS...

"...AND ROLLED HIM DOWN INTO THE WATER.

"THE UNCONSCIOUS BHEEMA SANK, DOWN, DOWN...

"...DOWN TO THE DEPTHS OF THE NAGA* KINGDOM.

* ACCORDING TO MANY SCHOLARS THE NAGAS WERE A RACE OF PEOPLE WITH WHOM THE ARYANS FREELY MIXED.

" THE NAGAS ATTACKED HIM BY THE THOUSANDS AND BIT HIM, RELEASING THE DEADLY POISON FROM THEIR FANGS.

" THE SNAKE-POISON ACTED AS AN ANTIDOTE AND BHEEMA REGAINED HIS SENSES.

" HE SNAPPED THE REEDS THAT BOUND HIM AND...

"...KILLED THE SNAKES BY DASHING THEM TO THE GROUND.

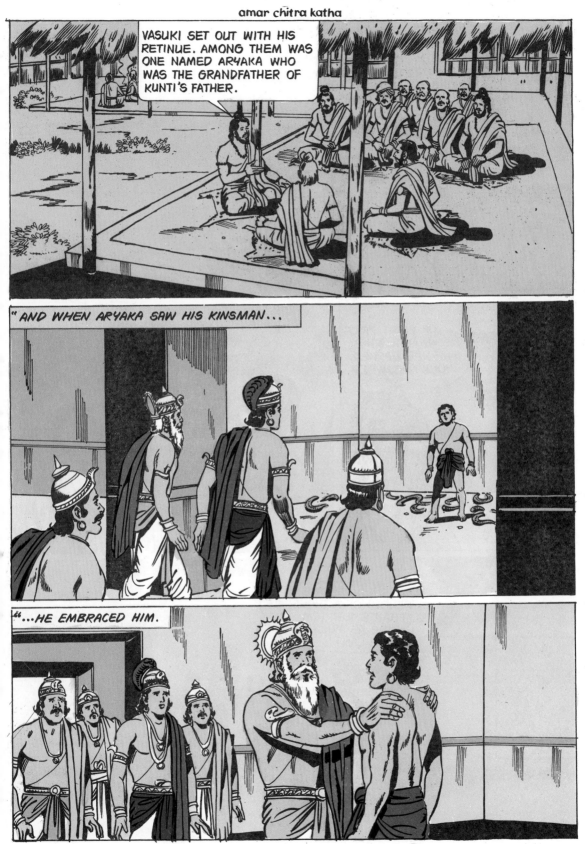

VASUKI SET OUT WITH HIS RETINUE. AMONG THEM WAS ONE NAMED ARYAKA WHO WAS THE GRANDFATHER OF KUNTI'S FATHER.

"AND WHEN ARYAKA SAW HIS KINSMAN...

"...HE EMBRACED HIM.

WHEN VASUKI GAVE HIS ASSENT, THE SERPENTS PREPARED BHEEMA FOR THE CEREMONY.

"THEN BHEEMA SAT FACING THE EAST, READY TO IMBIBE THE ESSENCE.

" HE FINISHED THE CONTENTS OF ONE VESSEL AT ONE GULP.

" AND THUS DID HE FINISH EIGHT OF THEM, ONE AFTER THE OTHER.

"THEN HE LAY HIMSELF DOWN ON THE SPECIAL BED THE NAGAS HAD MADE FOR HIM.

"MEANWHILE, AFTER HAVING HAD THEIR SURFEIT OF PLAY, THE PANDAVAS AND KAURAVAS LEFT THE CAMP.

"THE PANDAVAS BELIEVED THAT BHEEMA HAD GONE AHEAD OF THEM, AND DURYODHANA WAS FULL OF GLEE THAT BHEEMA WAS NOT WITH THEM.

THE HONEST YUDHISHTHIRA, O MONARCH, BELIEVED OTHERS TO BE AS HONEST AS HIMSELF.

"THEREFORE, WHEN HE REACHED THE PALACE, HE SAID TO HIS MOTHER:

WE THOUGHT THAT BHEEMA WAS ALREADY HERE. WHERE IS HE? HAS HE NOT COME BACK?

HAVE YOU SENT HIM ON AN ERRAND? HE WAS IN DEEP SLEEP WHEN WE SAW HIM LAST.

WAS IT SLEEP? OR WAS HE KILLED? I AM WORRIED.

"HEARING THIS, KUNTI CRIED OUT IN DISMAY:

I HAVE NOT SEEN BHEEMA.

"THEN SHE SUMMONED VIDURA AND SAID:

O VIDURA, BHEEMA IS MISSING. ALL THE OTHERS HAVE COME BACK.

DURYODHANA HATES HIM AND HE IS RECKLESS AND SPITEFUL.

HIS GREED FOR THE THRONE MIGHT EVEN HAVE PROMPTED HIM TO MURDER MY SON.

"VIDURA REPLIED:

O GOOD WOMAN, DO NOT SPEAK IN THIS MANNER. IF YOU ACCUSE DURYODHANA, HE MAY TURN ON YOUR OTHER SONS ALSO.

A LONG LIFE HAS BEEN PREDICTED FOR YOUR SONS. THEREFORE BHEEMA WILL CERTAINLY RETURN.

THE WISE VIDURA REASSURED KUNTI THUS, AND RETURNED HOME. BUT KUNTI WAS STILL TORMENTED BY ANXIETY.

"MEANWHILE BHEEMA ROSE FROM HIS SLEEP ON THE EIGHTH DAY, ALL THE MIGHTIER FOR THE POTENT ESSENCE WHICH HE HAD IMBIBED.

"AND THE NAGAS SAID TO HIM:
YOU HAVE ACQUIRED THE STRENGTH OF THOUSANDS OF ELEPHANTS. YOU WILL BE INVINCIBLE IN BATTLE.

PERFORM YOUR ABLUTIONS AND GO BACK TO YOUR BROTHERS WHO ARE DISTRESSED AT YOUR ABSENCE.

BHEEMA, PURE AFTER THE BATH, WEARING WHITE CLOTHES AND DECKED IN ORNAMENTS AND GARLANDS, ATE THE EXQUISITE FOOD SERVED BY THE NAGAS.

"THEN HE ACCEPTED AND RETURNED THE HOMAGE AND BENEDICTION OF THE NAGAS.

"THEN GUIDED BY THE NAGAS, HE ASCENDED THROUGH THE WATERS...

"...AND REACHED THE VERY GARDENS WHERE HE HAD AMUSED HIMSELF.

" AND THE NAGAS VANISHED FROM THE SCENE.

" THE MIGHTY BHEEMA THEN RAN IN HASTE...

"... TO HIS MOTHER AT HASTINAPURA.

"MOVED BY THE CLOSE AFFECTION FOR EACH OTHER THE PANDAVAS HAILED THEIR GOOD FORTUNE.

THEN BHEEMA RECOUNTED ALL THAT HAD HAPPENED TO HIM—THE GOOD AND THE BAD—DURING HIS NAGA EPISODE.

"THEN YUDHISHTHIRA SAID:

DO NOT SPEAK OF THIS INCIDENT TO ANYONE.

LET IT BE CONFINED TO OURSELVES.

THE PANDAVAS THENCEFORTH LED A PRUDENT LIFE AND IN THIS THEY WERE HELPED BY ADVICE FROM VIDURA.

DURYODHANA PERSISTED IN PLOTTING THE DEATH OF THE PANDAVAS. BUT HIS ATTEMPTS WERE FOILED BY YUYUTSU (DHRITARASHTRA'S SON BY A VAISHYA WOMAN) WHO IN HIS LOVE FOR THE PANDAVAS CAUTIONED THEM IN TIME.

MEANWHILE AS THE PRINCES WERE WHILING AWAY THEIR TIME IN IDLE PURSUITS, THEY WERE PLACED UNDER THE TUTELAGE OF GAUTAMA, WHOSE BIRTH HAD OCCURRED IN A CLUMP OF REED AND WHO WAS ALSO KNOWN AS KRIPA.

AND THUS ENDS THE FOURTH SESSION OF OUR RENDERING OF VAISHAMPAYANA'S NARRATION OF VYASA'S IMMORTAL ITIHASA, THE MAHABHARATA.

MAHABHARATA-5
Enter Drona

VEDA VYASA'S EPIC ON THE BHARATA RACE WAS FIRST RECITED IN PUBLIC, BY HIS DISCIPLE VAISHAMPAYANA, AT THE BEHEST OF THE AGELESS SEER VYASA HIMSELF.

THE RECITAL TOOK PLACE IN THE AUGUST PRESENCE OF KING JANAMEJAYA — GREAT-GRANDSON OF THE GRANDSON OF VYASA — AND THE MANY LEARNED SAGES WHO HAD ASSEMBLED FOR JANAMEJAYA'S SARPA SATRA.

THE FOURTH SESSION OF OUR RENDERING OF VAISHAMPAYANA'S RECITAL OF VYASA'S MAHABHARATA BEGAN WITH THE ARRIVAL OF KUNTI AND THE PANDAVAS AT HASTINAPURA; WENT ON TO DESCRIBE THE GROWING ANIMOSITY OF THE KAURAVA DURYODHANA TOWARDS HIS COUSINS THE PANDAVAS; AND ENDED WITH DHRITARASHTRA, THE FATHER OF DURYODHANA, PLACING ALL THE PRINCES UNDER THE TUTELEGE OF KRIPACHARYA.

FOR PRONUNCIATION AND MEANING OF SANSKRIT WORDS AND PROPER NAMES, PLEASE SEE PAGE 32.

O SAGE, TELL ME OF KRIPA AND HOW HE ACQUIRED HIS WEAPONS.

O MONARCH, KRIPA, AND HIS TWIN SISTER, KRIPI, WERE BORN IN A CLUMP OF REED FROM THE SEED OF SHARADWAN, THE SON OF GAUTAMA. ONE OF SHANTANU'S MEN FOUND THE TWINS AND BROUGHT THEM TO THE PALACE, WHERE THE KING REARED THEM AS HIS OWN CHILDREN.

"AND LATER WHEN SHARADWAN, AN EXCELLENT WIELDER OF WEAPONS HIMSELF, LEARNT WHERE THE TWINS WERE, HE CAME TO SHANTANU'S PALACE...

"...AND BECAME KRIPA'S INSTRUCTOR IN THE SCIENCE OF WEAPONS.

"KRIPA MASTERED THE SKILLS AND IN TIME TAUGHT THEM TO THE KAURAVAS, THE PANDAVAS, THE YADAVAS AND MANY OTHER PRINCES WHO CAME THERE FROM OTHER KINGDOMS.

BUT BHEESHMA, WHO WANTED ONLY THE BEST OF WARRIORS AS GURU FOR HIS GRANDSONS, APPOINTED DRONA AS THEIR INSTRUCTOR.

O SAGE, TELL ME OF DRONA AND HOW HE GAINED HIS SKILLS. HOW DID HE COME TO THE LAND OF THE KURUS? TELL ME IN DETAIL.

DRONA SPRANG FROM THE SEED OF THE MIGHTY SAGE BHARADWAJA, AND HE WAS NAMED DRONA BECAUSE HE WAS BORN IN ONE.

BHARADWAJA HAD IMPARTED THE SECRET OF THE FIERY AGNEYA MISSILE TO THE GREAT RISHI AGNIVESHA HIMSELF.

THE FIRE-BORN RISHI IN TIME TAUGHT DRONA THE SECRET OF THAT MISSILE AND MANY OTHER MISSILES.

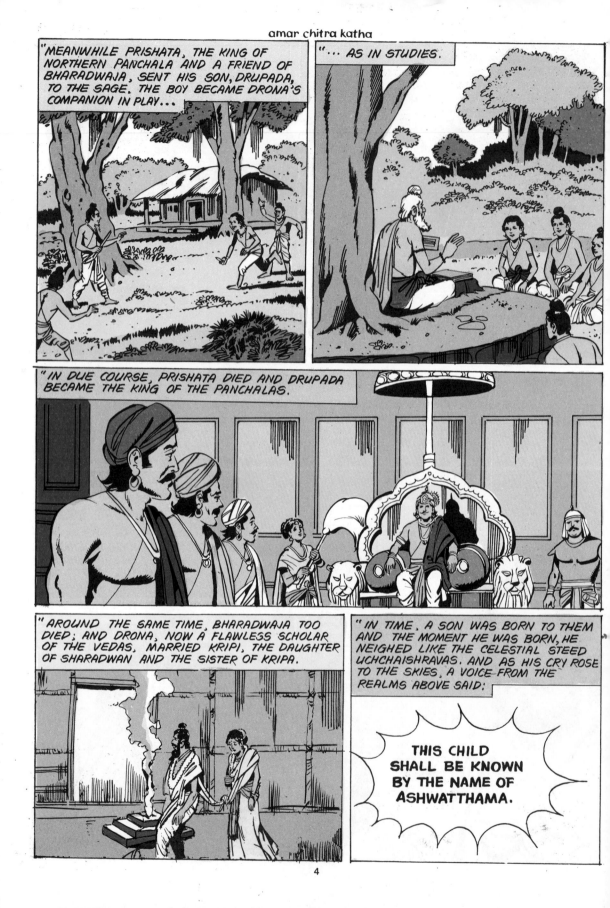

"MEANWHILE PRISHATA, THE KING OF NORTHERN PANCHALA AND A FRIEND OF BHARADWAJA, SENT HIS SON, DRUPADA, TO THE SAGE. THE BOY BECAME DRONA'S COMPANION IN PLAY...

"... AS IN STUDIES.

"IN DUE COURSE, PRISHATA DIED AND DRUPADA BECAME THE KING OF THE PANCHALAS.

"AROUND THE SAME TIME, BHARADWAJA TOO DIED; AND DRONA, NOW A FLAWLESS SCHOLAR OF THE VEDAS, MARRIED KRIPI, THE DAUGHTER OF SHARADWAN AND THE SISTER OF KRIPA.

"IN TIME, A SON WAS BORN TO THEM AND THE MOMENT HE WAS BORN, HE NEIGHED LIKE THE CELESTIAL STEED UCHCHAISHRAVAS. AND AS HIS CRY ROSE TO THE SKIES, A VOICE FROM THE REALMS ABOVE SAID:

THIS CHILD SHALL BE KNOWN BY THE NAME OF ASHWATTHAMA.

"THEN, O MONARCH, DRONA LEARNT THAT PARASHURAMA, THE SON OF JAMADAGNI, SUPREME IN LEARNING AS IN WARFARE, AND THE SCOURGE OF HIS ENEMIES, WAS GIVING AWAY HIS ACQUISITIONS TO DESERVING BRAHMANAS. MOVED BY HOPE AND AMBITION, DRONA SET OUT FOR THE MAHENDRA MOUNTAINS WHERE THE SAGE DWELT.

"AND WHEN HE ARRIVED THERE AND BEHELD PARASHURAMA...

"...HE FIRST PROSTRATED HIMSELF BEFORE THE SAGE...

"...AND THEN SAID:

I AM DRONA—A BRAHMANA BY BIRTH AND THE OFFSPRING OF SAGE BHARADWAJA, BUT NOT OF A WOMAN.

"ON HEARING HIS WORDS THE SAGE ASKED:

O BRAHMANA, WHAT DO YOU DESIRE?

"DRONA REPLIED:

I AM A SUPPLIANT FOR YOUR IMMENSE WEALTH.

"PARASHURAMA SAID:

I HAVE ALREADY DONATED ALL MY GOLD AND LAND. NOW LEFT ARE MY WEAPONS AND MY BODY.

CHOOSE, DRONA. WHICH ONE WOULD YOU HAVE?

"AND DRONA PROMPTLY ANSWERED:-

O SAGE, GIVE ME THE WEAPONS AND THE SECRETS OF WIELDING THEM.

PARASHURAMA ASSENTED AND GAVE HIS WEAPONS AND THEIR SECRETS TO DRONA. AND, EXULTING AT THE MARTIAL WEALTH IN HIS POSSESSION, DRONA REMEMBERED HIS OLD FRIEND DRUPADA.

"AND GOING TO PANCHALA, THE MIGHTY SON OF BHARADWAJA PRESENTED HIMSELF BEFORE DRUPADA AND SAID:

KNOW ME FOR YOUR FRIEND.

"BUT THE CHIEF OF THE PANCHALAS, INTOXICATED BY WEALTH AND POWER, ONLY SCOWLED AND SAID:

O BRAHMANA, YOUR INTELLIGENCE SEEMS CRUDE AND STUNTED. HOW ELSE COULD YOU PRESUME TO CLAIM ME AS YOUR FRIEND!

YOU ARE DIM-WITTED NOT TO KNOW THAT GREAT KINGS CAN NEVER BE FRIENDS WITH LUCKLESS, INDIGENT MEN LIKE YOU.

IT IS TRUE THAT LONG AGO WE WERE COMRADES WHEN WE WERE EQUAL IN CIRCUMSTANCES.

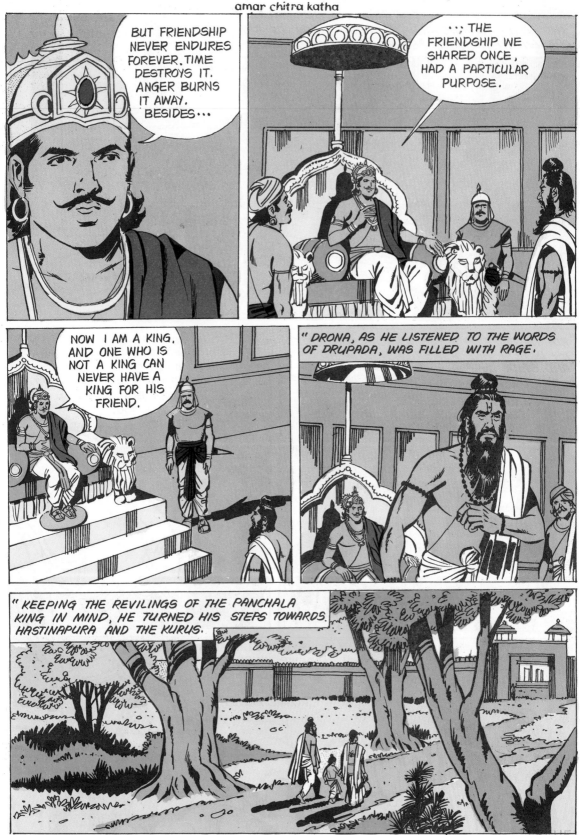

BUT FRIENDSHIP NEVER ENDURES FOREVER. TIME DESTROYS IT. ANGER BURNS IT AWAY. BESIDES...

...; THE FRIENDSHIP WE SHARED ONCE, HAD A PARTICULAR PURPOSE.

NOW I AM A KING, AND ONE WHO IS NOT A KING CAN NEVER HAVE A KING FOR HIS FRIEND.

" DRONA, AS HE LISTENED TO THE WORDS OF DRUPADA, WAS FILLED WITH RAGE.

" KEEPING THE REVILINGS OF THE PANCHALA KING IN MIND, HE TURNED HIS STEPS TOWARDS HASTINAPURA AND THE KURUS.

" AT HASTINAPURA, DRONA WITH KRIPI AND ASHWATTHAMA, LIVED UNKNOWN AND UNANNOUNCED FOR MANY YEARS IN THE HOUSE OF KRIPA, HIS BROTHER-IN-LAW.

"AND THEN, ONE DAY, THE PRINCES OF HASTINAPURA CAME OUT OF THE CITY TO PLAY VITA-DANDA.

"WHILE THEY WERE PLAYING, THE VITA FELL INTO A DEEP DRY WELL.

"THEY WERE UNABLE TO RETRIEVE IT AND LOOKED ABOUT, SHAMEFACED AND HELPLESS, WHEN THEY SPOTTED A BRAHMANA.

"THEY IMMEDIATELY SURROUNDED HIM AND THE BRAHMANA, WHO WAS NONE OTHER THAN DRONA, SAID:

THE DESCENDANTS OF BHARATA AT A LOSS TO RECOVER THEIR VITA! FIE ON YOUR KSHATRIYA VALOUR, AND FIE ON YOUR ARCHERY!

IF YOU PROMISE ME FOOD, I WILL RETRIEVE NOT ONLY THE VITA YOU LOST...

...BUT THIS RING TOO, WHICH I WILL NOW THROW INTO THE WELL.

"AND DRONA THREW HIS RING DOWN INTO THE WELL.

"THEN YUDHISHTHIRA THE ELDEST PANDAVA SAID:

O BRAHMANA, IF KRIPACHARYA PERMITS, PLEASE RECEIVE ALMS FROM US EVERY DAY.

"DRONA ONLY SMILED AND, UPROOTING A CLUMP OF REED, SAID:

I WILL INVEST THIS WITH THE POWER OF WEAPONS BY MY MANTRAS.

NOW I WILL PIERCE ONE REED WITH ANOTHER, AND THAT WITH ANOTHER, AND WITH THE CHAIN THUS MADE TAKE YOUR VITA OUT.

"AND WHEN DRONA BROUGHT THE VITA OUT, THE PRINCES OPENED THEIR EYES WIDE IN WONDER AND SAID:

O BRAHMANA, PLEASE RECOVER THE RING AS WELL.

"DRONA PIERCED THE RING WITH AN ARROW FROM HIS BOW, AND BROUGHT IT OUT OF THE WELL...

"...AND CALMLY GAVE IT TO THE ASTOUNDED PRINCES.

"AND THEY SAID:

WE SALUTE YOU, O BRAHMANA. SUCH PROWESS IS UNIQUE. WHO ARE YOU? WHAT COULD WE DO FOR YOU?

"DRONA REPLIED:

GO TO BHEESHMA AND DESCRIBE ME AND MY ACTIONS EXACTLY AS YOU HAVE WITNESSED. HE WILL KNOW ME.

WHEN BHEESHMA HEARD THE PRINCES' DESCRIPTION, HE KNEW THE BRAHMANA TO BE DRONA. DECIDING THAT HE WOULD BE THE BEST GURU FOR THE PRINCES, BHEESHMA WENT IN PERSON TO WELCOME HIM, AND LED HIM TO THE PALACE.

"THEN THE DISCERNING BHEESHMA ASKED HIM THE REASON FOR HIS BEING THERE.

"AND DRONA REPLIED:

O BHEESHMA, LONG AGO I HAD GONE TO RISHI AGNIVESHA TO BE INSTRUCTED IN THE SCIENCE OF WEAPONS.

DRUPADA, THE PANCHALA PRINCE, MY COMPANION IN STUDIES RIGHT FROM CHILDHOOD, WAS ALSO THERE.

"AND THERE HE WOULD OFTEN PLEASE ME BY SAYING:

O DRONA, WHEN I SUCCEED MY FATHER TO THE THRONE OF PANCHALA, MY WEALTH SHALL BE YOURS AS WELL. THIS IS A SOLEMN PROMISE.

"MANY YEARS LATER, ASHWATTHAMA, MY SON, ONE DAY CRIED FOR MILK. HE HAD SEEN THE RICH CHILDREN DRINKING IT.

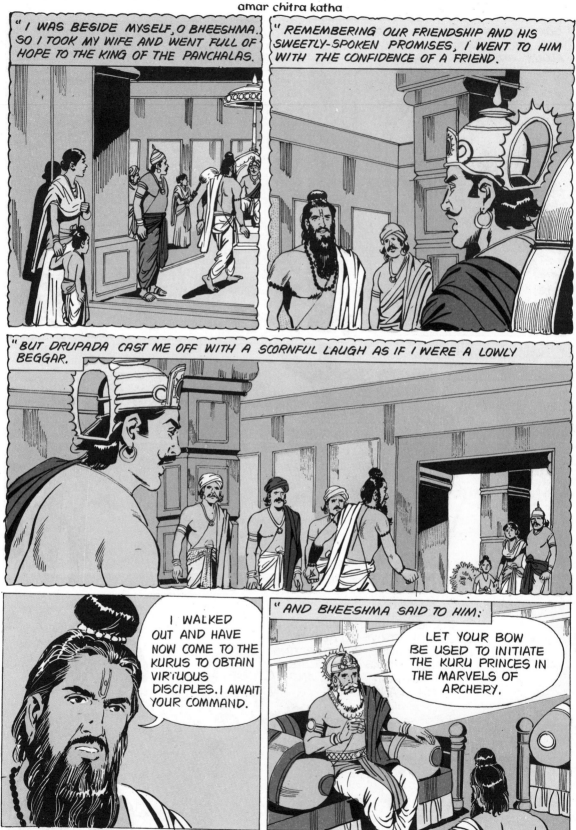

" I WAS BESIDE MYSELF, O BHEESHMA. SO I TOOK MY WIFE AND WENT FULL OF HOPE TO THE KING OF THE PANCHALAS.

" REMEMBERING OUR FRIENDSHIP AND HIS SWEETLY-SPOKEN PROMISES, I WENT TO HIM WITH THE CONFIDENCE OF A FRIEND.

" BUT DRUPADA CAST ME OFF WITH A SCORNFUL LAUGH AS IF I WERE A LOWLY BEGGAR.

I WALKED OUT AND HAVE NOW COME TO THE KURUS TO OBTAIN VIRTUOUS DISCIPLES. I AWAIT YOUR COMMAND.

" AND BHEESHMA SAID TO HIM:

LET YOUR BOW BE USED TO INITIATE THE KURU PRINCES IN THE MARVELS OF ARCHERY.

YOU ARE THE LORD OF ALL THE WEALTH OF THE KURUS. THE KURUS WILL EVER STAND BY YOU. O BRAHMANA, CONSIDER YOUR WISH AS ALREADY FULFILLED.

INDEED, WE LOOK UPON YOUR ARRIVAL HERE AS A BLESSING PORTENDING GOOD FORTUNE FOR US.

"AND BHEESHMA GAVE DRONA A HOUSE PROVIDED WITH ALL COMFORTS AND FILLED WITH GRAINS AND OTHER WEALTH.

"AND THEN HE ENTRUSTED HIS GRAND-SONS TO DRONA, ALONG WITH RICH GIFTS.

"DRONA JOYFULLY ACCEPTED THE PRINCES AND THEN SAID TO THEM:

I HAVE A PARTICULAR AIM. PROMISE ME THAT YOU WILL ACCOMPLISH IT WHEN I TRANSFORM YOU INTO EXPERT WARRIORS.

"WHILE THE OTHER KURU PRINCES REMAINED SILENT, ARJUNA PROMISED TO ACCOMPLISH IT, IRRESPECTIVE OF WHAT IT WAS. AND DRONA CLASPED HIM TO HIS BOSOM AND SHED TEARS OF JOY.

THEN THE VALOROUS DRONA IMPARTED HIS KNOWLEDGE OF WEAPONS, BOTH WORLDLY AND OCCULT, TO THE PANDAVAS. AND ALONG WITH THE PRINCES OF THE NEIGHBOURING KINGDOMS, KARNA THE FOSTER-SON OF THE CHARIOTEER ALSO CAME TO HIM.

AND, O MONARCH, WHEN ALL THE DISCIPLES WERE GIVEN WATERPOTS FOR PROCURING DRINKING WATER, ASHWATTHAMA WAS GIVEN A POT WITH A WIDER MOUTH, TO ENABLE HIM TO FILL IT FAST AND RETURN EARLY. AND IN THAT PERIOD DRONA WOULD IMPART SPECIAL SKILLS TO HIS SON.

ARJUNA KNEW THIS. SO, TO KEEP ABREAST OF THE SON OF HIS GURU, HE WOULD INVOKE THE VARUNA MISSILE TO FILL HIS POT, AND WOULD RETURN AT THE SAME TIME AS ASHWATTHAMA.

"AND BEHOLDING THIS STEADFAST DEVOTION OF ARJUNA TO ARCHERY, DRONA SUMMONED THE COOK AND TOLD HIM:

DON'T EVER GIVE ARJUNA HIS FOOD IN THE DARK. AND DON'T TELL HIM THAT I HAVE TOLD YOU THIS.

"A FEW DAYS LATER, IT SO HAPPENED THAT WHILE ARJUNA WAS AT HIS DINNER, A WIND AROSE AND PUT OUT THE LAMP.

"BUT ARJUNA CONTINUED TO EAT, HIS HAND REACHING HIS MOUTH BY FORCE OF HABIT.

"AND REALIZING SUDDENLY THE POTENTIAL OF HABITS...

"...ARJUNA STARTED PRACTISING WITH HIS BOW IN THE DARK. DRONA HEARD THE TWANG OF THE BOW-STRING AT NIGHT AND GOING UP TO ARJUNA...

"...CLASPED HIM IN AFFECTION AND SAID:

MARK MY WORDS. I SHALL MAKE YOU UNEQUALLED AMONG THOSE WHO WIELD THE BOW.

THUS STARTED THE LESSONS FOR ARJUNA, IN COMBATS AND FIGHTS ON THE GROUND OR ASTRIDE ANIMALS OR RIDING A CHARIOT, WITH WEAPONS AS DIVERSE AS THE MACE, THE SPEAR, THE SWORD AND THE DART.

AND AS FAME OF ARJUNA'S PROWESS SPREAD, MANY FROM FAR AND NEAR FLOCKED TO DRONA TO BE INSTRUCTED. ONE AMONG THEM WAS EKALAVYA, THE SON OF A NISHADA KING.

DRONA, HOWEVER, IN DEFERENCE TO THE STATUS OF THE KURU PRINCES AND AWARE OF THE RULES OF RIGHT CONDUCT, DID NOT ACCEPT HIM AS HIS PUPIL.

BUT EKALAVYA PAID HOMAGE TO DRONA BY TOUCHING THE GURU'S FEET WITH HIS HEAD...

"...AND THEN WENDED HIS WAY INTO THE FOREST. THERE HE MADE A CLAY IMAGE OF DRONA...

"...WORSHIPPED IT AS IF IT WERE HIS GURU...

"...AND PRACTISED ARCHERY BEFORE IT WITH UNSWERVING DILIGENCE AND INTENSE DEVOTION.

AND BEFORE LONG, BECAUSE OF HIS EXCEPTIONAL REVERENCE FOR HIS GURU AND HIS DEVOTION TO HIS GOAL, HE EXCELLED IN ALL THE VARIOUS ASPECTS OF ARCHERY.

"THEN ONE DAY, THE KURU PRINCES CAME TO THAT FOREST ON A HUNT FOLLOWED BY THEIR ATTENDANTS AND A DOG.

"THE DOG, STRAYING FROM THE GROUP, CAME UPON EKALAVYA AND BEGAN TO BARK LOUDLY.

"EKALAVYA THEREUPON SENT SEVEN ARROWS IN QUICK SUCCESSION INTO THE DOG'S MOUTH.

"THE GAPING DOG WENT RUNNING TOWARDS THE PANDAVAS, FILLED WITH WONDER...

"... THOSE PRINCES SCANNED THE FOREST FOR THE ONE WHO POSSESSED SUCH SKILL.

"AND THEY SOON FOUND THE WOODSMAN AT HIS CEASELESS PRACTICE.

"THEY DID NOT RECOGNIZE THE MAN OF UNKEMPT LOOKS AND ASKED HIM:

WHO ARE YOU?

HE REPLIED:

O VALIANT MEN, I AM THE SON OF HIRANYADHANUSH, KING OF THE NISHADAS. I AM ALSO A PUPIL OF DRONA, PERFECTING THE ART OF ARCHERY.

THE PANDAVAS LEARNT ALL ABOUT HIM AND, RETURNING HOME, NARRATED TO DRONA THE UNEXPECTED TURN OF EVENTS IN THE FOREST.

"ARJUNA PONDERED FOR LONG OVER EKALAVYA'S SKILL AND THEN, IN A PRIVATE AUDIENCE WITH HIS WELL-LOVED GURU, SAID:

CLASPING ME TO YOUR BOSOM, YOU HAD PREDICTED THAT YOU WOULD MAKE ME THE FOREMOST OF YOUR DISCIPLES.

HOW IS IT THEN THAT ANOTHER PUPIL OF YOURS, THIS SON OF THE NISHADA KING, IS SUPERIOR TO ME?

"DRONA REFLECTED FOR SOME TIME AND, IN A RESOLUTE MOVE, WENT TO THE NISHADA PRINCE TAKING ARJUNA WITH HIM. AND THERE HE SAW EKALAVYA OF UNKEMPT APPEARANCE AND DETERMINED WILL.

"AS SOON AS EKALAVYA SAW HIS GURU, HE WENT FORWARD AND PROSTRATED HIMSELF AT HIS FEET.

"THEN JOINING HIS HANDS IN REVERENCE HE STOOD BEFORE HIM. AND DRONA SAID:

O BRAVE ONE, IF YOU REALLY ARE MY PUPIL, GIVE ME MY GURU-DAKSHINA.

"GRATIFIED AT THESE WORDS, EKALAVYA SAID IN REPLY:

O WISE PRECEPTOR, I HAVE NOTHING WITH ME WHICH IS NOT FOR MY GREAT GURU.

COMMAND ME.

"AND DRONA SAID:

GIVE ME THE THUMB OF YOUR RIGHT HAND.

AT THESE CRUEL WORDS OF DRONA, EKALAVYA WHO WAS STEADFAST IN THE PATH OF TRUTH, CUT OFF HIS RIGHT THUMB; AND CHEERFUL AS EVER, GAVE IT TO DRONA.

AFTER THIS, THE NISHADA PRINCE PRACTISED SHOOTING ARROWS WITH HIS FOUR FINGERS BUT NEVER REGAINED HIS EARLIER AGILITY.

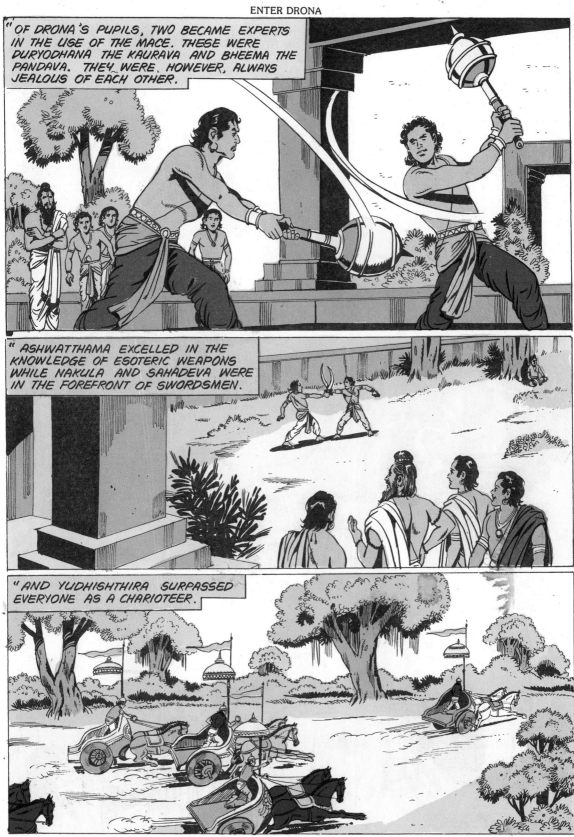

"OF DRONA'S PUPILS, TWO BECAME EXPERTS IN THE USE OF THE MACE. THESE WERE DURYODHANA THE KAURAVA AND BHEEMA THE PANDAVA. THEY WERE, HOWEVER, ALWAYS JEALOUS OF EACH OTHER.

"ASHWATTHAMA EXCELLED IN THE KNOWLEDGE OF ESOTERIC WEAPONS WHILE NAKULA AND SAHADEVA WERE IN THE FOREFRONT OF SWORDSMEN.

"AND YUDHISHTHIRA SURPASSED EVERYONE AS A CHARIOTEER.

BUT ARJUNA ALONE WAS VERSATILE IN HIS SKILLS. IN INTELLIGENCE, IN CONCENTRATION, IN STRENGTH, IN PRESENCE OF MIND AND IN DEVOTION TO HIS GURU, HE WAS ABOVE ALL OTHERS. THUS THOUGH THE INSTRUCTION WAS THE SAME FOR ALL, ARJUNA LEFT ALL OTHERS BEHIND, AND BECAME JUSTLY FAMOUS THROUGHOUT THE LAND.

"WHEN THE PRINCES HAD LEARNT ALL THAT WAS TO BE TAUGHT, DRONA, WISHING TO TEST THEIR PROWESS, HAD A WOODEN BIRD PLACED AS A TARGET ON THE TOP OF THE TREE.

"THEN, SUMMONING ALL THE PRINCES TO THE SPOT, HE SAID:

TAKE UP YOUR BOWS AND ARROWS AT ONCE AND BE READY TO SEVER THE HEAD OF THAT BIRD.

"THEN DRONA AGAIN ASKED HIM:

DO YOU SEE ME, THE TREE AND YOUR BROTHERS?

" YUDHISHTHIRA ANSWERED:

YES. I SEE YOU, THE TREE, MY BROTHERS AND THE BIRD. EACH DISTINCT AND CLEAR.

"VEXED WITH YUDHISHTHIRA'S ANSWER, DRONA SAID:

STAND BACK. YOU WILL NOT BE ABLE TO HIT THE TARGET.

THEN DRONA PUT THE SAME QUESTION TO DURYODHANA AND THE OTHER SONS OF DHRITARASHTRA, ONE AFTER THE OTHER, AS ALSO TO BHEEMA AND THE REST OF THE PRINCES. ALL OF THEM SAID THAT THEY SAW DRONA, THE TREE, THEIR BROTHERS AND THE BIRD. AND ALL OF THEM WERE DISQUALIFIED.

"THIS GLADDENED THE HEART OF DRONA AND HE GAVE THE ORDER:

SHOOT!

"THE ARROW FLEW FROM ARJUNA'S BOW...

"...HIT THE HEAD OF THE WOODEN BIRD... AND BROUGHT IT DOWN.

"AND DRONA HELD ARJUNA CLOSE AND THOUGHT THAT DRUPADA WAS AS GOOD AS VANQUISHED.

"AFTER A FEW DAYS, DRONA AND HIS DISCIPLES WENT FOR A BATH IN THE SACRED RIVER GANGA.

"AS DRONA ENTERED THE STREAM, A HUGE CROCODILE SEIZED HIM BY THE THIGH.

"THOUGH HE WAS CAPABLE OF FREEING HIMSELF, HE CALLED OUT IN APPARENT ALARM:

SLAY THIS MONSTER, AND SAVE ME!

"EVEN AS HE SPOKE, ARJUNA HIT THE MONSTER WITH FIVE SHARP ARROWS WHILE THE OTHER DISCIPLES STOOD STILL IN SHOCK AND CONFUSION.

"ARJUNA'S ARROWS CUT THE MONSTER INTO PIECES AND DRONA WAS SET FREE.

" IMMENSELY PLEASED HE SAID TO ARJUNA:

RECEIVE FROM ME THE SUPERIOR AND IRRESISTIBLE MISSILE, BRAHMASHIRAS, ALONG WITH THE SECRETS OF ITS USE.

THIS WEAPON IS UNIQUE IN ALL THE THREE WORLDS, THEREFORE YOU MUST KEEP YOUR MIND AND BODY IN CONTROL WHEN YOU RECEIVE IT.

THIS IS NOT TO BE USED AGAINST ANY HUMAN BEING. IF USED ON COMMON FOES IT COULD SET AFIRE THE WHOLE UNIVERSE.

YOU MAY USE IT ONLY TO KILL A FOE WHO IS NOT OF THE HUMAN KIND.

ARJUNA RECEIVED THE GREAT WEAPON IN ALL HUMILITY AND VOWED THAT HE WOULD ABIDE BY THE PRECEPTS OF THE GURU. DRONA ONCE AGAIN SAID TO HIM:

IN THIS WORLD THERE WILL BE NO ONE EQUAL TO YOU AS AN ARCHER. YOU SHALL BE INVINCIBLE AND FAMOUS.

SO DID DRONA ACQUIRE, SELECT, AND TRAIN DISCIPLES WHO WOULD ASSIST HIM IN AVENGING THE INSULT OF DRUPADA, HIS CHILD-HOOD FRIEND.

THUS ENDS THE FIFTH SESSION OF OUR RENDERING OF VAISHAMPAYANA'S RECITAL OF VYASA'S IMMORTAL ITIHASA, *THE MAHABHARATA.*

Mahabharata-6
ENTER KARNA

VEDA VYASA'S EPIC ON THE BHARATA RACE WAS FIRST RECITED IN PUBLIC, BY HIS DISCIPLE VAISHAMPAYANA, AT THE BEHEST OF THE AGELESS SEER VYASA HIMSELF.

THE RECITAL TOOK PLACE IN THE AUGUST PRESENCE OF KING JANAMEJAYA — GREAT-GRANDSON OF THE GRANDSON OF VYASA — AND THE MANY LEARNED SAGES WHO HAD ASSEMBLED FOR JANAMEJAYA'S SARPA SATRA.

THE FIFTH SESSION OF OUR RENDERING OF VAISHAMPAYANA'S RECITAL OF VYASA'S MAHABHARATA SPOKE OF HOW DRONA, SCORNED BY DRUPADA THE KING OF PANCHALA, CAME TO HASTINAPURA; OF HOW BHEESHMA APPOINTED HIM GURU OF THE PRINCES; AND OF HOW ARJUNA BY HIS PROWESS IN ARMS BECAME THE GURU'S FAVOURITE, TO THE CHAGRIN OF KARNA.

FOR PRONUNCIATION AND MEANING OF SANSKRIT WORDS AND PROPER NAMES, PLEASE SEE PAGE 32

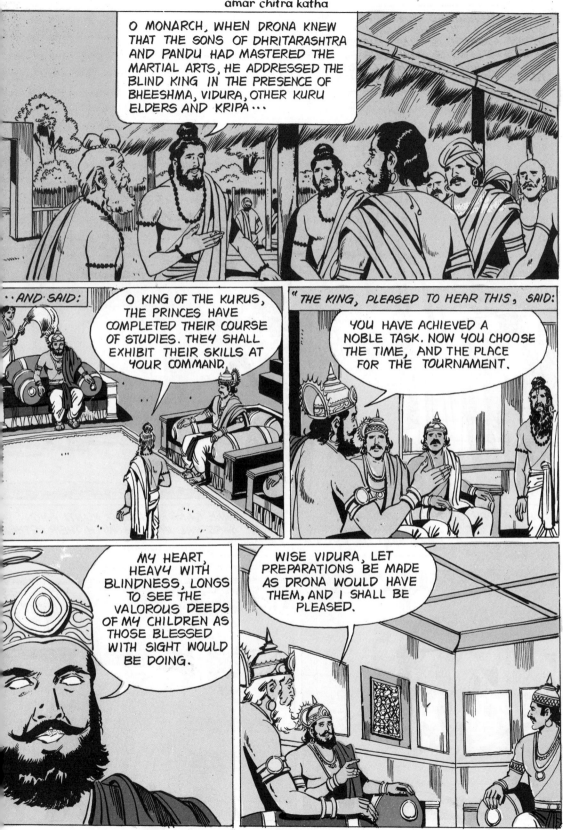

O MONARCH, WHEN DRONA KNEW THAT THE SONS OF DHRITARASHTRA AND PANDU HAD MASTERED THE MARTIAL ARTS, HE ADDRESSED THE BLIND KING IN THE PRESENCE OF BHEESHMA, VIDURA, OTHER KURU ELDERS AND KRIPA···

··AND·SAID:

O KING OF THE KURUS, THE PRINCES HAVE COMPLETED THEIR COURSE OF STUDIES. THEY SHALL EXHIBIT THEIR SKILLS AT YOUR COMMAND.

"THE KING, PLEASED TO HEAR THIS, SAID:

YOU HAVE ACHIEVED A NOBLE TASK. NOW YOU CHOOSE THE TIME, AND THE PLACE FOR THE TOURNAMENT.

MY HEART, HEAVY WITH BLINDNESS, LONGS TO SEE THE VALOROUS DEEDS OF MY CHILDREN AS THOSE BLESSED WITH SIGHT WOULD BE DOING.

WISE VIDURA, LET PREPARATIONS BE MADE AS DRONA WOULD HAVE THEM, AND I SHALL BE PLEASED.

"DRONA MEASURED OUT A PIECE OF SUITABLE LAND AND HAD IT SANCTIFIED AT AN AUSPICIOUS TIME. THERE THE CRAFTSMEN BUILT PAVILIONS FOR THE ROYALTY; AND WEALTHY CITIZENS HAD TENTS PITCHED FOR THEMSELVES.

"ON THE DAY OF THE TOURNAMENT, THE KING MADE HIS ENTRY ACCOMPANIED BY BHEESHMA, KRIPA AND THE RETINUE OF MINISTERS.

"THEN CAME GANDHARI AND KUNTI AND OTHER IMPERIAL WOMEN WITH THEIR RETINUE OF MAIDS.

"AND MEN AND WOMEN OF DIVERSE STATIONS AND ORDERS, EAGER TO WITNESS THE FEATS OF THE PRINCES, THRONGED THE SPOT TILL IN A SHORT WHILE THERE GATHERED A VAST ASSEMBLY.

"THEN DRONA, CLAD IN WHITE, ENTERED THE ARENA ACCOMPANIED BY HIS SON, ASHWATTHAMA.

"AFTER DRONA HAD CONDUCTED THE ACT OF CONSECRATION, SOME MEN CARRYING WEAPONS MADE THEIR ENTRY.

" AND THEN THOSE MAGNIFICENT PRINCES CAME UP, IN ORDER OF AGE, WITH YUDHISHTHIRA AT THEIR HEAD.

"EVEN AS THEY DISPLAYED THEIR EQUESTRIAN SKILLS, THE PRINCES HIT TARGETS WITH ARROWS THAT CARRIED THEIR NAMES.

"AND THE SPECTATORS EXCLAIMED:

WELL DONE!

WELL DONE!

"PROGRESSIVELY THE PRINCES EXHIBITED THEIR SKILL IN ARCHERY, IN CHARIOT RALLIES, IN FIGHTS ASTRIDE ELEPHANTS AND HORSES, AND IN FREE-HAND COMBATS. LAST OF ALL THEY DISPLAYED THEIR SWORDSMANSHIP.

WITH THE SWORD AND THE BUCKLER, O MONARCH, THEY REVEALED THROUGH WELL-WROUGHT BODIES THEIR FIRM STANCE, STRONG GRIP AND NIMBLE TURNS.

" AND THEN THE CONSTANT RIVALS, BHEEMA AND DURYODHANA, MOVED INTO THE ARENA.

" THEY FOUGHT, MOVING NOW TO THE LEFT, NOW TO THE RIGHT, NOW IN A CIRCLE AND NOW ALL OVER, LIKE TWO ENRAGED ELEPHANTS. AND VIDURA DESCRIBED EACH MOVE TO DHRITARASHTRA AND KUNTI TO GANDHARI.

"THE FIGHT BETWEEN THE TWO SPLIT THE CROWD. SOME CHEERED ONE, SOME THE OTHER.

HAIL DURYODHANA!

HAIL BHEEMA!

" AND PERCEIVING THIS, THE CLEVER DRONA SAID TO HIS SON:

STOP THE TWO BRAVE FIGHTERS LEST THE CROWD SHOULD GET INTOXICATED BY PARTISAN SPIRITS.

"ASHWATTHAMA RUSHED INTO THE ARENA AND RESTRAINED THE TWO WARRIORS.

"THEN DRONA CAME INTO THE ARENA AND, ORDERING THE MUSIC TO BE STOPPED, SAID IN A RINGING VOICE:

HERE COMES ARJUNA WHO IS DEARER TO ME THAN MY SON! HE IS THE SON OF INDRA, IS SUPREME IN ALL MARTIAL ARTS AND EQUALS VISHNU IN VALOUR.

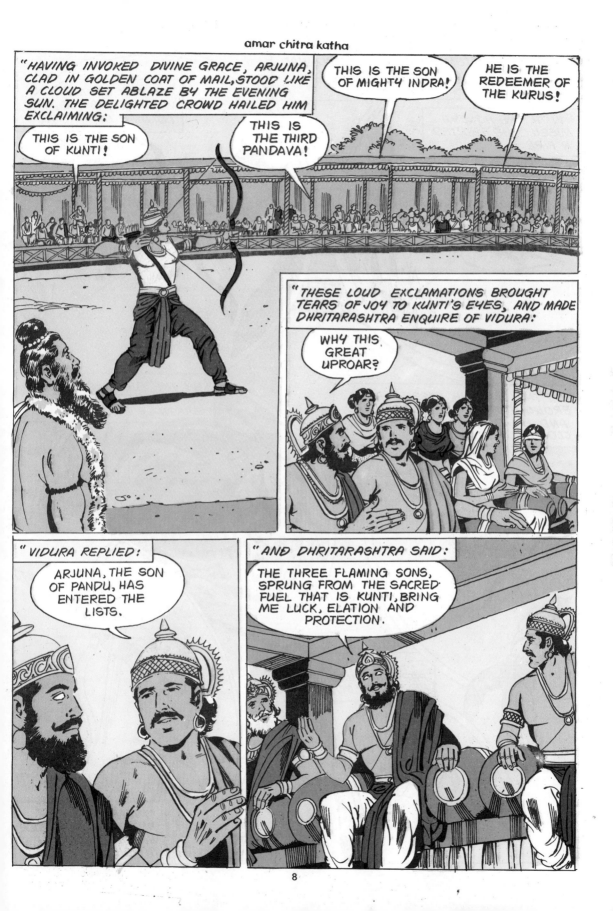

"HAVING INVOKED DIVINE GRACE, ARJUNA, CLAD IN GOLDEN COAT OF MAIL, STOOD LIKE A CLOUD SET ABLAZE BY THE EVENING SUN. THE DELIGHTED CROWD HAILED HIM EXCLAIMING:

THIS IS THE SON OF KUNTI!

THIS IS THE THIRD PANDAVA!

THIS IS THE SON OF MIGHTY INDRA!

HE IS THE REDEEMER OF THE KURUS!

"THESE LOUD EXCLAMATIONS BROUGHT TEARS OF JOY TO KUNTI'S EYES, AND MADE DHRITARASHTRA ENQUIRE OF VIDURA:

WHY THIS GREAT UPROAR?

"VIDURA REPLIED:

ARJUNA, THE SON OF PANDU, HAS ENTERED THE LISTS.

"AND DHRITARASHTRA SAID:

THE THREE FLAMING SONS, SPRUNG FROM THE SACRED FUEL THAT IS KUNTI, BRING ME LUCK, ELATION AND PROTECTION.

"ONCE THE EXCITEMENT OF THE CROWD HAD SUBSIDED, ARJUNA BEGAN TO DISPLAY HIS RESILIENCE TO HIS GURU.

"WITH THE AGNEYA MISSILE HE STARTED A FIRE...

"...AND BY THE VARUNA MISSILE, A COLUMN OF WATER.

"BY THE VAYAVYA MISSILE HE BROUGHT FORTH A GALE OF WIND, AND BY THE PARJANYA MISSILE, CLOUDS.

"BY THE BHAUMA MISSILE HE ENTERED INTO THE EARTH...

"...AND BY THE PARVATA MISSILE HE SET UP MOUNTAINS.

"THEN WITH THE ANTARDHANA MISSILE HE MADE HIMSELF INVISIBLE.

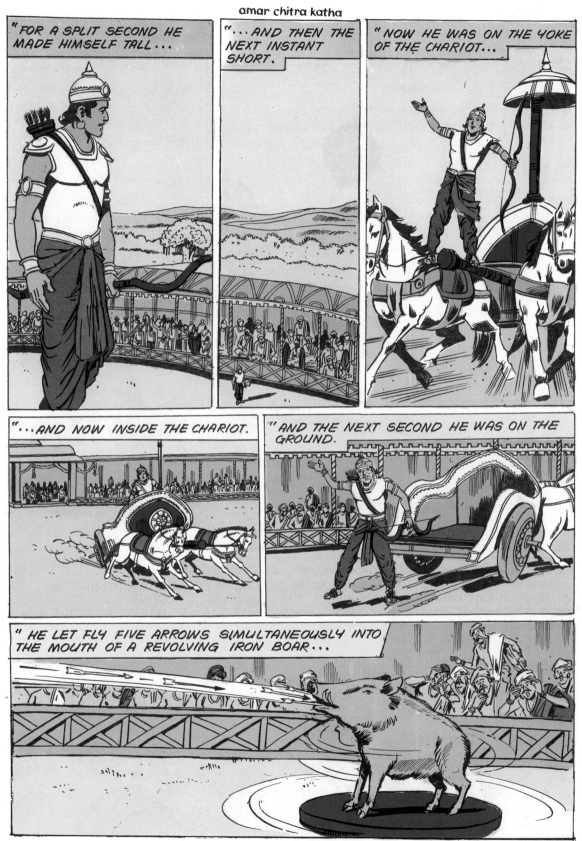

"...AND FOUND THE MARK FOR TWENTY-ONE OF HIS FLYING ARROWS, IN ONE SHOT, IN THE HOLLOW OF A SWINGING HORN.

"THEN ARJUNA EXHIBITED ALL THE COMPLEX MOVES IN FIGHTS WITH THE MACE AND THE SWORD.

"WHEN THE EVENTS WERE ALMOST OVER, WHEN THE INTEREST HAD WANED AND WHEN THE MUSIC WAS STILLED, THERE CAME FROM THE GATES THE SOUND OF THE SLAPPING OF ARMS, MIGHTY LIKE THE THUNDERBOLT SIGNIFYING IMMENSE STRENGTH, AND AT ONCE A THOUGHT PASSED THROUGH THE CROWD:

ARE THE MOUNTAINS CRACKING OR IS THE EARTH SPLITTING OR IS THE SKY ECHOING THE JOSTLE OF HEAVY CLOUDS?

"THEN THE SPECTATORS TURNED TOWARDS THE GATE. MEANWHILE THE PANDAVAS HAD TAKEN THEIR STANCE AROUND DRONA; AND THE KAURAVAS AND ASHWATTHAMA AROUND DURYODHANA.

"KARNA THEN STRODE IN, EVEN AS THE WONDER-STRUCK SPECTATORS MADE WAY FOR HIM. THAT HERO, GLORIOUS IN HIS CONGENITAL ARMOUR AND EARRINGS, BOW IN HAND AND SWORD AT HIS WAIST...

"...ENTERED THE ARENA LIKE A MASSIVE MOUNTAIN ON THE MOVE.

O MONARCH, KARNA THE SPLENDROUS ISSUE OF SURYA AND THE SON OF KUNTI STOOD TOWERING IN ALL HIS COUNTLESS ACCOMPLISHMENTS LIKE A GOLDEN PALM-TREE.

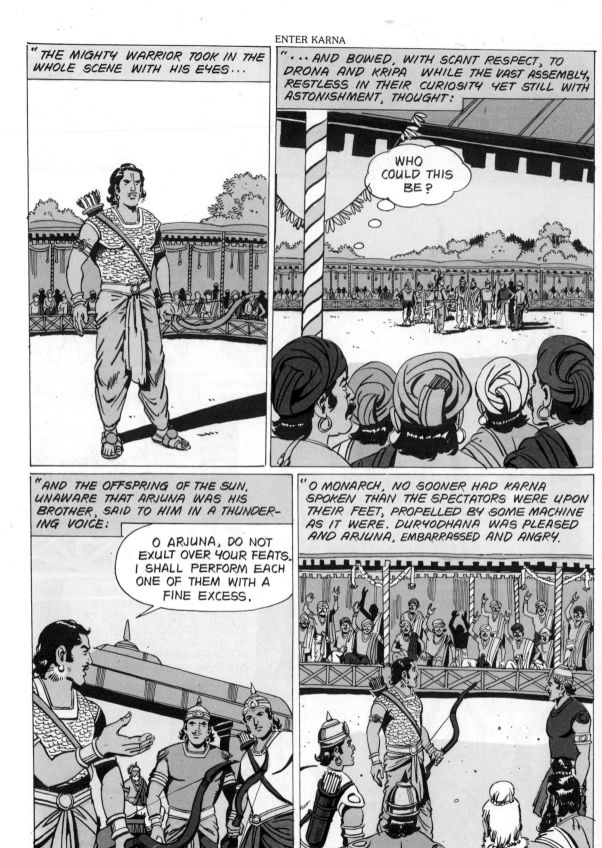

"THE MIGHTY WARRIOR TOOK IN THE WHOLE SCENE WITH HIS EYES...

"...AND BOWED, WITH SCANT RESPECT, TO DRONA AND KRIPA WHILE THE VAST ASSEMBLY, RESTLESS IN THEIR CURIOSITY YET STILL WITH ASTONISHMENT, THOUGHT:

WHO COULD THIS BE?

"AND THE OFFSPRING OF THE SUN, UNAWARE THAT ARJUNA WAS HIS BROTHER, SAID TO HIM IN A THUNDER- ING VOICE:

O ARJUNA, DO NOT EXULT OVER YOUR FEATS. I SHALL PERFORM EACH ONE OF THEM WITH A FINE EXCESS.

"O MONARCH, NO SOONER HAD KARNA SPOKEN THAN THE SPECTATORS WERE UPON THEIR FEET, PROPELLED BY SOME MACHINE AS IT WERE. DURYODHANA WAS PLEASED AND ARJUNA, EMBARRASSED AND ANGRY.

13

THEN KARNA, WITH PERMISSION FROM DRONA, DID ALL THAT ARJUNA HAD DONE BEFORE.

"AND, DELIGHTED, DURYODHANA HELD KARNA CLOSE AND SAID TO HIM:

WELCOME, O MIGHTY WARRIOR. IT IS MY GOOD FORTUNE THAT YOU ARE WITH ME. I AM AT YOUR COMMAND AND THE KINGDOM OF THE KURUS YOURS TO ENJOY.

" KARNA REPLIED:

I TAKE YOUR WORDS AS ALREADY FULFILLED. I LONG FOR A BOUT OF COMBAT WITH ARJUNA.

" DURYODHANA SAID:

PARTAKE OF THE GOOD THINGS OF LIFE WITH ME. BE GOOD TO YOUR COMPANIONS AND BRING DOWN YOUR FOOT ON YOUR ENEMIES.

" FEELING DISGRACED, ARJUNA SAID TO KARNA WHO STOOD LIKE A ROCK AMONGST THE BROTHERS:

O KARNA, SLAIN BY ME IN COMBAT, YOU SHALL GAIN THE REALM RESERVED FOR TRESPASSERS AND FOR THE BRAGGART.

"KARNA REPLIED:

WHY SPAR WITH WORDS LIKE THE WEAK? LET YOUR ARROWS SPEAK FOR YOU. AND I SHALL SEVER YOUR HEAD WITH MY ARROWS UNDER THE VERY WATCHFUL EYE OF YOUR GURU.

"PERMITTED BY DRONA...

"...AND EMBRACED BY HIS BROTHERS...

."...ARJUNA STEPPED FORWARD FOR THE FIGHT AND KARNA READIED HIS BOW AND ARROWS.

"THEN WITH STREAKS OF LIGHTNING AND THE RADIANT BOW OF INDRA, DARK CLOUDS CAME AND COVERED THE SKY. AND PERCEIVING INDRA WATCHING THE ARENA WITH AFFECTION...

"....SURYA SCATTERED THE CLOUDS AROUND HIM. AND KARNA WAS BRILLIANTLY VISIBLE UNDER A BENIGN SUN WHILE ARJUNA STOOD SHADED BY THE CLOUDS.

"BESIDE KARNA WERE DURYODHANA AND HIS BROTHERS...

...WHILE DRONA, KRIPA AND BHEESHMA WERE WITH ARJUNA.

"THE ENTIRE ASSEMBLY, INCLUDING THE WOMEN, WAS DIVIDED.

" KUNTI, AWARE OF THE FACTS, FELL UNCONSCIOUS.

" AND VIDURA, WITH THE HELP OF HER MAIDS, REVIVED KUNTI BY SPRINKLING AROMATIC WATER ON HER.

" ON REGAINING CONSCIOUSNESS, KUNTI SAW HER TWO BELLICOSE SONS AND BECAME AGITATED.

"THEN KRIPA, WHO KNEW WELL THE RULES OF DUELS, SURVEYED THE CONTENDING WARRIORS READY WITH BOW AND ARROWS AND SAID TO KARNA:

THIS PANDAVA HERE IS THE THIRD SON OF KUNTI AND IS OF THE KURU RACE. HE WILL ENGAGE YOU IN A DUEL. BUT...

...YOU TELL US OF WHICH ROYAL LINE YOU ARE AND WHO YOUR FATHER AND MOTHER ARE.

AND THEN ARJUNA MAY OR MAY NOT CHOOSE TO FIGHT WITH YOU. PRINCES NEVER FIGHT WITH MEN OF INFERIOR DESCENT

"KARNA'S FACE FELL AT KRIPA'S WORDS LIKE A LOTUS FLOWER WILTING UNDER PELTING RAIN. AND DURYODHANA SAID:

IT IS AVERRED THAT MEN OF NOBLE DESCENT, MEN OF VALOUR AND MEN WHO COMMAND ARMIES CAN ASPIRE TO KINGSHIP.

IF ARJUNA WILL NOT FIGHT ONE WHO IS NOT A KING, I SHALL CROWN KARNA KING OF ANGA.

"AT THAT VERY MOMENT, KARNA WAS INSTALLED ON A SEAT OF GOLD AND CROWNED KING OF ANGA, WITH CEREMONIAL GRAINS AND FLOWERS, BY MEN WHO KNEW THE MANTRAS. AND THE ROYAL UMBRELLA WAS RAISED OVER HIS HEAD WITH A BURST OF CHEERS OF APPROVAL.

"THEN KARNA SAID TO DURYODHANA:

WHAT MATCHING GIFT CAN I GIVE YOU IN RETURN FOR THE KINGDOM DONATED TO ME?

"AND DURYODHANA SAID TO HIM:

I LOOK FORWARD TO YOUR STAUNCH FRIENDSHIP.

"AND KARNA SAID:

SO BE IT.

"AND HAPPY AT THE TURN OF EVENTS THE TWO EMBRACED EACH OTHER.

"AND THEN CAME ADHIRATHA ON THE SCENE, WITH HIS CLOTHES ALL ASKEW, SUPPORTING HIS TREMBLING, PERSPIRING SELF ON A STAFF.

"AS SOON AS KARNA SAW HIM HE LEFT HIS WEAPONS AND:...

...IN FILIAL PIETY, BOWED HIS HEAD WHICH WAS STILL WET FROM ANOINTING.

MY SON!

"THE CHARIOTEER HELD HIS FOSTER-SON CLOSE AND SHED TEARS OF JOY.

"BHEEMA, WATCHING THE EVENTS, TOOK KARNA TO BE THE CHARIOTEER'S OFFSPRING AND SAID IN WORDS OF SLIGHT:

YOU, O SON OF A CHARIOTEER, DESERVE NOT DEATH AT THE HANDS OF ARJUNA. GO AND TAKE THE WHIP IN KEEPING WITH YOUR STATION.

NEITHER ARE YOU WORTHY OF REIGNING OVER ANGA, EVEN AS A CUR IS NOT WORTHY OF PARTAKING THE SACRAMENT BY THE SACRIFICIAL FIRE.

"WHEN KARNA HEARD THIS, HE DREW A DEEP BREATH AND WITH LIPS QUIVERING EVER SO LITTLE, SHOT A GLANCE AT THE SUN IN THE SKY.

" DURYODHANA THEN ROSE UP IN RAGE, LIKE AN ELEPHANT IN RUT, AND ROARED:

O BHEEMA, SUCH WORDS DO NOT BECOME YOU. MIGHT IS THE PRIME VIRTUE OF A KSHATRIYA.

THE ORIGIN OF HEROES LIKE THE SOURCE OF RIVERS REMAINS MYSTERIOUS.

THE ORIGIN OF THE MATCHLESS WARRIOR, OUR GURU DRONA, IS TO BE SOUGHT IN A WATER-POT; AND OF KRIPA IN A CLUMP OF REEDS. AND O PANDAVAS, I KNOW THE STORY OF YOUR BIRTH.

THIS KARNA HERE, WHO ALONG WITH HIS CONGENITAL ARMOUR BEARS EVERY AUSPICIOUS TRAIT, DESERVES TO BE THE KING NOT ONLY OF ANGA...

...BUT OF THE WHOLE WORLD.

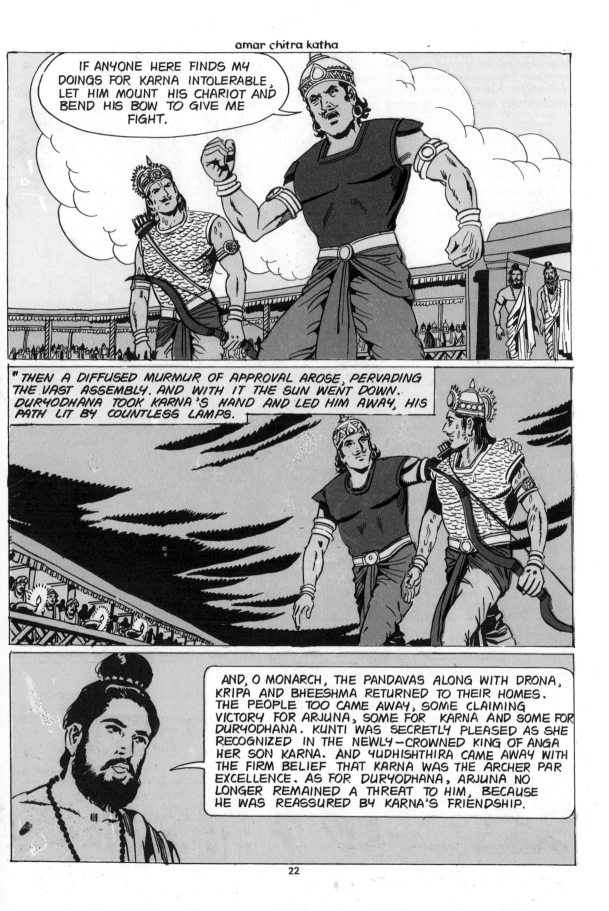

IF ANYONE HERE FINDS MY DOINGS FOR KARNA INTOLERABLE, LET HIM MOUNT HIS CHARIOT AND BEND HIS BOW TO GIVE ME FIGHT.

"THEN A DIFFUSED MURMUR OF APPROVAL AROSE, PERVADING THE VAST ASSEMBLY. AND WITH IT THE SUN WENT DOWN. DURYODHANA TOOK KARNA'S HAND AND LED HIM AWAY, HIS PATH LIT BY COUNTLESS LAMPS.

AND, O MONARCH, THE PANDAVAS ALONG WITH DRONA, KRIPA AND BHEESHMA RETURNED TO THEIR HOMES. THE PEOPLE TOO CAME AWAY, SOME CLAIMING VICTORY FOR ARJUNA, SOME FOR KARNA AND SOME FOR DURYODHANA. KUNTI WAS SECRETLY PLEASED AS SHE RECOGNIZED IN THE NEWLY-CROWNED KING OF ANGA HER SON KARNA. AND YUDHISHTHIRA CAME AWAY WITH THE FIRM BELIEF THAT KARNA WAS THE ARCHER PAR EXCELLENCE. AS FOR DURYODHANA, ARJUNA NO LONGER REMAINED A THREAT TO HIM, BECAUSE HE WAS REASSURED BY KARNA'S FRIENDSHIP.

"PERCEIVING THE PANDAVAS AND THE KAURAVAS TO BE COMPLETE WARRIORS, DRONA THOUGHT THE TIME HAD COME TO DEMAND THE TEACHER'S DUES. AND, O MONARCH, HE SAID TO THEM ONE DAY:

I DEMAND AS MY FEE, DRUPADA, THE KING OF PANCHALA OVERCOME IN BATTLE AND BROUGHT TO ME.

"ACCEDING TO THE DEMAND, THE PUGNACIOUS PRINCES MARCHED OUT ACCOMPANIED BY DRONA.

"THEY FOUGHT THE PANCHALAS IN THEIR WAY...

"...AND SURROUNDED THE CAPITAL OF DRUPADA.

"WHEN ARJUNA SAW DURYODHANA AND HIS BROTHERS AND KARNA AND YUYUTSU VYING WITH ONE ANOTHER TO LEAD THE ATTACK, HE SAID TO DRONA:

THEY WILL NOT BE ABLE TO SEIZE DRUPADA IN BATTLE. WE SHALL MOVE IN WHEN THEY HAVE EXPENDED THEIR ENERGY

"AND ARJUNA AND HIS BROTHERS WAITED OUTSIDE THE CITADEL.

"THE OTHER PRINCES, SPEEDING IN THEIR CHARIOTS AT THE HEELS OF THE CAVALRY, BROKE INTO THE CITY AND THUNDERED UP THE STREETS. MEANWHILE THE KING OF THE PANCHALAS, HEARING THE RUMBLE AND EYEING THE MARCHING ARMY...

"...CAME OUT OF HIS PALACE ACCOMPANIED BY HIS BROTHERS...

"...AND ASSAILING THE KURUS FROM HIS WHITE CHARIOT, BOMBARDED THEM WITH A VOLLEY OF ARROWS. THEN DURYODHANA AND HIS BROTHER DUHSHASANA, STUNG TO THE QUICK, SHOWERED ARROWS UPON THE ENEMY.

"THE MIGHTY BOWMAN DRUPADA, THOUGH LACERATED, RETALIATED WITH FORCE.

COURSING THROUGH THE BATTLEFIELD, LIKE A WHEEL OF FIRE, DRUPADA SHROUDED DURYODHANA, KARNA AND THE OTHER PRINCES WITH ARROWS.

THOUGH HE WAS FIGHTING SINGLEHANDED, O MONARCH, THE RAPIDITY WITH WHICH HE MOVED, STRUCK TERROR AMONG THE KURUS. THEY THOUGHT THEY WERE FIGHTING NOT ONE BUT MANY DRUPADAS. THE SHARP ARROWS OF THAT KING CAME FAST AND FIERCE, TILL THE PANCHALAS IN THEIR HOMES, BEAT THE DRUMS AND BLEW THE CONCHES OF VICTORY.

" ALL THE CITIZENS, YOUNG AND OLD, RUSHED OUT, AND THEY ADDED THEIR LEONINE ROAR TO THE RESONANCE OF THEIR BOW-STRINGS, AS THEY FELL UPON THE KAURAVAS.

" AND THE BATTLE-SCARRED KAURAVAS CAME WAILING TO THE PANDAVAS.

" WHEN THE PANDAVAS HEARD THE TERRIBLE LAMENT, THEY SALUTED DRONA...

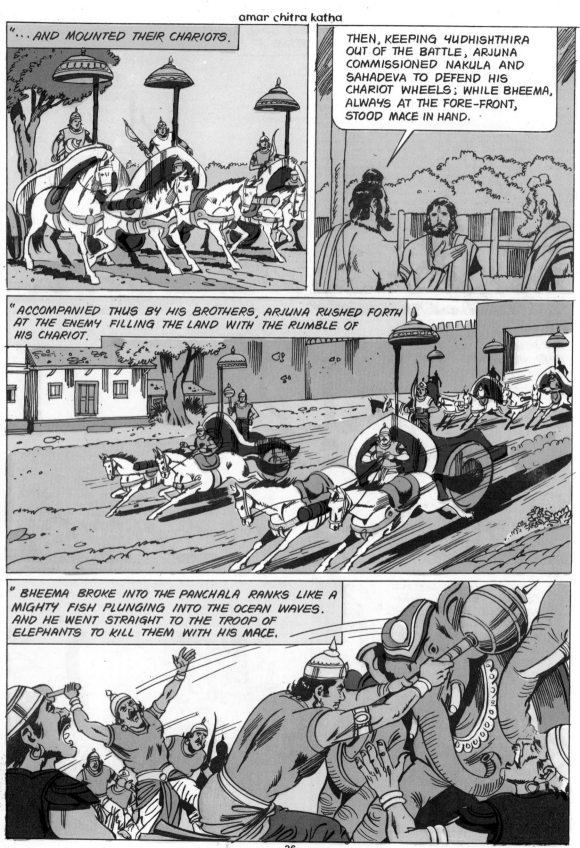

"...AND MOUNTED THEIR CHARIOTS.

THEN, KEEPING YUDHISHTHIRA OUT OF THE BATTLE, ARJUNA COMMISSIONED NAKULA AND SAHADEVA TO DEFEND HIS CHARIOT WHEELS; WHILE BHEEMA, ALWAYS AT THE FORE-FRONT, STOOD MACE IN HAND.

"ACCOMPANIED THUS BY HIS BROTHERS, ARJUNA RUSHED FORTH AT THE ENEMY FILLING THE LAND WITH THE RUMBLE OF HIS CHARIOT.

" BHEEMA BROKE INTO THE PANCHALA RANKS LIKE A MIGHTY FISH PLUNGING INTO THE OCEAN WAVES. AND HE WENT STRAIGHT TO THE TROOP OF ELEPHANTS TO KILL THEM WITH HIS MACE.

"MEANWHILE ARJUNA, INTENT ON PLEASING HIS GURU, MOVED TOWARDS DRUPADA, SHOOTING ARROWS AT HIM CEASELESSLY.

" THEN THE PANCHALAS, ROARING LIKE LIONS, ATTACKED ARJUNA FROM ALL SIDES. ENRAGED BY THE SHOUTS, HE STIFLED THEM WITH HIS NEVER-ENDING ARROWS.

O MONARCH, THE BATTLE BECAME TERRIBLE AND WONDROUS. IF THERE WAS A GAP BETWEEN THE AIMING AND DISPATCH OF ARJUNA'S ARROWS, THE OBSERVERS MISSED IT. CHEERING SOUNDS MINGLED WITH THOSE OF CHALLENGE.

" THEN THE KING OF PANCHALA RACED TOWARDS ARJUNA, LIKE SHAMBARA, THE ASURA DID TOWARDS INDRA IN DAYS OF YORE. EVEN AS DRUPADA COVERED ARJUNA WITH ARROWS...

"...THE PANDAVA PRINCE CUT THE KING'S BOW, AND HIS FLAGSTAFF INTO TWO...

"...AND FELLED HIS HORSES AND CHARIOTEER WITH FIVE ARROWS.

" AS THE KING STOOD GROPING FOR ANOTHER BOW, ARJUNA ABANDONED HIS OWN...

"...UNSHEATHED HIS SWORD, AND ROARING LIKE A LION, LEAPT OUT OF HIS CHARIOT...

"...ONTO THAT OF HIS ENEMY...

"...AND CAPTURED HIM. SEEING THIS...

"...THE PANCHALA ARMY FLED. ARJUNA WHO HAD PROVED HIS MIGHT TO ALL, LET OUT A ROAR OF TRIUMPH...

"...AND MADE HIS RETURN.

"THE PRINCES SEEING ARJUNA RETURNING THUS, BEGAN TO SLAY DRUPADA'S MEN.

"THEN ARJUNA SAID:

DRUPADA, THE VALIANT KING, IS RELATED TO THE KURU HEROES. THEREFORE, BHEEMA, DO NOT KILL HIS SOLDIERS. LET US GO AND PAY OUR GURU DAKSHINA.

O MONARCH, WHEN ARJUNA RESTRAINED HIM THUS, BHEEMA TURNED BACK THOUGH HIS YEARNING FOR BATTLE REMAINED UNFULFILLED.

AND THE PRINCES THEN OFFERED THE CAPTIVE KING TO THEIR GURU.

"DRONA, SEEING DRUPADA CAPTIVE, INDIGENT AND HUMILIATED, AND REMEMBERING THE KING'S EARLIER ARROGANCE, SAID:

I HAVE LAID DESOLATE YOUR KINGDOM AND CAPITAL. YOUR LIFE IS AT THE MERCY OF YOUR FOE. WOULD YOU REVIVE AN OLD FRIENDSHIP?

"WITH A SLIGHT SMILE HE CONTINUED:

WE BRAHMANAS ARE EVER-FORGIVING. AND MY AFFECTION FOR YOU WAS NURTURED BY OUR DAYS OF CHILDHOOD FUN IN THE ASHRAMA. THEREFORE, O KING, I SEEK YOUR FRIENDSHIP ONCE AGAIN.

I AM NOW GIVING HALF YOUR KINGDOM BACK TO YOU AS A GIFT. A KING, IT WAS SAID, COULD HAVE ONLY ANOTHER KING AS HIS FRIEND. THAT WAS WHY I STROVE FOR YOUR KINGDOM.

ALL THE TERRITORY TO THE SOUTH OF BHAGIRATHI SHALL BE YOUR KINGDOM, AND ALL THAT TO THE NORTH, MINE.

AND I SHALL REMAIN YOUR FRIEND, IF YOU CHOOSE IT TO BE SO.

"DRUPADA SEETHED WITHIN, BUT REPLIED:

SUCH MAGNANIMITY IN ONE WHO IS VALIANT AND NOBLE, LIKE YOU, IS NOT SURPRISING. I AM PLEASED WITH YOU, AND WISH TO HAVE YOUR LASTING FRIENDSHIP.

AFTER THIS, O MONARCH, DRONA RELEASED THE KING AND PRESENTED HIM WITH HALF HIS KINGDOM. DRUPADA, SAD IN MIND, CHOSE TO STAY IN THE CITY OF KAMPILYA IN THE PROVINCE OF MAKANDI, AND RULED OVER SOUTHERN PANCHALA UP TO THE RIVER CHARMANWATI.

THEN, CONVINCED THAT HIS KSHATRIYA MIGHT WAS NO MATCH AGAINST DRONA, DRUPADA WANDERED ALL OVER THE EARTH WITH THE HOPE OF OBTAINING A MIGHTY SON.

AND DRONA REIGNED OVER THE LAND NAMED AHICHCHHATRA—THE LAND WON BY ARJUNA IN WAR AND BESTOWED UPON HIS GURU. WITH ITS TOWNS AND ITS POPULACE.

THUS ENDS THE SIXTH SESSION OF OUR RENDERING OF VAISHAMPAYANA'S RECITAL OF VYASA'S IMMORTAL ITIHASA, **THE MAHABHARATA.**

Mahabharata – 7
THE CONSPIRACY

VEDA VYASA'S EPIC ON THE BHARATA RACE WAS FIRST RECITED IN PUBLIC BY HIS DICIPLE VAISHAMPAYANA AT THE BEHEST OF THE AGELESS SEER VYASA HIMSELF.

THE RECITAL TOOK PLACE IN THE AUGUST PRESENCE OF KING JANAMEJAYA—GREAT-GRANDSON OF THE GRANDSON OF VYASA— AND THE MANY LEARNED SAGES WHO HAD ASSEMBLED FOR JANAMEJAYA'S SARPA SATRA.

THE SIXTH SESSION OF OUR RENDERING OF VAISHAMPAYANA'S RECITAL OF VYASA'S MAHABHARATA INCLUDED THE INCIDENTS THAT LED TO KARNA'S SWEARING ETERNAL LOYALTY TO DURYODHANA. IT ALSO TOLD OF HOW DRONA, THROUGH HIS VALOROUS DISCIPLE ARJUNA, AVENGED THE HUMILIATION HE HAD SUFFERED AT THE HANDS OF DRUPADA, THE PANCHALA KING.

ONE DAY, SOON AFTER HE HAD HUMBLED DRUPADA, DRONA ADDRESSED ARJUNA IN THE PRESENCE OF THE KURU PRINCES.

"HE SAID:

WITH DEEP DILIGENCE, I RECEIVED THE BRAHMASHIRAS FROM RISHI AGNIVESHA WHO HAD ACQUIRED IT FROM RISHI AGASTYA.

AND I HAVE PASSED ON THAT WEAPON WHICH CAN ANNIHILATE THE EARTH TO YOU, BECAUSE YOU ALONE DESERVE IT.

IT IS ONLY PROPER THAT YOU NOW GIVE ME MY FEE IN THE PRESENCE OF YOUR COUSINS.

"WHEN ARJUNA GAVE HIS ASSENT THE GURU SAID:

IF EVER I ENGAGE YOU IN COMBAT YOU MUST FIGHT WITH ME — WITHOUT A MOMENT'S HESITATION.

"AND A YEAR AFTER DRONA HAD HUMBLED DRUPADA, DHRITARASHTRA HAVING OBSERVED YUDHISHTHIRA TO BE FIRM, YET TOLERANT AND SCRUPULOUSLY HONEST, INSTALLED HIM AS THE HEIR-APPARENT.

WITHIN A SHORT TIME, YUDHISHTHIRA, THE SON OF KUNTI, WITH HIS GOOD BEHAVIOUR, SAGACITY AND DISCERNMENT, EXCELLED HIS FATHER, PANDU, IN FAME.

"BHEEMA, THE SECOND PANDAVA, TOOK INSTRUCTIONS FROM BALARAMA IN WIELDING THE SWORD AND THE MACE, AND IN STEERING THE CHARIOT IN THE BATTLEFIELD; AND YET LIVED IN PEACEFUL ACCORD WITH HIS BROTHERS.

"ARJUNA WAS RENOWNED FOR HIS STRONG GRIP, AGILITY, MARKSMANSHIP AND PROFICIENCY WITH DIVERSE WEAPONS. HE WAS CONSIDERED UNRIVALLED BY DRONA.

"SAHADEVA LEARNT ALL THE PRECEPTS OF MORALS AND MANNERS FROM DRONA WHO WAS IN SPIRITUAL LORE AKIN TO BRIHASPATI, THE GURU OF THE DEVAS...

"...AND LIVED IN PEACEFUL ACCORD WITH HIS BROTHERS.

"NAKULA, THE FAVOURITE OF HIS BROTHERS, EARNED FAME AS A WIELDER OF UNUSUAL WEAPONS AND AS AN ATIRATHA.

✳ A warrior who is a past master in the art of charioteering.

"INDEED, ARJUNA AND HIS BROTHERS BECAME MIGHTY ENOUGH TO SLAY SAUVIRA, WHO DURING HIS THREE-YEAR-LONG YAGNA HAD KEPT EVEN THE INVADING GANDHARVAS AT BAY.

" AND ARJUNA VANQUISHED THE YAVANA KING WHOM EVEN PANDU IN DAYS GONE BY, COULD NOT.

" THEN VIPULA, WHO HAD SHOWN SCANT RESPECT FOR THE KURUS, WAS ALSO SLAIN.

" AND AFTER SUMITRA, ALSO KNOWN AS DATTAMITRA AND RENOWNED FOR HIS POWER IN BATTLES, WAS SUBDUED...

"...THE THIRD PANDAVA, IN HIS SINGLE CHARIOT AND WITH BHEEMA IN SUPPORT, PUT TO ROUT THE KINGS OF THE EAST AND THEIR TEN THOUSAND CHARIOTS. IN THE SAME WAY, HE CONQUERED THE SOUTH AND BROUGHT AMPLE BOOTY TO THE LAND OF THE KURUS.

THUS DID THE PANDAVAS, HAVING SUBJUGATED ALL OTHER TERRITORIES, EXTEND THEIR EMPIRE."

" BUT THE TIDINGS OF THE GAINFUL MIGHT OF THE PANDAVAS EMBITTERED DHRITARASHTRA.

"HE SAW THE BROODING JACKAL AND SAID:

HOW IS IT THAT YOU WHO ARE SO CLEVER LOOK VEXED? LET US FEAST OURSELVES ON THIS FLESH.

"THE JACKAL REPLIED:

O FEROCIOUS ONE, THE MOUSE CLAIMS THAT HIS MIGHT FELLED THE STAG. AND IT IS HIS MIGHT THAT WILL FEED YOU, THE KING OF BEASTS.

HIS BOASTFUL WORDS HAVE MADE THIS MEAL DISTASTEFUL TO ME.

"THE TIGER REPLIED:

IF THOSE ARE HIS WORDS, I SHALL KILL MY PREY WITH MY OWN HANDS AND THEN EAT.

THE TIGER WENT A-STALKING AND THE MOUSE REACHED THE SPOT. THE JACKAL SAID TO HIM:

LISTEN TO WHAT THE MONGOOSE HAS SAID TO ME.

HE SAID: THIS CARCASS IS POISONED BY THE TIGER'S CLAWS. I WILL NOT EAT OF IT. INSTEAD, O JACKAL, IF YOU PERMIT, I SHALL MAKE A MEAL OF THE MOUSE.

THUS, O KING, SHOULD YOUR ENEMIES BE SUBDUED.

YOU ARE A SUPERIOR PERSON OF AMPLE RESOURCES. BUT THE PANDAVAS ARE MEN OF MIGHT. PROTECT YOUR-SELF FROM THEM.

SHAPE YOUR CONDUCT TO SAFEGUARD YOURSELF AND YOUR CHILDREN FROM THE PANDAVAS. ACT IN ACCORDANCE WITH POLITY SO THAT YOU DO NOT HAVE TO REPENT.

"AND HAVING COUNSELLED DHRITARASHTRA THUS, O MONARCH, KANIKA RETURNED TO HIS ABODE.

AND THE MEN AND WOMEN, WHO WERE WITNESSES TO THE DEEDS OF THE PANDAVAS, SPOKE OPENLY ABOUT THEIR EXCELLENCE, INSIDE THE ASSEMBLIES OR OUTSIDE IN THE STREETS, THE CITIZENS TOOK THE NAME OF YUDHISHTHIRA AS THE MOST PROMISING RULER FOR THE KINGDOM.

" AND THEY SAID:

IF DHRITARASHTRA COULD NOT REIGN EARLIER BECAUSE OF HIS BLINDNESS. HOW CAN HE BE THE KING NOW?

BUT BHEESHMA, THE HONEST ONE, HAVING ALREADY GIVEN UP THE KINGDOM WILL REMAIN ADAMANT IN HIS VOW.

LET THE FIRST PANDAVA RULE THE KINGDOM. LET US INSTALL HIM ON THE THRONE. HE IS YOUNG, TRUTHFUL AND A FAVOURITE WITH THE ELDERS.

YES. HE WILL KEEP BHEESHMA AND DHRITARASHTRA AND THE LATTER'S CHILDREN IN HAPPINESS.

"DURYODHANA HEARD OF THESE REMARKS AND WAS SORELY VEXED BY THE PREFERENCE SHOWN FOR YUDHISHTHIRA. INTOLERANT AND JEALOUS HE WENT TO DHRITARASHTRA AND SAID:

O FATHER, CASTING YOU AND BHEESHMA ASIDE, THE CITIZENS WOULD HAVE YUDHISHTHIRA FOR THEIR KING. BHEESHMA WILL APPROVE OF THIS BECAUSE HE HAS RENOUNCED THE THRONE.

IN DAYS GONE BY, PANDU ACQUIRED THE KINGDOM BY VIRTUE OF HIS EXCELLENCE, AND YOU DID NOT ON ACCOUNT OF YOUR BLINDNESS.

IF PANDU'S SON ACQUIRES THE KINGDOM AS AN INHERITANCE FROM PANDU, THEN THE SONS BORN IN HIS FAMILY WILL CLAIM THE THRONE IN THE LINEAL PATTERN.

AND WE ALONG WITH OUR CHILDREN, SHALL REMAIN THE LOWLY ONES IN THE ROYAL LINE. O KING, WE SHALL BE THE ONES SPURNED BY THE WORLD.

THE CITIZENS ARE OUT TO CAST US INTO DIFFICULT TIMES.

IF SOVEREIGNTY HAD BEEN YOURS, WE WOULD HAVE INHERITED IT EVEN IF THE SUBJECTS WERE NOT IN FAVOUR.

THEREFORE, O KING, YOUR RULE MUST SPARE US THE HELL OF LIFELONG DEPENDENCE ON OTHER MEN'S CHARITY.

DHRITARASHTRA, WHOSE PERCEPTION WAS LIMITED BY THE TIDINGS HE HEARD, PONDERED OVER THE WORDS OF HIS SON AND KANIKA. AND HE WAS DISTURBED.

AND DURYODHANA, DUHSHASANA, KARNA AND SHAKUNI CONFERRED AMONG THEMSELVES.

"THEN DURYODHANA CAME TO DHRITARASHTRA AND SAID:

IF YOU CAN SEND THE PANDAVAS TO THE CITY OF VARANAVATA UNDER SOME PRETEXT WE SHALL BE RID OF THE FEAR OF THEM.

"DHRITARASHTRA THOUGHT OVER THE WORDS OF HIS SON AND SAID:

THE VIRTUOUS PANDU WAS EVER DUTIFUL TO HIS KINSMEN AND MORE SO TO ME. THERE WAS NO JOY THAT HE DID NOT SHARE WITH ME. HE GAVE ME HIS VERY EMPIRE.

PANDU'S SON IS EQUALLY VIRTUOUS AND THEREFORE HELD IN HIGH ESTEEM BY OUR SUBJECTS.

THE ACCUMULATED HERITAGE OF ROYAL POWER GIVES HIM MANY ALLIES.

THE COUNSELLORS AND THE SOLDIERS ARE ALL EITHER PANDU'S MEN OR THE OFF-SPRING OF PANDU'S MEN. THE CITIZENS TOO HAD BEEN CHERISHED BY PANDU.

WILL THEY NOT SLAY US FOR THE SAKE OF YUDHISHTHIRA?

16

"DURYODHANA REPLIED: I HAVE ALREADY FORESEEN THIS TURN OF EVENTS.

AND I HAVE WON OVER THE POWERFUL ONES WITH GIFTS AND ENDOWMENTS.

THE TREASURY AND THE COUNSELLORS ARE NOW UNDER OUR SWAY.

THEREFORE, O KING, ENSURE THE REMOVAL OF THE PANDAVAS TO VARANAVATA BY SOME SUBTLE PLAN.

WHEN MY HOLD ON THE DOMINION IS MADE FIRM, KUNTI AND HER CHILDREN MAY BE BROUGHT BACK.

" DHRITARASHTRA SAID: THE SAME THOUGHT HAS CROSSED MY MIND TOO. BUT I DID NOT SPEAK IT OUT LEST IT SHOULD BE DEEMED WICKED.

BESIDES, BHEESHMA, DRONA, VIDURA, KRIPA — NOT ONE OF THEM WILL AGREE TO SEND THE PANDAVAS AWAY.

WE AND THE PANDAVAS ARE EQUAL IN THE EYES OF THOSE MORAL SEERS WHO KNOW NO PARTIALITY.

AND THEREFORE HOW CAN WE ESCAPE BEING THE TARGETS OF THE IRE OF THESE ELDERS AS WELL AS OF THE CITIZENS?

"DURYODHANA ANSWERED:

BHEESHMA WILL EVER REMAIN NEUTRAL.

DRONA UNDOUBTEDLY WILL BE WHERE HIS SON IS AND HIS SON, ASHWATTHAMA, IS WITH ME.

KRIPA WILL BE WITH THESE TWO. HE WILL NEVER ABANDON HIS NEPHEW AND DRONA.

VIDURA IS DEPENDENT ON US THOUGH IN HIS HEART HE IS WITH OUR FOES. HIS LONE HELP TO THE PANDAVAS IS NO THREAT.

THEREFORE, REMOVE THE PANDAVAS AND THEIR MOTHER, AND WITH IT, THE TERRIBLE HURT THAT ROBS US OF OUR SLEEP.

THEN DURYODHANA AND HIS BROTHERS BEGAN WINNING THE PEOPLE OVER WITH WEALTH AND ESTATES.

AND WITH CLEVER PROMPTING FROM DHRITARASHTRA SOME COURTIERS BEGAN PRAISING VARANAVATA.

"AND THEY SAID:

THE FESTIVAL OF PASHUPATI, FAMOUS ALL OVER FOR ITS SPARKLING GLORY, IS TO BE HELD AT VARANAVATA.

THESE REPORTS KINDLED THE DESIRE OF THE PANDAVAS TO ATTEND THE FESTIVAL.

"WHEN THE KING CAME TO KNOW OF THE INTEREST AROUSED IN THE PANDAVAS, HE SAID TO THEM:

I AM REPEATEDLY BEING TOLD OF THE ATTRACTIONS OF VARANAVATA.

IF YOU WISH TO WITNESS THE FESTIVAL THERE, PROCEED TO VARANAVATA WITH YOUR FRIENDS IN A BEFITTING MANNER.

BE FREE WITH GIFTS TO THE BRAHMANAS AND MUSICIANS THERE.

HAVE YOUR FILL OF THE PLEASURES THERE AND THEN COME BACK TO HASTINAPURA.

" YUDHISHTHIRA SAW THROUGH THE EAGERNESS OF DHRITARASHTRA BUT KNOWING HIMSELF TO BE POWERLESS SAID:

SO BE IT.

" DURYODHANA THEN SECRETLY SUMMONED PUROCHANA, A TRUSTED COUNSELLOR, AND SAID:

THIS EARTH, RICH IN RESOURCES, IS AS MUCH YOURS AS MINE. SO GUARD IT CAREFULLY.

WHEN THE MANSION IS BUILT, INVITE KUNTI, HER SONS AND THEIR FRIENDS TO STAY IN IT. PROVIDE THEM WITH VEHICLES, SOFT BEDS, AND EXQUISITE FURNITURE AS WOULD PLEASE DHRITARASHTRA.

THEN WAIT FOR THE RIGHT MOMENT. AND CONDUCT EVERYTHING IN SUCH A MANNER THAT NOBODY GETS WISE TO OUR SCHEME.

IN DUE COURSE, WHEN THE PANDAVAS START SLEEPING IN TRUSTFUL CONFIDENCE, SET FIRE TO THE MANSION AT THE ENTRANCE.

WHEN THEY ARE FOUND DEAD IN THE FIRE PEOPLE WILL NOT BLAME US.

ASSENTING TO DURYODHANA'S INSTRUCTIONS, PUROCHANA WENT TO VARANAVATA AND CARRIED OUT THE ORDERS OF THE PRINCE.

"MEANWHILE ADDRESSING BHEESHMA, VIDURA AND DRONA AND KRIPA AND ASHWATTHAMA AND GANDHARI, YUDHISHTHIRA SAID IN ALL HUMILITY:

WE AND OUR RETINUE ARE GOING TO THE PLEASANT TOWN OF VARANAVATA AT THE COMMAND OF DHRITARASHTRA. SEE US OFF WITH WORDS OF GOODWILL AND FACES AGLOW WITH SMILES. YOUR BLESSINGS WILL WARD OFF ANY DANGER THERE FOR US.

"THE KURU ELDERS, PLEASED IN MIND, BLESSED THEM SAYING:

LET ALL THE ELEMENTS BE FAVOURABLE TO YOU ON YOUR WAY. NOTHING INCLEMENT SHALL BEFALL YOU.

THEN THE PANDAVAS BADE FAREWELL TO THE ELDERS, EMBRACED THEIR CONFRERES, ACCEPTED THE COURTEOUS REGARD OF THE CHILDREN, CIRCUMAMBULATED THE VENERABLE LADIES, AND TOUCHED THE FEET OF BHEESHMA, DHRITARASHTRA, DRONA, KRIPA, VIDURA AND OTHER ELDERS.

"THEN THE DISTRAUGHT PRINCES MOUNTED THEIR CHARIOTS WITH HORSES THAT WERE AS SWIFT AS A STORM.

"AND WITH VIDURA PRECEDING THEM, THE CITIZENS FOLLOWED THE PRINCES AS THEY DROVE OUT.

"THE DISTRESS OF THE PANDAVAS, HOWEVER, AFFECTED THE CITIZENS WHO FOLLOWED THEM.

"ON HEARING THESE SAD WORDS OF THE CITIZENS, YUDHISHTHIRA REFLECTED FOR A MOMENT AND THEN SAID TO THEM WITH A HEAVY HEART:

IT IS OUR DUTY TO CARRY OUT THE KING'S COMMAND BECAUSE THE KING IS TO BE REVERED AS THE FATHER AND THE PROTECTOR.

YOU ARE OUR FRIENDS. LEAVE YOUR BLESSINGS WITH US AND RETURN TO YOUR HOMES.

AND AT THE OPPORTUNE MOMENT DO FOR US ALL THAT IS BENEFICIAL TO US.

"AND THE CITIZENS TOOK LEAVE OF THEM AND RETURNED TO THEIR HOMES.

" AFTER THE CITIZENS HAD DEPARTED, THE WISE VIDURA SPOKE TO YUDHISHTHIRA IN THE DIALECT OF THE MLECHCHHAS WHICH WAS UNFAMILIAR TO ALL BUT YUDHISHTHIRA. HE SAID:

THE BLIND ONE KNOWS NOT THE DIRECTION. REMEMBER THAT ONE WHOSE BASE IS NOT FIRM LOSES ALL SENSE OF VALUES.

HE WHO IS AWARE OF THE PLANNED SCHEMES OF FOES SHOULD PROTECT HIMSELF FROM FORESEEN CALAMITIES.

HE WHO ACTS IN THE KNOWLEDGE THAT IT IS NOT WEAPONS OF METAL ALONE THAT PROVE FATAL, STANDS BEYOND THE PALE OF DANGER.

GO FORTH AND YOU SHALL FIND THE PATH. FOR, ONE WHO HAS POWER OVER THE FIVE SENSES WILL NEVER BE OVERPOWERED.

"AND YUDHISHTHIRA SAID:

I HAVE UNDERSTOOD.

AND VIDURA HAVING CAUTIONED THEM THUS RETURNED TO THE CITY.

"AND THEN KUNTI SAID TO YUDHISHTHIRA:

VIDURA SPOKE TO YOU WORDS WHICH DID NOT SAY ANYTHING.

YET YOU AGREED TO WHAT HE SAID. AND WE HAVE NOT UNDERSTOOD ANYTHING.

IF IT IS PROPER FOR US TO KNOW, THEN WE WOULD LIKE TO KNOW ALL THAT WAS SAID.

30

"YUDHISHTHIRA SAID:

FIRST OF ALL HE WARNED US OF FIRE IN THE MANSION BUILT FOR US. HE ALSO INFORMED ME THAT NO PATH OF ESCAPE SHALL REMAIN UNKNOWN TO US. AND···

···THAT THOSE WHO CAN SUBJUGATE THEIR SENSES WILL RULE THE WORLD.

I REPLIED THAT I UNDERSTOOD.

AND THE PANDAVAS, ARMED WITH THE COUNSEL OF VIDURA, MADE THEIR WAY TO VARANAVATA.

AND THUS ENDS THE SEVENTH SESSION OF OUR RENDERING OF VAISHAMPAYANA'S RECITAL OF VYASA'S IMMORTAL ITIHASA THE MAHABHARATA.

Mahabharata–8
THE ESCAPE

VEDA VYASA'S EPIC ON THE BHARATA RACE WAS FIRST RECITED IN PUBLIC, BY HIS DISCIPLE VAISHAMPAYANA, AT THE BEHEST OF THE AGELESS SEER VYASA HIMSELF.

THE RECITAL TOOK PLACE IN THE AUGUST PRESENCE OF KING JANAMEJAYA— GREAT-GRANDSON OF VYASA—AND THE MANY LEARNED SAGES WHO HAD ASSEMBLED FOR JANAMEJAYA'S SARPA SATRA.

THE SEVENTH SESSION OF OUR RENDERING OF VAISHAMPAYANA'S RECITAL OF VYASA'S MAHABHARATA RECOUNTED HOW THE ASCENDANCY OF THE SONS OF PANDU OVER HIS OWN, ROUSED THE ENVY OF DHRITARASHTRA; AND HOW HE, ADVISED BY HIS POLITICAL MENTOR KANIKA AND ABETTED BY HIS SON DURYODHANA, PLOTTED THE EXILE OF THE PANDAVAS TO THE CITY OF VARANAVATA.

AS THE PANDAVAS ARRIVED AT VARANAVATA, THEY WERE WELCOMED JOYFULLY AND CEREMONIALLY BY THE PEOPLE THERE, AND THE ENTIRE CITY WENT GAY.

THE PANDAVAS RECIPROCATED BY VISITING THE HOMES OF PEOPLE OF DIVERSE STATIONS. THEN PUROCHANA LED THEM TO A PALACE.

FOR TEN DAYS THEY STAYED IN THAT PALACE ATTENDED BY PUROCHANA AND THE CITIZENS. THEN PUROCHANA SPOKE TO THE PRINCES OF THE MANSION EXCLUSIVELY BUILT FOR THEM. AT HIS INSTANCE THE PANDAVAS LEFT THE PALACE...

"...AND ENTERED THE MANSION. AND YUDHISHTHIRA SENSING THE AROMA OF GHEE AND FAT AND LACQUER...

"...LATER SAID TO BHEEMA:

THIS HOUSE IS BUILT OF INFLAMMABLE MATERIALS. PUROCHANA, THE WICKED HENCHMAN OF DURYODHANA, IS WAITING TO BURN ME TO DEATH.

WISE VIDURA KNEW OF IT AND HAD WARNED ME ABOUT IT.

OUR YOUNGEST UNCLE, EVER WISHING US WELL, TOLD ME THAT THIS HOUSE OF RUIN WAS BUILT AS COMMANDED BY DURYODHANA.

EVEN IF OUR DEATH BY FIRE MAKES GRAND-FATHER BHEESHMA ANGRY, WHY WOULD HE SHOW IT AND INCUR THE WRATH OF THE KAURAVAS?

OR PERHAPS HE AND THE OTHER ELDERS MIGHT SHOW IT ONLY TO APPEAR RIGHTEOUS.

"THEN BHEEMA SAID:

IF YOU KNOW THIS TO BE AN INFLAMMABLE HOUSE, LET US RETURN TO THE PALACE WHERE WE FIRST STAYED.

" AND YUDHISHTHIRA REPLIED:

I THINK WE SHOULD CONTINUE TO LIVE HERE SIMULATING INNOCENCE AND YET BE CAUTIOUS AND ALERT.

IF PUROCHANA KNOWS THAT WE HAVE READ HIS DESIGNS, HE MAY STRAIGHT AWAY BURN US TO DEATH.

IF WE FLEE THIS PLACE, DURYODHANA WITH HIS SPIES WILL CERTAINLY STALK US TO DEATH.

HE HAS THE POWER OF RANK. HE HAS ALLIES. HE HAS THE FULL TREASURY. WE HAVE NONE OF THESE.

WILL HE NOT PLOT OUR DEATH BY DEVIOUS MEANS?

LET US THEREFORE DISSEMBLE OUR INTENTIONS AND SPEND OUR DAYS ROAMING OVER THIS LAND AND HUNTING. THEN THE PATHS OF ESCAPE WILL BE FAMILIAR TO US.

WE SHALL LIVE HERE GUARDING OUR SAFETY AND PLANNING OUR ESCAPE, BUT ALL CONCEALED FROM PUROCHANA AND THE PEOPLE. WE SHALL ALSO HAVE AN UNDER-GROUND OUTLET FROM OUR CHAMBER, DUG IN SECRECY.

IF WE ACT IN THIS WAY, NO FIRE WILL BE ABLE TO CONSUME US.

"THEN ONE DAY, A FRIEND OF VIDURA'S CAME TO THE PANDAVAS SECRETLY AND SAID:

VIDURA HAS SENT ME, AN EXPERT MINER, TO BE OF HELP TO THE PANDAVAS.

"HEARING HIS WORDS, YUDHISHTHIRA SAID:

I NOW KNOW YOU TO BE VIDURA'S FAITHFUL FRIEND. LOOK AFTER US AS VIDURA ALWAYS DOES.

RESCUE US FROM THE DISASTER OF WHICH VIDURA HAD SPOKEN AND WHICH IS AT OUR DOOR NOW.

O SAVE US WITHOUT THE KNOWLEDGE OF PUROCHANA.

THE MINER CONCURRED, O MONARCH, AND STARTED DIGGING A SECRET TUNNEL.

"THE MOUTH OF THE TUNNEL WAS IN THE CENTRE OF THE MANSION ON A LEVEL WITH ITS FLOOR...

"...AND WAS COVERED AND CONCEALED.

"AT NIGHT THE PANDAVAS, READY WITH THEIR WEAPONS, SLEPT WITHIN. AND DURING THE DAY THEY WENT A-HUNTING FROM FOREST TO FOREST.

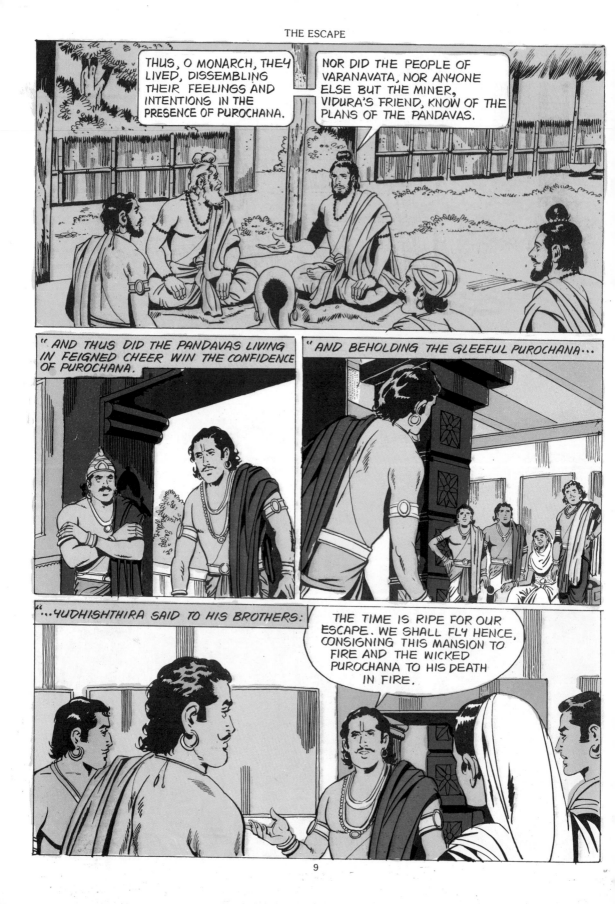

THUS, O MONARCH, THEY LIVED, DISSEMBLING THEIR FEELINGS AND INTENTIONS IN THE PRESENCE OF PUROCHANA.

NOR DID THE PEOPLE OF VARANAVATA, NOR ANYONE ELSE BUT THE MINER, VIDURA'S FRIEND, KNOW OF THE PLANS OF THE PANDAVAS.

"AND THUS DID THE PANDAVAS LIVING IN FEIGNED CHEER WIN THE CONFIDENCE OF PUROCHANA.

"AND BEHOLDING THE GLEEFUL PUROCHANA...

"...YUDHISHTHIRA SAID TO HIS BROTHERS:

THE TIME IS RIPE FOR OUR ESCAPE. WE SHALL FLY HENCE, CONSIGNING THIS MANSION TO FIRE AND THE WICKED PUROCHANA TO HIS DEATH IN FIRE.

"THEN DURING AN ALMSGIVING RITUAL, KUNTI ARRANGED TO HAVE BRAHMANAS FED.

"SEEKING FOOD, A NISHADA WOMAN AND HER FIVE SONS CAME THERE, PROMPTED AS IT WERE BY A DESTINY OF DOOM.

"O MONARCH, THE SIX OF THEM, SENSELESS WITH A SURFEIT OF WINE, SLEPT INSIDE THE MANSION LIKE THE DEAD.

"AND IN THE NIGHT, WHEN ALL WERE ASLEEP, AND WHEN STRONG WINDS WERE BLOWING...

"...BHEEMA SET FIRE TO THAT PART OF THE MANSION WHERE PUROCHANA LAY SLEEPING...

"...AND THEN, TO ITS ENTRANCE...

"...AND THEN, TO ITS VARIOUS PARTS.

WHEN THE SONS OF PANDU SAW THAT THE MANSION WAS ALL AND WELL ABLAZE...

"...THEY WITH THEIR MOTHER ENTERED THE TUNNEL.

THEN, O MONARCH, THE CITIZENS WERE AWAKENED BY THE RAGING FIRE AND ITS ROARING FLAMES.

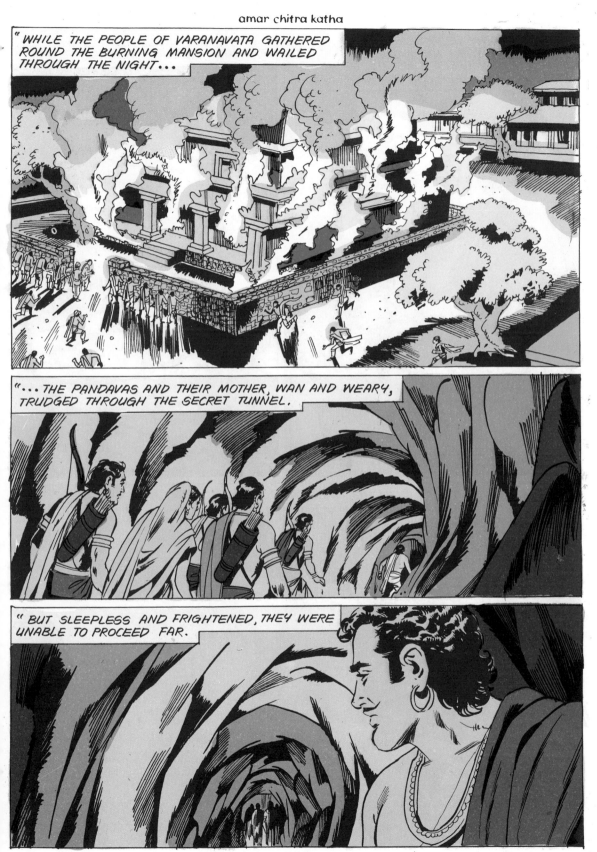

"WHILE THE PEOPLE OF VARANAVATA GATHERED ROUND THE BURNING MANSION AND WAILED THROUGH THE NIGHT...

"...THE PANDAVAS AND THEIR MOTHER, WAN AND WEARY, TRUDGED THROUGH THE SECRET TUNNEL.

"BUT SLEEPLESS AND FRIGHTENED, THEY WERE UNABLE TO PROCEED FAR.

" THEN, O MONARCH, THE VALIANT BHEEMASENA, WITH HIS IMMENSE STRENGTH AND SPEED, CARRIED UPON HIMSELF HIS MOTHER AND HIS BROTHERS...

"...AND CONTINUED ON HIS WAY PUSHING THROUGH THE DARKNESS...

"...FELLING THE TREES WITH HIS CHEST AND SHAKING THE EARTH UNDER HIS FOOTFALL.

"AT THIS JUNCTURE THERE ARRIVED, IN THAT FOREST ON THE BANKS OF THE GANGA, A TRUSTED SERVANT SENT BY THE FORESIGHTED VIDURA.

" HE CAME UPON THE PANDAVAS AND THEIR MOTHER CHECKING THE DEPTH OF THE WATER TO CROSS THE RIVER.

"HE SAID:

O YUDHISHTHIRA, HERE ARE THE WORDS SPOKEN TO YOU ONCE BY VIDURA.

HE WILL SURVIVE WHO PRESERVES HIMSELF WITH THE KNOWLEDGE THAT FIRE WHICH BURNS UP FORESTS AND WARDS OFF WINTER WILL NOT SINGE THOSE IN FOREST HIDEOUTS.

"HE THEN LED THE ANGUISHED PANDAVAS AND THEIR MOTHER INTO THE BOAT.

" AND AS HE FERRIED THEM ACROSS THE RIVER HE SAID:

VIDURA IN HIS AMPLE AFFECTION FOR YOU SAYS THAT...

...YOU MUST CAST OFF YOUR GLOOM AND CONTINUE YOUR JOURNEY WITH AN EVEN MIND.

"AND WHEN THEY REACHED THE OPPOSITE BANK...

"...HE RETURNED THE WAY HE HAD COME.

MEANWHILE SOON AFTER THE PANDAVAS HAD ESCAPED, THE MINER SENT BY VIDURA HAD, EXPECTING A THOROUGH SEARCH LATER, CONCEALED THE ENTRANCE TO THE TUNNEL BY CLEVER LEVELLING.

AND WHEN THE NIGHT CAME TO AN END, THE VAST ASSEMBLY OF CITIZENS RUMMAGED THE EMBERS FOR THE REMAINS OF THE PANDAVAS.

AND THEY FOUND THE CHARRED REMAINS OF THE POOR NISHADA WOMAN AND HER SONS.

AND THEY SAW THAT THE MANSION WAS OF LACQUER AND THAT PUROCHANA HAD DIED BY FIRE.

"AND THEY SAID:

THAT WRETCHED KNAVE PUROCHANA, INDUCED BY DURYODHANA, BUILT A HOUSE OF RUIN AND GOT HIMSELF BURNT IN IT.

IT IS MEET THAT THE VILLAIN WHO KILLED THE TRUSTFUL AND NOBLE PANDAVAS BY FIRE MET HIS OWN END IN THAT FIRE.

LET DHRITARASHTRA BE INFORMED THAT HIS GOAL IS ACHIEVED! THAT THE PANDAVAS ARE BURNT!

AND THE TIDINGS WERE CARRIED TO DHRITARASHTRA.

"WHEN DHRITARASHTRA HEARD OF THE DEATH OF THE PANDAVAS HE WAILED IN DEEP SORROW AND SAID:

I SUFFER THE AGONY OF PANDU'S DEATH TODAY, IN THE DEATH OF THOSE HEROES AND THEIR MOTHER.

LET THEIR KINSMEN AND FRIENDS, AND MY MEN, GO WITHOUT DELAY TO VARANAVATA FOR THE FUNERAL RITES OF THE DAUGHTER OF KUNTIBHOJA AND THOSE VALIANT ONES.

LET ALL THAT MUST BE DONE BY ME FOR THE GOOD OF KUNTI AND THE PANDAVAS BE ACCOMPLISHED BY MY WEALTH.

"HAVING SAID THIS, DHRITARASHTRA ALONG WITH HIS KINSMEN MADE LIBATIONS OF WATER TO THE SONS OF PANDU.

"AND THEN ALL OF THEM CRIED OUT IN MOURNING:

OH, YUDHISHTHIRA! OH, YUVARAJA OF THE KURU RACE!

OH, BHEEMA! OH, ARJUNA!

OH NAKULA! OH SAHADEVA! OH KUNTI!

THE CITIZENS TOO MOURNED FOR THE PANDAVAS. ONLY VIDURA MOURNED LITTLE BECAUSE HE WAS IN THE KNOW.

"MEANWHILE THE PANDAVAS, GUIDED BY THE STARS, HAD TAKEN THE PATH SOUTHWARD.

"AND, AFTER MUCH TRAVAIL, THEY REACHED A THICK FOREST.

"THEY WERE TIRED AND THIRSTY AND NEAR-BLIND WITH SLEEP. THEN YUDHISHTHIRA SAID TO BHEEMA:

WE DO NOT KNOW WHETHER PUROCHANA IS BURNT OUT OR NOT.

COULD THERE BE ANYTHING MORE DIRE THAN THAT?

"...WENT FORTH UNDAUNTED. AND AS HE SPED THROUGH THE FOREST, WITH THE FORCE OF VAYU HIMSELF, THE PANDAVAS ALMOST FAINTED.

"SPANNING WIDE TURBULENT STREAMS...

"...AND TRAVERSING CRAGGY TERRAIN...

TOWARDS EVENING HE REACHED A DESOLATE JUNGLE WHERE ROAMED PREDATORY BEASTS AND WHERE THERE WAS SCANT WATER OR FRUITS OR ROOTS.

"AS DARKNESS CREPT UPON THE TWILIGHT, THE HOWL OF ANIMALS TURNED MORE RAUCOUS; AND AN UNTIMELY WIND BEGAN TO BLOW WHICH, TEARING THROUGH THE JUNGLE, SCATTERED THE DRIED LEAVES EVEN AS IT GROUNDED STURDY TREES.

"THE PANDAVAS, WEIGHED DOWN BY SLEEP, WERE UNABLE TO GO ON. THEY SAT DOWN THERE. THEN KUNTI, OPPRESSED BY THIRST, SAID TO HER SONS:

I AM THE MOTHER OF FIVE PANDAVAS. I AM IN THE MIDST OF THEM AND YET I AM RACKED BY THIRST.

THESE WORDS OF HIS MOTHER, O MONARCH, SCORCHED THE HEART OF BHEEMA AND HE SET OUT.

26

"AS HE WOUND HIS WAY THROUGH THE THICK, DESERTED JUNGLE, HE SAW A BEAUTIFUL, SPREADING BANYAN TREE.

"HE SET HIS MOTHER AND BROTHERS DOWN, AND SAID TO THEM:

I CAN HEAR THE CALL OF WATER-BIRDS. THERE MUST BE A POOL NEAR BY.

YOU REST HERE WHILE I GO IN SEARCH OF WATER.

" BHEEMA WENT IN THE DIRECTION OF THE CRIES OF THE WATER-BIRDS...

"... AND SOON ARRIVED AT A LAKE.

"... WHERE HE SLAKED HIS THIRST AND THEN BATHED.

" THEN SOAKING HIS UPPER CLOTH...

"... HE SPED BACK...

"... TO HIS MOTHER AND BROTHERS.

"FINDING THEM SLEEPING ON THE BARE EARTH, HE WAS OVERCOME BY GRIEF AND CRIED:

ACCURSED THAT I AM, I AM FORCED TO SEE THIS MOST PAINFUL SIGHT OF MY MOTHER SLEEPING ON THIS RUDE GROUND!

KUNTI. THE DAUGHTER OF KUNTIBHOJA, THE DAUGHTER-IN-LAW OF VICHITRAVEERYA, THE WIFE OF KING PANDU TO SLEEP THUS ON BARE EARTH!

KUNTI WHO HAS BORNE THE SONS OF DHARMA, INDRA AND VAYU! SHE WHO RECLINED ON THE SOFT BEDS OF ROYAL CHAMBERS, LYING HERE ON THE CRUDE EARTH!

O WHAT CAN BE MORE DISTRESSING THAN TO WATCH THESE PRINCES AMONG MEN ASLEEP ON THE DUSTY EARTH.

HE WHO HAS NO RELATIVES TO TAINT THE FAMILY WITH JEALOUSY, IS HAPPY IN THIS WORLD, LIKE THE SOLITARY FRUIT-BEARING TREE WHICH COMES TO BE REVERED AS SACRED BY ALL BECAUSE IT IS UNIQUE.

THOSE WHO ABOUND IN RELATIVES WHO ARE JUST AND VALIANT ARE ALSO HAPPY IN THIS WORLD.

THOSE WHO ARE POWERFUL WITH AMPLE WEALTH, AND AN ABUNDANCE OF FRIENDS AND RELATIVES, STAND TALL LIKE THE TREES OF A FOREST.

AS FOR US, IT HAS BEEN EXILE AT THE HANDS OF WICKED DHRITARASHTRA AND HIS SONS; AND A FORTUITOUS ESCAPE FROM A FIERY DEATH.

O DURYODHANA, YOUR VISION IS IMPAIRED. YOU REMAIN SMUG IN THE THOUGHT THAT THE GODS ARE WITH YOU.

BUT IF YOU ARE ALIVE IT IS ONLY BECAUSE YUDHISHTHIRA DOES NOT GET ANGRY WITH YOU AND COMMAND ME TO KILL YOU.

OTHERWISE, IN MY FULL RAGE, I WOULD SEND YOU AND YOUR BROTHERS AND KARNA AND SHAKUNI TO THE REALMS OF THE DEAD.

"HAVING SAID THIS, BHEEMA WRUNG HIS HANDS IN RAGE AND LET OUT A SIGH AND SAID:

THERE MUST BE A TOWN NOT FAR AWAY FROM THIS JUNGLE.

THEY ARE ASLEEP WHILE THEY SHOULD BE ALERT. WELL...I SHALL KEEP AWAKE. WHEN THEY GET UP REFRESHED THEY CAN QUENCH THEIR THIRST WITH THIS.

SAYING THIS BHEEMA SAT THERE AWAKE, ALONE.

THUS DID THE PANDAVAS, WITH THE HELP OF VIDURA, ESCAPE THE FIERY DEATH THAT THE KAURAVAS HAD DESIGNED FOR THEM AT VARANAVATA.

AND THUS ENDS THE EIGHTH SESSION OF OUR RENDERING OF VAISHAMPAYANA'S RECITAL OF VYASA'S IMMORTAL ITIHASA, *THE MAHABHARATA*.

Mahabharata – 9
The Birth of Ghatotkacha

VEDA VYASA'S EPIC ON THE BHARATA RACE WAS FIRST RECITED IN PUBLIC, BY HIS DISCIPLE VAISHAMPAYANA, AT THE BEHEST OF THE AGELESS SEER VYASA HIMSELF.

THE RECITAL TOOK PLACE IN THE AUGUST PRESENCE OF KING JANAMEJAYA — GREAT GRANDSON OF THE GRANDSON OF VYASA — AND THE MANY LEARNED SAGES WHO HAD ASSEMBLED FOR JANAMEJAYA'S SARPA SATRA*.

THE EIGHTH SESSION OF OUR RENDERING, OF VAISHAMPAYANA'S RECITAL, OF VYASA'S MAHABHARATA DESCRIBED HOW THE PANDAVAS AND THEIR MOTHER, KUNTI, ESCAPED FROM THE FIERY END AT VARANAVATA, PLANNED FOR THEM BY THEIR COUSIN AND RIVAL DURYODHANA. IT ENDED WITH BHEEMA WATCHING OVER HIS SLEEPING MOTHER AND BROTHERS, IN A FOREST ON THE OPPOSITE BANK OF THE GANGA.

* 12-YEAR-LONG SNAKE SACRIFICE

ON A TREE, NOT FAR FROM WHERE THE PANDAVAS AND KUNTI LAY ASLEEP, DWELT A HUGE RAKSHASA NAMED HIDIMBA WHO ATE HUMAN FLESH.

"FAMISHED, HE WAS LONGING FOR FOOD WHEN HE SCENTED MAN. HE SHOOK HIMSELF UP, RAN HIS FINGERS THROUGH HIS DRY LOCKS AND LOOKED AROUND. AND HE BEHELD THE SONS OF PANDU ASLEEP ON THE GROUND.

"AT THE BIDDING OF HER BROTHER, THE RAKSHASI HIDIMBAA WENT, O MONARCH...

"...AND SHE BEHELD THE SLEEPING SONS OF PANDU AND THEIR MOTHER, GUARDED BY THE INVINCIBLE BHEEMA.

"AND BEHOLDING BHEEMA, THE RAKSHASI FELL IN LOVE WITH HIM. AND SHE SAID TO HERSELF:

THIS PERSON OF MIGHTY ARMS AND RADIANT HUE, OF LEONINE SHOULDERS AND SHAPELY NECK, IS FIT TO BE MY HUSBAND.

ONCE SLAIN, HE WILL YIELD SOME MOMENTARY PLEASURE. IF HE LIVES, ENDURING PLEASURES WILL BE MINE.

I SHALL NOT OBEY THE CRUEL COMMAND OF MY BROTHER. A WOMAN'S LOVE FOR HER HUSBAND FAR EXCEEDS THAT FOR HER BROTHER.

MAKE ME YOURS, O MAN OF RUGGED MIGHT, AND I SHALL SAFEGUARD YOU FROM THE CANNIBAL RAKSHASA.

I CAN TRAVEL AT WILL THROUGH THE SKIES. AS HUSBAND AND WIFE WE SHALL LIVE IN THE SECRET CAVERNS OF HIGH MOUNTAIN RANGES.

"LISTENING TO THESE WORDS, BHEEMA SAID:

WOULD A MAN LIKE ME ABANDON HIS SLEEPING MOTHER AND BROTHERS? WOULD HE, SMITTEN WITH LUST, LEAVE THEM TO BE A MEAL FOR THE RAKSHASA?

"HIDIMBAA REPLIED:

WAKE THEM UP. I SHALL SAVE ALL OF YOU FROM THE RAKSHASA.

"BHEEMA THEN SAID:

I WILL NOT AWAKEN MY MOTHER AND BROTHERS FROM THEIR PEACEFUL SLEEP FOR FEAR OF YOUR BROTHER.

7

" AND HIDIMBA OF BLOOD-SHOT EYES, GNASHED HIS TEETH AND RAN TOWARDS HER TO KILL HER. AND BHEEMA, BEHOLDING THE CHARGING RAKSHASA, CRIED:

STOP, YOU WICKED WRETCH! YOU SHALL NOT HARM A WOMAN IN MY PRESENCE.

COME AND FIGHT WITH ME. DO NOT SLAY THE WOMAN, ESPECIALLY WHEN THE CULPRIT IS SOMEONE ELSE.

YOU SENT YOUR SISTER HERE. IF IMPELLED BY THE PROMPTINGS OF KAMADEVA, SHE NOW DESIRES ME, THE FAULT IS NOT HERS.

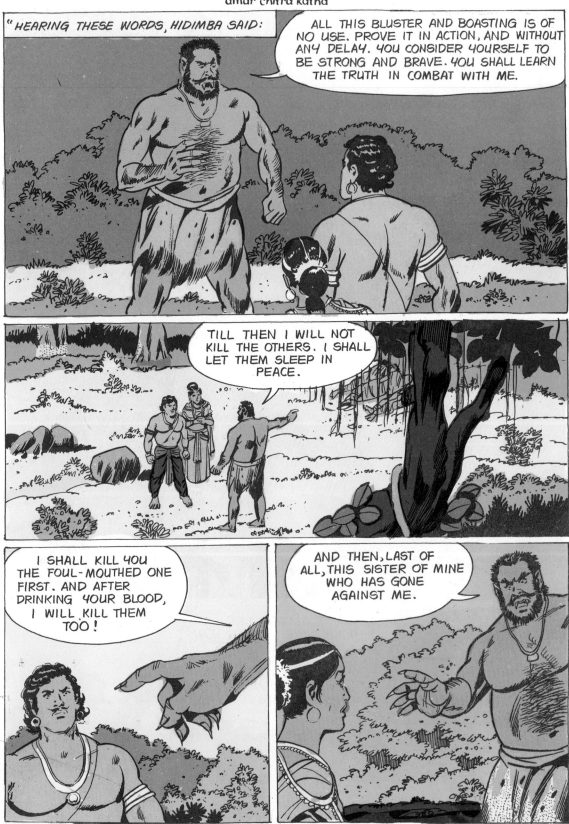

"HEARING THESE WORDS, HIDIMBA SAID:

ALL THIS BLUSTER AND BOASTING IS OF NO USE. PROVE IT IN ACTION, AND WITHOUT ANY DELAY. YOU CONSIDER YOURSELF TO BE STRONG AND BRAVE. YOU SHALL LEARN THE TRUTH IN COMBAT WITH ME.

TILL THEN I WILL NOT KILL THE OTHERS. I SHALL LET THEM SLEEP IN PEACE.

I SHALL KILL YOU THE FOUL-MOUTHED ONE FIRST. AND AFTER DRINKING YOUR BLOOD, I WILL KILL THEM TOO!

AND THEN, LAST OF ALL, THIS SISTER OF MINE WHO HAS GONE AGAINST ME.

"AND THE RAKSHASA, RAISING HIS ARMS IN WRATH, RUSHED FORTH TOWARDS BHEEMA.

"BHEEMA LAUGHINGLY CAUGHT HOLD OF HIS OUTSTRETCHED HANDS...

"...AND DRAGGED THE DESPERATELY STRUGGLING RAKSHASA A FULL THIRTY-TWO CUBITS, LIKE A LION DRAGGING SOME SMALL ANIMAL.

"SEIZED THUS BY BHEEMA, THE RAKSHASA TURNED FURIOUS AND HE LET OUT A FEARSOME YELL.

E-E-A-AH

THE MIGHTY BHEEMA THEN DRAGGED THE RAKSHASA FARTHER AWAY, O MONARCH, LEST HIS YELLS SHOULD DISTURB THE SLEEP OF HIS BROTHERS.

"THEY THEN BEGAN UPROOTING THE TREES AND TEARING APART THE MAZE OF CREEPERS.

"LIKE TWO FULL-GROWN, FURIOUS ELEPHANTS ...

"... BHEEMA AND HIDIMBA GRAPPLED AND STRUGGLED.

E-E-A-H!

" THE SOUNDS WOKE UP THE SLEEPING PANDAVAS AND THEIR MOTHER, AND THEY SAW HIDIMBAA STANDING BEFORE THEM. WONDERING AT THE BEAUTY OF THE GIRL, KUNTI ASKED HER:

WHO ARE YOU? ARE YOU A FOREST-SPRITE? ARE YOU AN APSARA? O FAIR ONE, FROM WHERE ARE YOU COME? WHAT IS THE ERRAND THAT BRINGS YOU HERE?

"HIDIMBAA ANSWERED HER QUESTIONS AND THEN SAID:

...BUT WHEN I SAW YOUR MIGHTY SON, INDUCED BY LORD MANMATHA* WHO HOLDS THE HEARTSTRINGS OF ALL THINGS CREATED, I CAME UNDER HIS SPELL AND CHOSE HIM AS MY HUSBAND.

AND THE RAKSHASA, IRKED BY MY DELAY CAME HERE TO KILL ALL YOUR SONS. THEN YOUR MIGHTY SON DRAGGED HIM AWAY FROM HERE.

BEHOLD THEM, THE ROARING RIVALS, THE MAN AND THE RAKSHASA, MATCHING THEIR MIGHT IN COMBAT.

*E*E*

* THE GOD OF LOVE (KAMADEVA)

"HEARING THESE WORDS, YUDHISHTHIRA, ARJUNA, NAKULA AND SAHADEVA ROSE AT ONCE AND BEHELD THE COMBATANTS EAGER TO OVERPOWER EACH OTHER.

"THE DUST THEY RAISED SPREAD UP LIKE THE SMOKE OF A FOREST FIRE. THEIR BODIES COVERED WITH DUST STOOD OUT LIKE MOUNTAINS WITH A MANTLE OF MIST.

"THEN ARJUNA, PERCEIVING BHEEMA TO BE UNDER STRAIN, SAID WITH A QUIET SMILE:

BE NOT AFRAID, BHEEMA. WE DID NOT KNOW OF YOUR STRENUOUS DUEL. I AM HERE TO HELP YOU. I SHALL FELL THIS RAKSHASA. NAKULA AND SAHADEVA WILL GUARD OUR MOTHER.

"HEARING HIM BHEEMA SAID:

YOU WATCH THIS FIGHT AS A MERE SPECTATOR. BE NOT ANXIOUS. HAVING COME WITHIN MY GRIP, THE RAKSHASA SHALL NOT ESCAPE ALIVE.

"THEN ARJUNA SAID:

WHY ARE YOU EXTENDING HIS LIFE? ENOUGH OF SPARRING WITH HIM. WE HAVE TO GO FARTHER AND CANNOT STAY ON HERE. SLAY HIM WITHOUT DELAY.

THE EAST IS AGLOW WITH THE RED OF DAWN AND SOON THE MORNING TWILIGHT WILL SET IN. THE TWILIGHT HOURS REINFORCE THE STRENGTH OF THE RAKSHSAS. THEREFORE HASTEN, O BHEEMA.

"THEN, INFLAMED WITH RAGE, BHEEMA SUMMONED ALL HIS LATENT MIGHT, WHICH RESEMBLED THE MIGHT VAYU, HIS FATHER, RELEASES DURING THE DISSOLUTION OF THE UNIVERSE...

"...LIFTED THE RAKSHASA HIGH AND, WHIRLING HIM ALOFT A HUNDRED TIMES, SAID TO HIM:

O RAKSHASA, YOUR CANNIBALISTIC STRENGTH, YOUR GROWTH, YOUR INTELLIGENCE HAVE ALL BEEN FUTILE. THERE-FORE DO YOU SEEK TODAY A FUTILE END TO YOUR FUTILE LIFE.

"AT THIS JUNCTURE ARJUNA SAID:

IF YOU CONSIDER THIS RAKSHASA FORMIDABLE IN COMBAT, I SHALL HELP YOU TO SLAY HIM WITHOUT DELAY.

OTHERWISE I SHALL SLAY HIM MYSELF. YOU ARE EXHAUSTED BY THE TASK AND NEED TO REST FOR A WHILE.

"INFURIATED BY THESE WORDS, BHEEMA HURLED THE RAKSHASA...

"...TO HIS DEATH. AND THE MORTAL ROAR OF THE DYING RAKSHASA FILLED THE WIDE FOREST.

O MONARCH, THEN, WITH HIS BARE HANDS, THE MIGHTY BHEEMA BENT THE BODY OF THE RAKSHASA AND BROKE IT BY THE MIDDLE. THE FEAT PLEASED THE BROTHERS. AND THOSE BRAVE MEN CONGRATULATED THE VALOROUS CONQUEROR.

"THEN ARJUNA, WHO WAS ALL REVERENCE FOR HIS BROTHER OF RUGGED MIGHT, SAID:

I BELIEVE THERE IS A TOWN NOT FAR FROM THIS FOREST. LET US GO ONWARD SOON SO THAT DURYODHANA DOES NOT TRACE US.

" AS ALL THOSE VALIANT MEN PROCEEDED WITH THEIR MOTHER, HIDIMBAA FOLLOWED THEM.

" SEEING THIS, BHEEMA SAID:

RAKSHASAS ARE VINDICTIVE AND USE SORCERY TO WREAK VENGEANCE.

THEREFORE O HIDIMBAA, YOU SHALL FOLLOW THE PATH OF YOUR BROTHER.

" THEN YUDHISHTHIRA SAID:

O BHEEMA, THOUGH ENRAGED YOU SHALL NOT KILL A WOMAN. OBSERVANCE OF ONE'S DHARMA IS SUPERIOR TO KEEPING ALIVE THE BODY.

HIDIMBA WHO CAME TO SLAY US HAS ALREADY BEEN SLAIN BY YOU.

WHAT CAN THIS SISTER OF THAT RAKSHASA, ANGERED THOUGH SHE BE, DO TO US?

"HIDIMBAA THEN PAID OBEISANCE TO KUNTI AND YUDHISHTHIRA AND SAID:

O NOBLE LADY, YOU KNOW THE PANGS OF LOVE WHICH WOMEN FEEL. I FEEL THEM NOW AND THE CAUSE IS BHEEMA.

FORSAKING MY FRIENDS, MY TRIBE AND MY TRADITION, I HAVE CHOSEN YOUR SON AS MY HUSBAND.

IF THAT HERO AND YOU DENY ME, I WILL NOT LIVE.

CONSIDER ME DEVOTED OR DIM-WITTED. OR KEEP ME AS YOUR MAID. BUT HAVE PITY ON ME. UNITE ME WITH YOUR SON, MY HUSBAND. LET ME GO TO THE PLACES I LIKE, WITH HIM.

"THEN YUDHISHTHIRA SAID:

WHAT YOU SAY IS PROPER BEYOND DOUBT. BUT YOU MUST BE TRUE TO YOUR WORDS.

DURING THE DAY, AFTER BHEEMA HAS CONCLUDED HIS ABLUTION, PRAYERS AND RITUAL OFFERINGS...

...YOU MAY ATTEND ON HIM AND. TAKE PLEASURE IN HIS COMPANY. BUT BRING HIM BACK TO US EVERY NIGHT.

" BHEEMA THEN SAID TO HIDIMBAA:

AND I SHALL STAY WITH YOU TILL A SON IS BORN TO YOU.

" THEN SAYING:

SO BE IT.

"...HIDIMBAA TOOK BHEEMA ON HER BACK, ROSE UP...

"...AND SPED THROUGH THE SKIES.

" SHE SPORTED WITH HIM ON MOUNTAIN SLOPES WHERE CELESTIALS ROAM AND WHERE THE BIRDS SING AND WHERE EVERY SIGHT IS STIMULATING.

" SHE DESCENDED WITH HIM ON LAKES COVERED WITH LOTUSES...

"...AND WALKED WITH HIM THROUGH WILD FORESTS OF STRANGE TREES AND DELICATE CREEPERS.

"SWIFT AS THE MIND IN HER MOBILITY, SHE SPORTED WITH BHEEMA IN VARIOUS PLACES TILL IN DUE COURSE SHE GAVE BIRTH TO A MIGHTY SON, BEGOTTEN BY THE PANDAVA. AND THE CHILD GREW INTO A YOUNG MAN THE INSTANT HE WAS BORN.

PERCEIVING HIS HEAD TO BE SMOOTH LIKE A WATER-POT HIS MOTHER NAMED HIM GHATOTKACHA.

AND THOUGH BEGOTTEN BY MAN, HE WAS SUPERHUMAN AND EXCELLED ALL THE RAKSHASAS AND PISHACHAS IN STRENGTH.

"THE MIGHTY SON SOON MASTERED THE SECRETS OF WIELDING WEAPONS OF ALL KINDS.

"AND GHATOTKACHA, WHO WAS FULL OF LOVE FOR THE PANDAVAS, WON THEIR AFFECTION AND CAME TO BE COUNTED ONE OF THEM.

"THEN HIDIMBAA SAID:

THE TERM OF MY STAY WITH MY HUSBAND HAS RUN OUT.

"AND SALUTING KUNTI AND THE PANDAVAS...

"...SHE WENT HER WAY.

"AND GHATOTKACHA, ASSURING THE PANDAVAS THAT HE WOULD ALWAYS BE WITH THEM WHEN NEEDED, SALUTED THEM..."

"...AND PROCEEDED NORTHWARDS.

O MONARCH, THOSE FORMIDABLE WARRIORS THEN TRAVERSED THE FORESTS KILLING ANIMALS OF VARIOUS TYPES.

THEY WORE THEIR HAIR IN MATTED LOCKS AND WERE CLAD IN TREE-BARKS AND ANIMAL-SKINS.

THEY MEDITATED ON THE VEDAS AND UPANISHADS AND RUMINATED OVER THE PRINCIPLES OF ETHICS.

"WHILE ENGAGED THUS, THEY SAW THEIR GRANDFATHER, MY GURU VEDA VYASA, AND HE SAID TO THEM:

I HAVE COME TO YOU BECAUSE I HAD DIVINED YOUR MISFORTUNE AT THE HANDS OF THE UNFAIR KAURAVAS. DO NOT GRIEVE BECAUSE ALL THIS WILL ULTIMATELY LEAD YOU TO HAPPINESS.

YOU AND THE KAURAVAS ARE EQUAL IN MY AFFECTIONS. YET MEN CARE MORE FOR CHILDREN AND FOR THOSE WHO ARE IN MISFORTUNE. THAT IS WHY I HOLD YOU IN GREATER AFFECTION NOW.

AND THEREFORE I SHALL WORK FOR YOUR PROSPERITY. THERE IS A DELIGHTFUL TOWN NEAR BY AND THERE YOU SHALL HAVE NO ANXIETIES.

" THUS CONSOLING THE PANDAVAS, MY GURU LED THEM TOWARD THE TOWN OF EKACHAKRA.

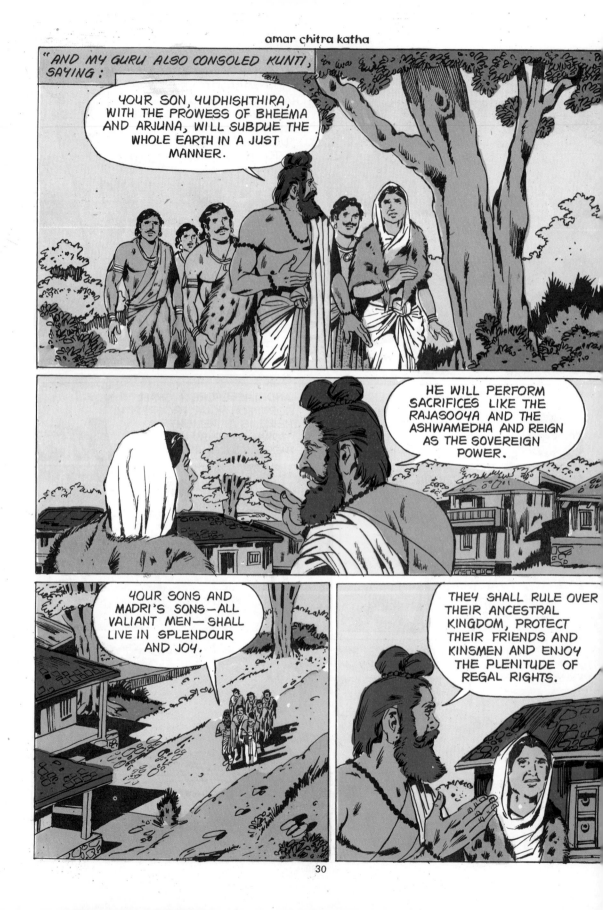

"AND MY GURU ALSO CONSOLED KUNTI, SAYING:

YOUR SON, YUDHISHTHIRA, WITH THE PROWESS OF BHEEMA AND ARJUNA, WILL SUBDUE THE WHOLE EARTH IN A JUST MANNER.

HE WILL PERFORM SACRIFICES LIKE THE RAJASOOYA AND THE ASHWAMEDHA AND REIGN AS THE SOVEREIGN POWER.

YOUR SONS AND MADRI'S SONS—ALL VALIANT MEN—SHALL LIVE IN SPLENDOUR AND JOY.

THEY SHALL RULE OVER THEIR ANCESTRAL KINGDOM, PROTECT THEIR FRIENDS AND KINSMEN AND ENJOY THE PLENITUDE OF REGAL RIGHTS.

"THEN MY GURU HAD THEM ACCOMMODATED IN A BRAHMANA'S HOUSE AND SAID TO YUDHISHTHIRA:

STAY HERE FOR A MONTH AND AWAIT MY RETURN. YOUR STAY HERE WILL BE HAPPY IF YOU ACT DISCERNING THE NEEDS OF THE PLACE AND THE TIMES.

"THEN THE PANDAVAS SALUTED THE RISHI WITH JOINED PALMS...

"... AND MY DIVINE GURU WENDED HIS WAY BACK.

IN THIS MANNER DID THE PANDAVAS, AFTER THE SLAYING OF HIDIMBA AND THE BIRTH OF GHATOTKACHA, ARRIVE AT EKACHAKRA.

THUS ENDS THE NINTH SESSION OF OUR RENDERING OF VAISHAMPAYANA'S RECITAL OF VYASA'S IMMORTAL ITIHASA, THE MAHABHARATA.

Mahabharata-10
THE PANDAVAS AT EKACHAKRA

VEDA VYASA'S EPIC ON THE BHARATA RACE WAS FIRST RECITED IN PUBLIC, BY HIS DISCIPLE VAISHAMPAYANA, AT THE BEHEST OF THE AGELESS SEER VYASA HIMSELF.

THE RECITAL TOOK PLACE IN THE AUGUST PRESENCE OF KING JANAMEJAYA — GREAT-GRANDSON OF THE GRANDSON OF VYASA — AND THE MANY LEARNED SAGES WHO HAD ASSEMBLED FOR JANAMEJAYA'S SARPA SATRA*.

THE NINTH SESSION OF OUR RENDERING OF VAISHAMPAYANA'S RECITAL OF VYASA'S MAHABHARATA NARRATED THE ADVENTURES OF THE PANDAVAS AFTER THEIR ESCAPE FROM VARANAVATA. IT CONCLUDED WITH THEIR ARRIVAL AT THE HOUSE OF A BRAHMANA IN EKACHAKRA, A NEARBY TOWN.

* 12-YEAR-LONG SNAKE SACRIFICE

O SAGE, WHAT DID THE PANDAVAS DO AFTER ARRIVING AT EKACHAKRA?

THE PANDAVAS, SAGE-LIKE IN APPEARANCE, LIVED IN THE HOUSE OF THE BRAHMANA AT EKACHAKRA AND LED THE LIFE OF MENDICANTS. AND WITH THEIR VIRTUOUS BEARING, THEY ENDEARED THEMSELVES TO THE PEOPLE OF THE TOWN.

"AT SUNSET THEY WOULD SUBMIT THE ALMS THEY HAD COLLECTED TO KUNTI...

"...AND EACH WOULD TAKE THE SHARE APPORTIONED TO HIM BY HER.

"WHILE ONE HALF ALWAYS WENT TO MIGHTY BHEEMA, THE OTHER WAS SHARED BY THE REST.

IN THIS MANNER, O MONARCH, THE PANDAVAS LIVED THERE FOR SOME TIME.

THEN ONE DAY IT SO HAPPENED THAT WHILE THE OTHERS WENT OUT SEEKING ALMS, BHEEMA STAYED AT HOME WITH KUNTI.

"AND KUNTI HEARD A LOUD, DISTRESSING WAIL OF SORROW COMING FROM WITHIN THE HOUSE.

AYE-EE-OH--

"THEN KUNTI, O MONARCH, SAID TO BHEEMA:

AYE-EE-OH-

BEYOND DOUBT SOME TERRIBLE GRIEF HAS BEFALLEN THE BRAHMANA. IF WE COULD HELP HIM WE WOULD BE RENDERING HIM A FAVOUR.

LIKE THOSE WHO LIVE HAPPILY IN ANOTHER'S HOUSE, I ALWAYS THINK OF THE GOOD I SHOULD DO TO HIM.

HE IS A MAN WHO RETURNS IN INCREASED MEASURE A FAVOUR RECEIVED.

"THEN BHEEMA SAID:

FIND OUT WHAT HIS GRIEF IS AND THE SOURCE OF IT. HOWEVER DIFFICULT THE TASK, I SHALL APPLY MYSELF TO IT.

"THEN KUNTI ENTERED THE INNER CHAMBER OF THE HOUSE AND BEHELD THE BRAHMANA SITTING DOWNCAST WITH HIS WIFE AND DAUGHTER AND SON BESIDE HIM.

"AND SHE HEARD HIM SAY:

FIE ON THIS WORLDLY LIFE WHICH IS HOLLOW AND FUTILE; WHICH IS ROOTED IN PAIN AND HELD IN CHAINS; WHICH METES OUT ONLY MISERY.

O MY WIFE, I HAD WANTED TO MOVE TO SOME SAFER PLACE, BUT YOU DID NOT PAY ANY HEED TO ME THEN.

YOU TURNED DOWN MY FREQUENT REQUESTS SAYING: I WAS BORN HERE AND I GREW UP HERE AND SO DID MY FATHER. LOVE FOR YOUR KIN TURNED YOU DEAF TO MY WORDS.

5

" AT THIS THE BRAHMANA CRIED OUT:

I CANNOT ABANDON YOU. YOU ARE MY HELP-MATE IN VIRTUOUS DEEDS. MATERNAL IN YOUR SELF-EFFACING LOVE, YOU ARE ALSO A GOD-GIVEN COMPANION TO ME, AND THE MAINSTAY OF MY LIFE.

" THE WIFE REPLIED:

WISE MEN OF ETHICS HAVE DECREED THAT WOMEN SHOULD NEVER BE SLAIN AND RAKSHASAS ARE SAID TO FOLLOW ETHICAL CODES.

THEREFORE, WHILE THE RAKSHASA WILL CERTAINLY KILL A MAN, IT IS DOUBTFUL IF HE WILL, A WOMAN.

BESIDES, HAVING DISCHARGED MY DUTIES AND HAVING BORNE YOUR CHILDREN, I HAVE FULFILLED THE WANTS OF LIFE. DEATH HOLDS NO PAIN FOR ME NOW.

SO IT BEHOVES YOU TO SEND ME TO THE RAKSHASA.

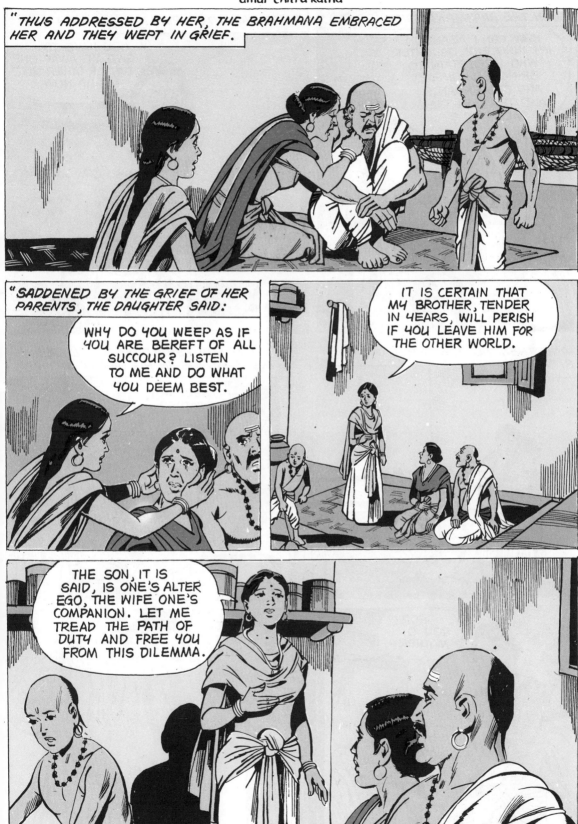

"THUS ADDRESSED BY HER, THE BRAHMANA EMBRACED HER AND THEY WEPT IN GRIEF.

"SADDENED BY THE GRIEF OF HER PARENTS, THE DAUGHTER SAID:

WHY DO YOU WEEP AS IF YOU ARE BEREFT OF ALL SUCCOUR? LISTEN TO ME AND DO WHAT YOU DEEM BEST.

IT IS CERTAIN THAT MY BROTHER, TENDER IN YEARS, WILL PERISH IF YOU LEAVE HIM FOR THE OTHER WORLD.

THE SON, IT IS SAID, IS ONE'S ALTER EGO, THE WIFE ONE'S COMPANION. LET ME TREAD THE PATH OF DUTY AND FREE YOU FROM THIS DILEMMA.

9

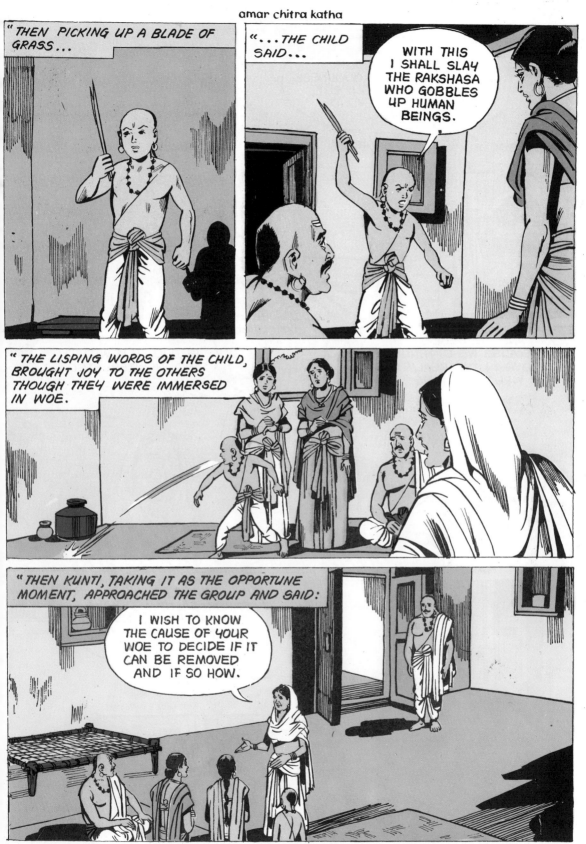

"THEN PICKING UP A BLADE OF GRASS...

"...THE CHILD SAID...

WITH THIS I SHALL SLAY THE RAKSHASA WHO GOBBLES UP HUMAN BEINGS.

"THE LISPING WORDS OF THE CHILD, BROUGHT JOY TO THE OTHERS THOUGH THEY WERE IMMERSED IN WOE.

"THEN KUNTI, TAKING IT AS THE OPPORTUNE MOMENT, APPROACHED THE GROUP AND SAID:

I WISH TO KNOW THE CAUSE OF YOUR WOE TO DECIDE IF IT CAN BE REMOVED AND IF SO HOW.

"THE BRAHMANA REPLIED:

O ASCETIC LADY, YOUR WORDS MATCH THE GOODNESS OF PEOPLE LIKE YOU. BUT OUR GRIEF IS BEYOND HUMAN REPAIR.

AND WE DESERVE IT BECAUSE WE CONTINUE TO LIVE IN THE REALM OF A WRETCHED KING.

AS OUR KING IS DULL, DIM-WITTED AND DISINTERESTED...

...A MIGHTY RAKSHASA NAMED BAKA, A CANNIBAL, RULES AND PROTECTS OUR TOWN AND OUR LAND.

11

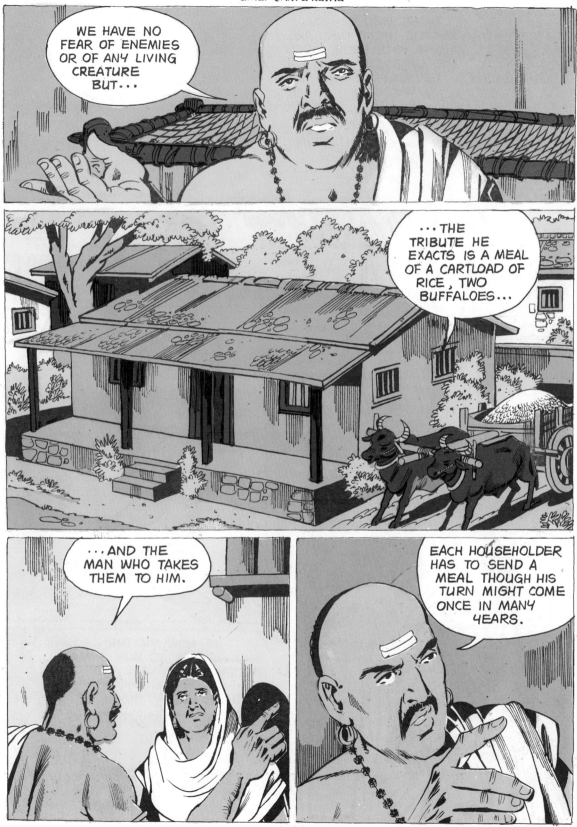

12

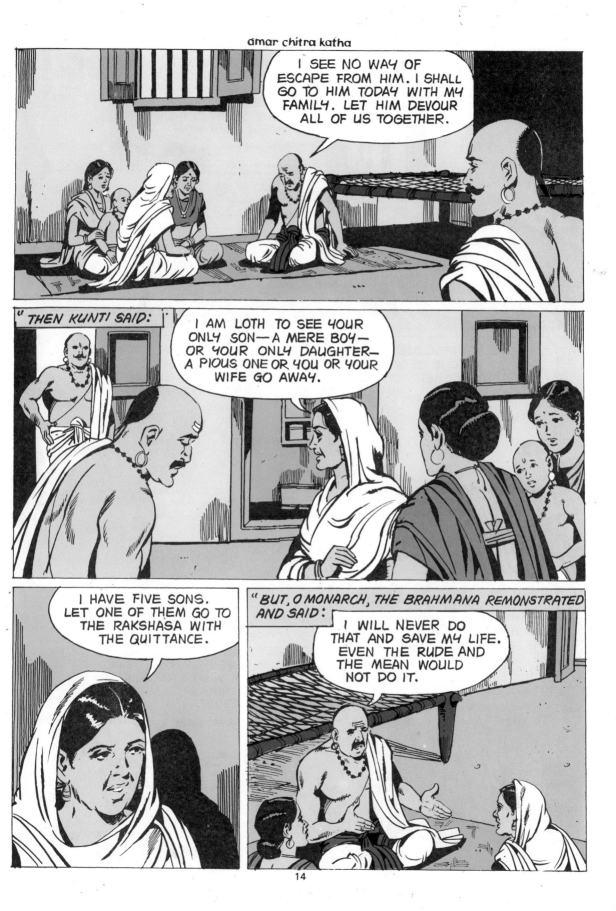

14

"THEN KUNTI SAID:

THE RAKSHASA CANNOT SLAY MY SON. HE IS VALOROUS AND BEARS A CHARMED LIFE. I HAVE SEEN MANY RAKSHASAS SLAIN IN THEIR ENCOUNTER WITH HIM.

BUT DO NOT DISCLOSE THIS TO ANYONE BECAUSE CURIOUS SEEKERS OF SKILLS WILL PESTER HIM.

AND IF MY SON IMPARTS THE SKILL WITHOUT HIS GURU'S SANCTION...

...THEN THE SKILL WILL BE BLUNTED IN EFFECT.

THUS ADDRESSED BY KUNTI, O MONARCH, THE BRAHMANA AND HIS WIFE AGREED. THEN KUNTI AND THE BRAHMANA ASKED BHEEMA TO DO THE DEED. AND BHEEMA READILY CONSENTED.

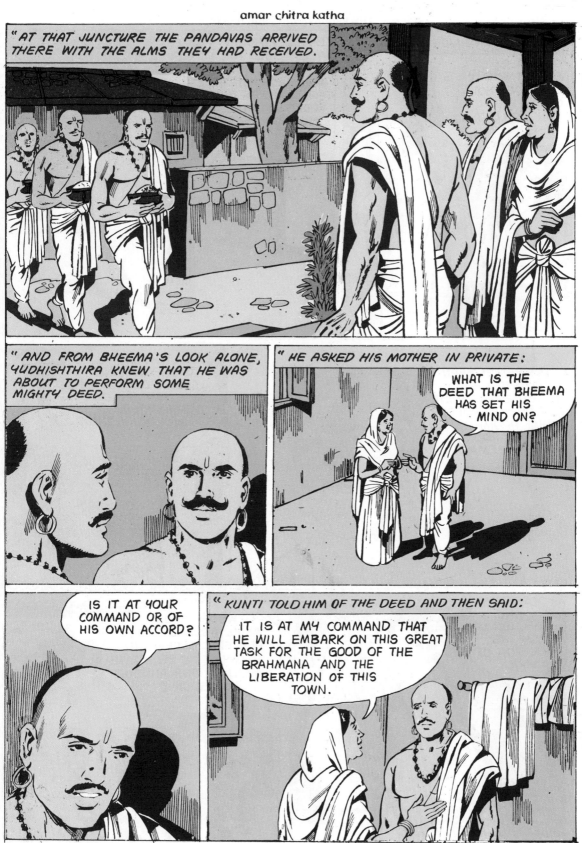

"AT THAT JUNCTURE THE PANDAVAS ARRIVED THERE WITH THE ALMS THEY HAD RECEIVED.

" AND FROM BHEEMA'S LOOK ALONE, YUDHISHTHIRA KNEW THAT HE WAS ABOUT TO PERFORM SOME MIGHTY DEED.

" HE ASKED HIS MOTHER IN PRIVATE:

WHAT IS THE DEED THAT BHEEMA HAS SET HIS MIND ON?

IS IT AT YOUR COMMAND OR OF HIS OWN ACCORD?

" KUNTI TOLD HIM OF THE DEED AND THEN SAID:

IT IS AT MY COMMAND THAT HE WILL EMBARK ON THIS GREAT TASK FOR THE GOOD OF THE BRAHMANA AND THE LIBERATION OF THIS TOWN.

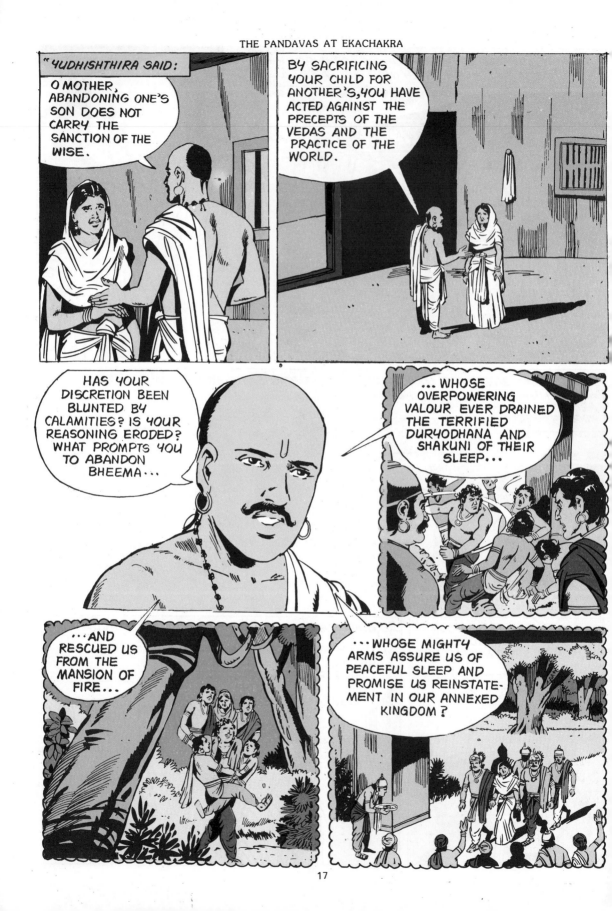

"YUDHISHTHIRA SAID:

O MOTHER, ABANDONING ONE'S SON DOES NOT CARRY THE SANCTION OF THE WISE.

BY SACRIFICING YOUR CHILD FOR ANOTHER'S, YOU HAVE ACTED AGAINST THE PRECEPTS OF THE VEDAS AND THE PRACTICE OF THE WORLD.

HAS YOUR DISCRETION BEEN BLUNTED BY CALAMITIES? IS YOUR REASONING ERODED? WHAT PROMPTS YOU TO ABANDON BHEEMA...

...WHOSE OVERPOWERING VALOUR EVER DRAINED THE TERRIFIED DURYODHANA AND SHAKUNI OF THEIR SLEEP...

...AND RESCUED US FROM THE MANSION OF FIRE...

...WHOSE MIGHTY ARMS ASSURE US OF PEACEFUL SLEEP AND PROMISE US REINSTATE-MENT IN OUR ANNEXED KINGDOM?

17

"KUNTI REPLIED:

YOU MUST NOT BE ANXIOUS ABOUT BHEEMA. AND MY RESOLVE WAS NOT THE RESULT OF A FATIGUED BRAIN.

THE POWER OF BHEEMA, WITNESSED BY ME DURING OUR ESCAPE FROM THAT MANSION OF FIRE AND ALSO IN THE SLAYING OF HIDIMBA, HAS REINFORCED MY FAITH IN HIM.

IT WAS HIS STRENGTH OF 10,000 ELEPHANTS WHICH CARRIED ALL OF YOU— EACH ONE AS STRONG AS AN ELEPHANT— FROM VARANAVATA.

AND YEARS AGO, SOON AFTER HE SLIPPED FROM MY LAP, HIS FALL HAD CRUSHED UP THE ROCK BELOW.

I KNOW FULL WELL HOW STRONG BHEEMA IS AND THEREFORE HAVE I ASSIGNED THIS TASK TO HIM. NEITHER IGNORANCE NOR GREED NOR FOOLHARDINESS IS BEHIND MY RESOLVE. MY VIRTUOUS DEED IS THE OUTCOME OF THOUGHTFUL REASONING.

THE MERIT OF THE DEED IS TWOFOLD — RECOMPENSE TO THE BRAHMANA FOR OUR STAY AND THE DISCHARGE OF A MOST VIRTUOUS DEED. A KSHATRIYA MUST PROTECT ONE IN DISTRESS. IF HE DOES SO HE IS ASSURED OF A NOBLE LINEAGE AND THE RESPECT OF KINGS.

"YUDHISHTHIRA THEN SAID:

YOUR DELIBERATE DECISION, O MOTHER, IS INDEED PROPER. BHEEMA WILL CERTAINLY SLAY THE CANNIBAL AND RETURN ALIVE.

BUT STRIVE WITH THE BRAHMANA TO KEEP THIS UNDISCLOSED TO THE PEOPLE OF THE TOWN.

"THEN, AS THE NIGHT PASSED, BHEEMA TOOK CHARGE OF THE FOOD FOR THE RAKSHASA AND SET OUT TO HIS ABODE.

"THE POWERFUL SON OF PANDU THEN ENTERED THE FOREST OF THE RAKSHASA, HELPING HIMSELF TO THE FOOD...

"...AND CALLING OUT:

BAKA— O BAKA— BAKA-A—

"IMMENSE IN SIZE AND STRENGTH, RED ALL ALIKE IN EYES, HAIR AND BEARD, BAKA WAS FEARSOME TO BEHOLD...

"...AND HE CAME WITH AN EARTH-SPLITTING TREAD. AND BEHOLDING BHEEMA EATING HIS FOOD...

"...THE RAKSHASA CAME UP IN FERVID FURY AND SAID:

WHO IS THIS VILLAIN EATING UP MY MEAL IN MY VERY PRESENCE AS IF HE IS KEEN TO BE SENT TO THE ABODE OF YAMA?

" BHEEMA, O MONARCH, ONLY SMILED IN DERISION...

"...AND CONTINUED TO EAT. BEHOLDING THIS...

"...THE CANNIBAL LET OUT A TERRIBLE ROAR...

E-EE-EA

".. AND WITH UPRAISED ARMS RUSHED TOWARDS BHEEMA INTENDING TO KILL HIM. BUT BHEEMA IN UTTER CONTEMPT WENT ON EATING THE RAKSHASA'S FOOD.

"OVERCOME BY RAGE THE RAKSHASA BROUGHT DOWN HIS FISTS ON BHEEMA, FROM BEHIND.

"BUT BHEEMA CONTINUED TO EAT WITHOUT SO MUCH AS A GLANCE AT HIM."

" THEN THE RAKSHASA, BEYOND HIMSELF WITH ANGER, UPROOTED A TREE...

"...AND HURLED IT AT BHEEMA WHO HAVING FINISHED THE RICE STOOD CHEERFULLY READY FOR FIGHT.

"BHEEMA PLAYFULLY CAUGHT THE TREE IN HIS LEFT HAND ...

"...AND HURLED IT BACK AT THE RAKSHASA.

"THEN, O MONARCH, THE RAKSHASA UPROOTED MANY MORE TREES AND HURLED THEM AT BHEEMA...

...AND BHEEMA SMOTE HIM WITH AS MANY IN RETURN. THAT TERRIBLE COMBAT BETWEEN THE PRINCE AND THE CANNIBAL RAGED SO FIERCE THAT THE FOREST AROUND WAS SOON DENUDED OF TREES.

"THEN THE RAKSHASA SPRANG UPON BHEEMA AND SEIZED HIM. THE MIGHTY HERO ALSO HAD HIM IN HIS CLUTCHES.

"AND HE BEGAN DRAGGING HIM VIOLENTLY. THE CANNIBAL IN TURN PITTED HIS FORCE AGAINST THAT OF BHEEMA. THE VERY EARTH SEEMED TO TREMBLE UNDER THE FORCE UNLEASHED BY THE TWO.

"THEN BEHOLDING THAT THE CANNIBAL WAS OVERCOME BY FATIGUE, BHEEMA LAID HIM LOW AND PRESSED HIM DOWN WITH HIS KNEES.

"THEN HE SEIZED HIS NECK...

"...AND BENT HIM DOUBLE WITH ALL HIS MIGHT. THE CANNIBAL EXPELLED A ROAR OF PAIN...

"...AND FELL DEAD. AND THE KINSMEN OF THE RAKSHASA, TERRIFIED BY THE ROAR, CAME OUT WITH THEIR ATTENDANTS.

"WHEN BHEEMA SAW THE TERROR-STRUCK GROUP, HE COMFORTED THEM AND SAID:

NEVER SHALL YOU KILL A HUMAN BEING. IF YOU DO, THEN YOU TOO WILL BE SLAIN LIKE BAKA.

"THE RAKSHASAS CONSENTED, O MONARCH, TO ABIDE BY THE COMMANDMENTS OF BHEEMA. THEN BHEEMA CARRIED THE LIFELESS CANNIBAL...

"...TO THE TOWN GATES, DEPOSITED HIM THERE UNOBSERVED BY ANYONE...

"...AND RETURNED TO THE BRAHMANA'S HOUSE.

" THE NEXT MORNING, AS THEY CAME OUT OF THE TOWN, THE PEOPLE SAW THE RAKSHASA DEAD ON THE GROUND, GLUTTED IN GORE.

" THEY WENT BACK AND SPREAD THE TIDINGS.

" AND THOUSANDS OF MEN, YOUNG AND OLD WITH THEIR WIVES AND CHILDREN, THRONGED THE SPOT TO SEE BAKA DEAD AND WERE AMAZED AT THE SUPERHUMAN DEED.

THEY OFFERED PRAYERS TO THEIR DEITIES, AND THEN ASCERTAINED WHOSE TURN IT HAD BEEN TO CARRY THE MEAL.

" THEN THEY WENT TO THE HOUSE OF THE BRAHMANA...

"...AND QUESTIONED HIM. HE SAID TO THOSE IMPORTUNATE MEN:

WHILE I WAS LAMENTING MY FATE WITH MY RELATIVES, A BRAHMANA— NOBLE IN SPIRIT AND A MASTER OF OCCULT LORE— CAME TO ME AND SAID: I SHALL CARRY THE FOOD FOR THAT BRUTE TODAY. DO NOT FEAR FOR ME.

Mahabharata – 11
ENTER DRAUPADI

VEDA VYASA'S EPIC ON THE BHARATA RACE WAS FIRST RECITED IN PUBLIC BY HIS DISCIPLE VAISHAMPAYANA AT THE BEHEST OF THE AGELESS SEER VYASA HIMSELF.

THE RECITAL TOOK PLACE IN THE AUGUST PRESENCE OF KING JANAMEJAYA— GREAT-GRANDSON OF VYASA—AND THE MANY LEARNED SAGES WHO HAD ASSEMBLED FOR JANAMEJAYA'S SARPA SATRA*.

THE TENTH SESSION OF OUR RENDERING OF VAISHAMPAYANA'S RECITAL OF VYASA'S MAHA-BHARATA RECOUNTED HOW BHEEMA, AT THE BEHEST OF KUNTI, DELIVERED BOTH THEIR BRAHMANA HOST AND THE TOWN OF EKACHAKRA FROM THE CLUTCHES OF RAKSHASA BAKA, BY SLAYING THE TYRANT.

*12-YEAR-LONG SNAKE SACRIFICE

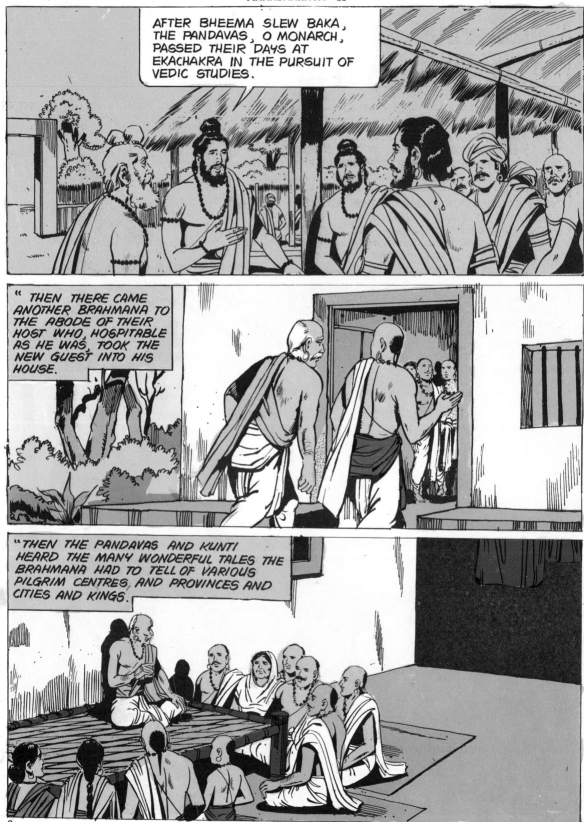

AFTER BHEEMA SLEW BAKA, THE PANDAVAS, O MONARCH, PASSED THEIR DAYS AT EKACHAKRA IN THE PURSUIT OF VEDIC STUDIES.

" THEN THERE CAME ANOTHER BRAHMANA TO THE ABODE OF THEIR HOST WHO, HOSPITABLE AS HE WAS, TOOK THE NEW GUEST INTO HIS HOUSE.

"THEN THE PANDAVAS AND KUNTI HEARD THE MANY WONDERFUL TALES THE BRAHMANA HAD TO TELL OF VARIOUS PILGRIM CENTRES, AND PROVINCES AND CITIES AND KINGS.

amar chitra katha

"WHEN HE SPOKE OF THE MARVELLOUS BIRTHS OF DHRISHTADYUMNA AND DRAUPADI AT THE YAGNA OF DRUPADA...

"...THE PANDAVAS ASKED:

WHY DID THIS EXTRAORDINARY BIRTH OF DHRISHTADYUMNA AND DRAUPADI TAKE PLACE, O BRAHMANA?

"THUS QUESTIONED, THE BRAHMANA NARRATED ALL THE EVENTS THAT LED TO THE HUMBLING OF DRUPADA AT THE HANDS OF DRONA, AND OF DRUPADA'S SUBSEQUENT DISTRESS. THEN HE SAID:

BENT ON TAKING REVENGE, DRUPADA WANDERED ABOUT IN SEARCH OF BRAHMANAS WHO EXCELLED IN ACHIEVING GOALS BY PERFORMING RITES.

"AND HE CAME UPON THE BRAHMANA BROTHERS, YAJA AND UPAYAJA, IN AN ASHRAMA ON THE BANKS OF THE GANGA AND YAMUNA.

"HE SAID TO YAJA:

O YAJA, MY HATRED FOR DRONA, THE SON OF BHARADWAJA AND THE GURU OF THE KURUS, BURNS ME UP.

A SUPREME SCHOLAR OF THE VEDAS AND AN EXPERT WIELDER OF THE BRAHMA MISSILE, HE HAS DEFEATED ME IN BATTLE. NO MAN ON EARTH CAN OVERCOME HIM.

OBTAIN AN INVINCIBLE SON FOR ME WHO WILL SLAY DRONA, AND I WILL GIVE YOU TEN THOUSAND KINE.

amar chitra katha

"THEN THERE SPRANG FROM THE FIRE AN AWESOME YOUTH RADIANT LIKE A CELESTIAL AND SPLENDIDLY ARRAYED WHO AS SOON AS HE CAME FORTH...

"...ASCENDED A CHARIOT...

"...AND DROVE IT AROUND. THEN A VOICE FROM THE REALMS ABOVE SAID:

THIS PRINCE IS BORN TO KILL DRONA, END THE SORROW OF THE KING AND BRING FAME TO THE PANCHALAS.

" THE MAGNITUDE OF THE EXULTATION OF THE PANCHALAS WHEN THEY HEARD THIS STRAINED THE VERY EARTH AS IT WERE.

" AND THEN THERE EMERGED, FROM THE MIDDLE OF THE SACRIFICIAL PLATFORM, A DAUGHTER FOR THE PANCHALA KING.

"AND A VOICE FROM ABOVE SAID:

THIS GIRL, DARK OF SKIN AND THE BEST OF WOMEN, WILL BE THE CAUSE OF THE FALL OF THE KSHATRIYAS. THROUGH HER THE WILL OF THE GODS SHALL COME TO PASS. SHE SHALL BE THE CAUSE OF MUCH TERROR TO THE KAURAVAS.

HER EYES WERE DARK AND LONG, HER HAIR WAS DARK AND CURLY. THE FRAGRANCE THAT EMANATED FROM HER, AS FROM A BLUE LOTUS, FILLED THE AIR. SHE WAS MATCHLESS IN BEAUTY.

"AND WHEN SHE CAME FORTH, THE QUEEN SAID TO YAJA:

LET THESE CHILDREN LOOK UPON ME AND NONE ELSE AS THEIR MOTHER.

"YAJA GAVE HIS ASSENT. THE BRAHMANA THEN SET ABOUT NAMING THE CHILDREN. HE SAID:

LET THIS SON OF DRUPADA FOR HIS DARING MANNER AND WEALTH OF ARMOUR BE NAMED DHRISHTADYUMNA.

AND THIS DAUGHTER, KRISHNAA, FOR HER DARK COMPLEXION.

THUS DID DRUPADA OBTAIN THE TWINS THROUGH THE GREAT YAGNA.

SOON AFTER THIS DRONA, IN DEFERENCE TO DESTINY, TOOK DHRISHTADYUMNA TO HIS ABODE AND INSTRUCTED HIM IN THE SCIENCE OF ARMS THUS SAFEGUARDING HIS OWN REPUTATION.

" SMITTEN BY ALL THAT THEY HAD HEARD, THE SONS OF KUNTI, THOSE MIGHTY HEROES, BECAME RESTLESS IN MIND.

"OBSERVING THE TROUBLED STATE OF HER SONS...

"...KUNTI SAID TO YUDHISHTHIRA :

WE HAVE BEEN LIVING IN THE ABODE OF THIS BRAHMANA FOR MANY DAYS. I THINK IT IS NOT PROPER TO STAY LONG AT ONE PLACE. IF YOU AGREE, LET US PROCEED TO PANCHALA.

" AND YUDHISHTHIRA REPLIED :

WHATEVER YOU SAY IS ALWAYS FOR OUR GOOD. YET···

SHE REQUESTED SHIVA TO GIVE HER A MOST VIRTUOUS HUSBAND AND SHE REPEATED THIS REQUEST AGAIN AND AGAIN.

"THEN SHIVA REPLIED:

YOU SHALL HAVE YOUR FIVE HUSBANDS.

"THE MAID THEN SAID:

O LORD, I DESIRE ONLY ONE HUSBAND.

"SHIVA REPLIED:

FIVE TIMES DID YOU REPEAT YOUR REQUEST FOR A HUSBAND. WHEN YOU TAKE ON THE NEXT LIFE YOU SHALL HAVE FIVE HUSBANDS.

THAT HEAVENLY MAIDEN HAS NOW BEEN BORN IN THE HOUSE OF DRUPADA. AND SHE IS DESTINED TO BE YOUR WIFE. THEREFORE GO TO PANCHALA AND TAKE UP YOUR RESIDENCE THERE.

BEYOND DOUBT YOU WILL WIN HER AND MUCH HAPPINESS.

HAVING ADVISED THE PANDAVAS THUS, MY GURU TOOK HIS LEAVE OF THEM AND WENT HIS WAY.

"THEN THE PANDAVAS BID THE BRAHMANA FAREWELL, SALUTED HIM...

"...AND SET OUT.

"TURNING THEIR STEPS NORTHWARDS, LED BY ARJUNA WHO HELD A TORCH ALOFT, THEY WALKED DAY AND NIGHT TILL...

"...THEY CAME TO THE BANKS OF THE GANGA. THERE IN THAT SECLUDED SPOT, THE KING OF THE GANDHARVAS WAS SPORTING WITH HIS WIVES IN THE WATERS OF THE RIVER.

"AND HE HEARD THEIR FOOTFALLS AS THEY CAME ALONG THE RIVERSIDE.

" WHEN THE PANDAVAS AND THEIR MOTHER CAME INTO HIS VIEW ...

"...HE SHOUTED:

STAY WHERE YOU ARE! THE TWILIGHT HOURS ARE EXCLUSIVELY FOR THE YAKSHAS, THE GANDHARVAS AND THE RAKSHASAS.

KEEP YOUR DISTANCE! FOOLISH MEN WHO VENTURE OUT DURING THESE HOURS ARE SLAIN BY US.

" TO THIS ARJUNA SAID:

O ROVER OF THE SKIES, THE RIGHT TO APPROACH GANGA IS NOT BARRED BY TIME. NO ONE CAN HAVE ANY EXCLUSIVE RIGHT TO THE OCEANS, THE HIMALAYAN RANGES OR TO GANGA— BE IT NIGHT OR DAY OR TWILIGHT.

" THE GANDHARVA REPLIED:

I CAN. I AM ANGARAPARNA AND MY STRENGTH IS MY FAITH. THIS FOREST— ALL MINE— IS NAMED AFTER ME. HERE, LEAVE ALONE MEN, EVEN THE DIVINES, THE RAKSHASAS AND SORCERERS FEAR TO TREAD.

amar chitra katha

"THE BLAZING MISSILE BURNT DOWN THE GANDHARVA'S CHARIOT AND STUNNED BY THE FORCE OF THAT WEAPON...

"...HE FELL HEADLONG FROM THE CHARIOT. AS HE FELL ARJUNA SEIZED HIM BY HIS HAIR...

"...AND DRAGGED HIM TOWARDS HIS BROTHERS.

"KUMBHEENASI, THE GANDHARVA'S WIFE, ALL ANXIOUS TO SAVE HER HUSBAND'S LIFE, RAN TOWARDS YUDHISHTHIRA AND PLEADED:

SAVE ME, O NOBLE ONE. SAVE MY HUSBAND AND SAVE ME. I AM KUMBHEENASI.

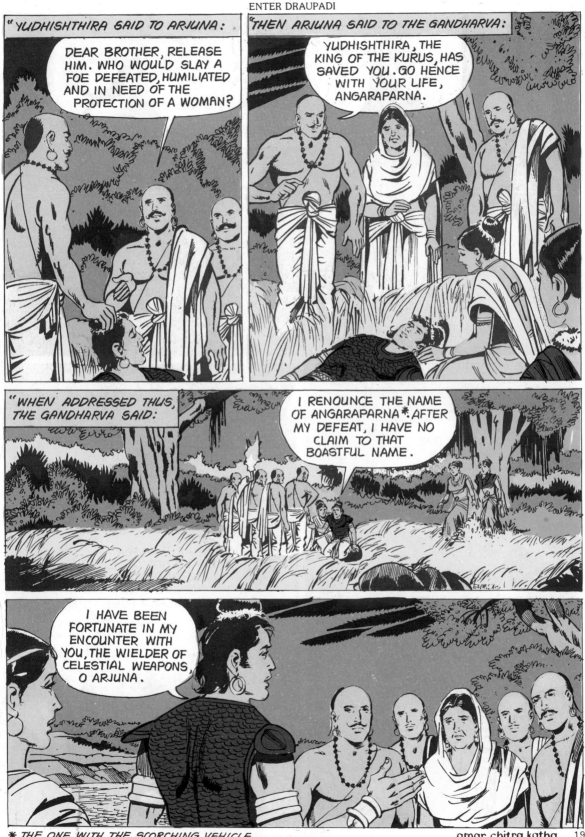

"YUDHISHTHIRA SAID TO ARJUNA:

DEAR BROTHER, RELEASE HIM. WHO WOULD SLAY A FOE DEFEATED, HUMILIATED AND IN NEED OF THE PROTECTION OF A WOMAN?

"THEN ARJUNA SAID TO THE GANDHARVA:

YUDHISHTHIRA, THE KING OF THE KURUS, HAS SAVED YOU. GO HENCE WITH YOUR LIFE, ANGARAPARNA.

"WHEN ADDRESSED THUS, THE GANDHARVA SAID:

I RENOUNCE THE NAME OF ANGARAPARNA.* AFTER MY DEFEAT, I HAVE NO CLAIM TO THAT BOASTFUL NAME.

I HAVE BEEN FORTUNATE IN MY ENCOUNTER WITH YOU, THE WIELDER OF CELESTIAL WEAPONS, O ARJUNA.

* THE ONE WITH THE SCORCHING VEHICLE

AND NOW I SHALL IMPART TO YOU THE SECRET LORE OF THE GANDHARVAS FOR MAGICAL POWERS. THE SECRET SCIENCE IS CALLED CHAKSHUSHI. IT ENABLES ONE TO PERCEIVE WHAT ONE DESIRES TO SEE, IN ALL THE THREE WORLDS.

IT IS THIS PERCEPTION THAT ELEVATES US TO THE LEVEL OF THE CELESTIALS, SUPERIOR TO THE MORTALS.

WHAT PROSPERITY DOES HE NOT DESERVE WHOSE MERCY SPARES THE LIFE OF A VANQUISHED FOE!

amar chitra katha

"THE GANDHARVA REPLIED:

A MEETING WITH A GREAT MAN IS ALWAYS A SOURCE OF GREAT JOY. OVERWHELMED BY WHAT YOU HAVE GIVEN ME, I WISH TO GIVE YOU MY SCIENCE.

TO CONFORM TO PROPRIETY, HOWEVER, I WILL RECEIVE FROM YOU THE AGNEYA MISSILE.

"THEN ARJUNA SAID:

I SHALL GIVE YOU THE MISSILE AND ACCEPT YOUR HORSES.

LET US REMAIN FRIENDS FOREVER.

O VIRTUOUS FRIEND, WE ARE SCHOLARS AND WE ARE WARRIORS. WHY DID YOU ATTACK US?

THE GANDHARVA REPLIED: NO MAN ESTEEMED FOR HIS MIGHT WILL SUFFER A SLIGHT IN THE PRESENCE OF WOMEN AND···

···YOU WANDER WITHOUT RITES AND WITHOUT RITUALS AND EVEN WITHOUT PRIESTS TO GUIDE YOU.

A KING SHOULD ALWAYS SELECT A CONSUMMATE PRIEST TO ACQUIRE WHAT HE SHOULD, AND TO PROTECT HIS ACQUISITIONS.

O TAPATYA, THAT BRAHMANA SHOULD BE INSTALLED AS PRIEST WHO IS A VEDIC SCHOLAR, WHO IS BLAMELESS, TRUTHFUL, DUTIFUL AND VIRTUOUS.

amar chitra katha

O TAPATYA, NO KING CAN EVER ASPIRE TO BE A WORLD CONQUEROR, HIS VALOUR AND PEDIGREE NOTWITHSTANDING, WITHOUT THE GUIDANCE OF A PRIEST.

" ARJUNA THEN SAID:

WHY DO YOU, O GANDHARVA, ADDRESS ME AS TAPATYA? AS THE SONS OF KUNTI WE ARE KAUNTEYAS. BUT WHO IS TAPATI TO US?

THUS ADDRESSED, O MONARCH, THE GANDHARVA TOLD HIM THE STORY OF RISHI VASISHTHA, WITH WHOSE GUIDANCE KING SAMVARANA REGAINED HIS LOST KINGDOM AND WON TAPATI THE DAUGHTER OF SURYA AS HIS BRIDE.

"AND THEN SAID:

THE SON BORN TO TAPATI AND KING SAMVARANA WAS YOUR ANCESTOR, KURU, AND THUS YOU ARE A TAPATYA.

"THEN ARJUNA ASKED:

O GANDHARVA, WITH YOUR VAST KNOWLEDGE, YOU TELL US WHICH BRAHMANA IS TO BE CHOSEN AS OUR PRIEST.

THE GANDHARVA REPLIED:

DHOUMYA WHO PRACTISES PENANCES IN THIS FOREST IS TO BE YOUR PRIEST.

THEN, PLEASED AT THE TURN OF EVENTS, ARJUNA GAVE THE SECRET OF THE AGNEYA MISSILE TO THE GANDHARVA IN ALL PROPRIETY...

"...AND SAID:

O NOBLE GANDHARVA, LET THESE HORSES BE WITH YOU. WE SHALL TAKE THEM IN THE TIME OF NEED.

"THEN THE PANDAVAS WENT TO THE ASHRAMA OF DHOUMYA WHO WELCOMED THEM WITH WILD FRUITS AND ROOTS...

"...AND CONSENTED TO BECOME THEIR PRIEST.

WITH DHOUMYA AS THEIR PRIEST, THE PANDAVAS REGARDED THEIR KINGSHIP AND THEIR KINGDOM AS ALREADY REGAINED, AND THE DAUGHTER OF PANCHALA ALREADY WON IN THE SWAYAMVARA.

AND THAT BRAHMANA DISCERNING THE INTELLIGENCE, VALOUR AND STEADFASTNESS OF THE SONS OF KUNTI, AKIN TO THAT OF THE IMMORTALS, REGARDED THEM AS ALREADY REINSTATED AS SOVEREIGN KINGS BY THEIR OWN VIRTUES.

"THEN THE KINGLY MEN ACCOMPANIED BY THEIR MOTHER AND DHOUMYA WALKED ON TO ATTEND THE SWAYAMVARA OF THE PANCHALA PRINCESS.

"ON THE WAY THEY CAME UPON A GROUP OF BRAHMANAS.

"AND THOSE BRAHMANAS, BEHOLDING THE PANDAVAS, ASKED THEM:

WHERE ARE YOU GOING?

WHERE DO YOU COME FROM?

YUDHISHTHIRA REPLIED:

WE ARE BROTHERS WHO HAVE COME HERE, WITH OUR MOTHER, FROM EKACHAKRA.

"THE BRAHMANAS THEN SAID:

WE ARE ON OUR WAY TO THE KINGDOM OF THE PANCHALAS WHERE A GRAND SWAYAMVARA IS TO BE HELD.

KINGS AND PRINCES WILL ASSEMBLE FROM FAR AND NEAR FOR THAT EVENT. THOSE MAGNIFICENT MEN EAGER TO WIN THE HAND OF DRUPADA'S DAUGHTER, DRAUPADI, WILL BE LAVISH WITH THEIR DONATIONS OF FOOD AND MONEY.

THERE WILL BE BARDS AND ACTORS AND DANCERS AND ATHLETES.

AT YOUR BEHEST, THIS HANDSOME BROTHER OF YOURS WITH HIS SINEWY ARMS COULD FETCH AMPLE WEALTH.

COME WITH US. ENJOY THE SIGHTS AND COLLECT THE GIFTS AND COME BACK.

WHO KNOWS? DRAUPADI MIGHT CHOOSE THE BEST OF YOU — ALL HANDSOME LIKE THE CELESTIALS.

"HEARING THESE WORDS, YUDHISHTHIRA REPLIED:

ALL OF US SHALL GO WITH YOU TO THE SWAYAMVARA.

"AND THE PANDAVAS THEN WALKED ON TOWARDS THE LAND OF THE SOUTHERN PANCHALAS RULED BY DRUPADA.

"RESTING NOW AND THEN IN FOREST BOWERS AND TARRYING BY THE SIDE OF LAKES ...

"...THEY FINALLY REACHED THE CITY OF DRUPADA.

AFTER SEEING THE CITY AND ITS RAMPARTS, THE PANDAVAS TOOK THEIR RESIDENCE IN THE HOUSE OF A POTTER AND LIVED LIKE MENDICANTS. NO ONE KNEW WHO THEY WERE.

AND THUS ENDS THE ELEVENTH SESSION OF OUR RENDERING OF VAISHAMPAYANA'S RECITAL OF VYASA'S IMMORTAL ITIHASA, *THE MAHABHARATA.*

Mahabharata–12
Draupadi's Swayamvara

VEDA VYASA'S EPIC ON THE BHARATA RACE WAS FIRST RECITED IN PUBLIC BY HIS DISCIPLE VAISHAMPAYANA AT THE BEHEST OF THE AGELESS SEER VYASA HIMSELF.

THE RECITAL TOOK PLACE IN THE AUGUST PRESENCE OF KING JANAMEJAYA—GREAT-GRANDSON OF THE GRANDSON OF VYASA—AND THE MANY LEARNED SAGES WHO HAD ASSEMBLED FOR JANAMEJAYA'S SARPA SATRA*

THE ELEVENTH SESSION OF OUR RENDERING OF **VAISHAMPAYANA'S** RECITAL OF VYASA'S MAHABHARATA SPOKE OF WHY THE PANDAVAS AND THEIR MOTHER SET OUT FOR DRUPADA'S CAPITAL AND HOW THEY ARRIVED THERE WITH DHOUMYA AS THEIR PRIEST. IT ENDED WITH THEIR LIVING UNRECOGNIZED IN THE HOUSE OF A POTTER.

*12-YEAR-LONG SNAKE SACRIFICE

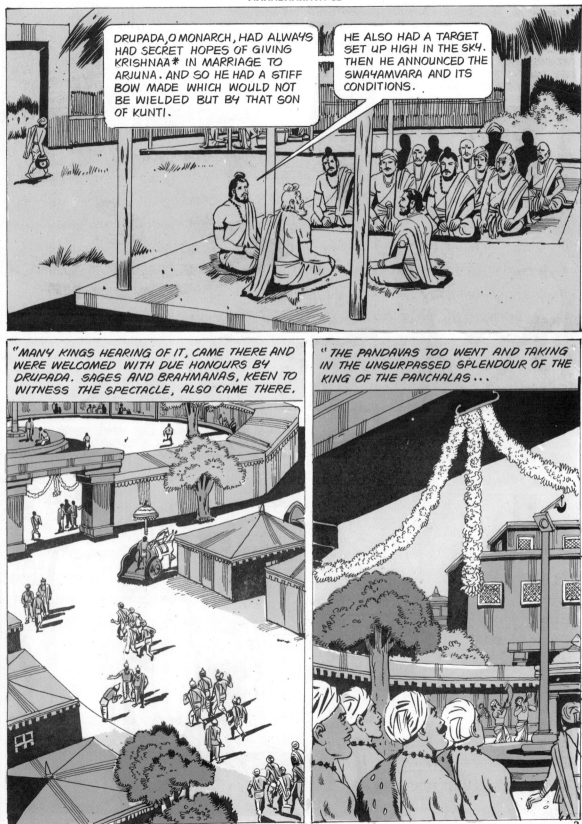

DRUPADA, O MONARCH, HAD ALWAYS HAD SECRET HOPES OF GIVING KRISHNAA* IN MARRIAGE TO ARJUNA. AND SO HE HAD A STIFF BOW MADE WHICH WOULD NOT BE WIELDED BUT BY THAT SON OF KUNTI.

HE ALSO HAD A TARGET SET UP HIGH IN THE SKY. THEN HE ANNOUNCED THE SWAYAMVARA AND ITS CONDITIONS.

"MANY KINGS HEARING OF IT, CAME THERE AND WERE WELCOMED WITH DUE HONOURS BY DRUPADA. SAGES AND BRAHMANAS, KEEN TO WITNESS THE SPECTACLE, ALSO CAME THERE.

"THE PANDAVAS TOO WENT AND TAKING IN THE UNSURPASSED SPLENDOUR OF THE KING OF THE PANCHALAS...

* DRAUPADI

"...TOOK THEIR PLACE AMONG THE BRAHMANAS. THE CONCOURSE OF MEN RECEIVING AMPLE DONATIONS AND WATCHING THE PERFORMING ARTISTES HAD SWELLED DAY BY DAY TILL, ON THE SIXTEENTH DAY, THE DAUGHTER OF DRUPADA, TASTEFULLY DRESSED AND AMPLY BEJEWELLED...

"...ENTERED THE ARENA.

" THEN A PRIEST, PURE IN BODY AND MIND, POURED LIBATIONS OF GHEE AS ORDAINED INTO THE SACRIFICIAL FIRE. HAVING HONOURED AGNI THUS AND WON THE BENEDICTION OF THE BRAHMANAS...

"... HE THEN SILENCED THE MANY INSTRUMENTS OF MUSIC PLAYING ALL AROUND. AND WHEN THAT VAST ASSEMBLY...

"...BECAME STILL AND SILENT, DHRISHTADYUMNA, THE SON OF DRUPADA, SAID:

LISTEN TO ME, O KINGS. MY SISTER DRAUPADI SHALL BECOME HIS WIFE WHO, DISTINGUISHED BY BIRTH LOOKS AND STRENGTH, CAN ACHIEVE THE FEAT...

...OF HITTING THAT TARGET, WITH FIVE ARROWS SHOT AT ONCE, THROUGH THE GAP IN THE MECHANISM.

" DHRISHTADYUMNA THEN ADDRESSED HIS SISTER THUS:

DURYODHANA, YUYUTSU AND OTHER MIGHTY SONS OF DHRITARASHTRA, KARNA, SHAKUNI, SHALYA, BALARAMA, KRISHNA, JAYADRATHA, SHISHUPALA, JARASANDHA AND MANY OTHER RENOWNED KSHATRIYAS HAVE ALL COME HERE FOR YOUR HAND.

THESE MIGHTY MEN ARE TO HIT THE TARGET. AND YOU SHALL WED THE ONE WHO HITS THE MARK.

amar chitra katha

"THEN THOSE KINGS, EACH VAIN OF HIS OWN PROWESS AND JEALOUS OF THE OTHERS, ALL SMITTEN BY THE DARTS OF KAMADEVA, ENTERED THE ARENA. AS THEY HAD EYES ONLY FOR DRAUPADI THEY DID NOT NOTICE THE PANDAVAS. KRISHNA THE YADAVA, HOWEVER, NOTICED THE FIVE BRAHMANAS DISTRAUGHT BY KAMADEVA'S SHAFTS AT THE SIGHT OF DRAUPADI. HE REFLECTED FOR A WHILE AND SAID TO BALARAMA:

THAT IS YUDHISHTHIRA. THAT IS BHEEMA AND ARJUNA AND OVER THERE THE TWINS. I HEARD THAT THEY ESCAPED THE BURNING HOUSE OF LACQUER.

"AND AS THE CELESTIALS FILLED THE SKIES, THE MANY KINGS, WHO COULD NOT STRING THAT STIFF BOW EVEN IN THEIR FANCY, STRAINED THEIR MIGHT TO WIN DRAUPADI. BUT THEY TURNED BACK DISPIRITED, THWARTED IN THEIR HOPES AS THEY WERE BY THE STIFF BOW.

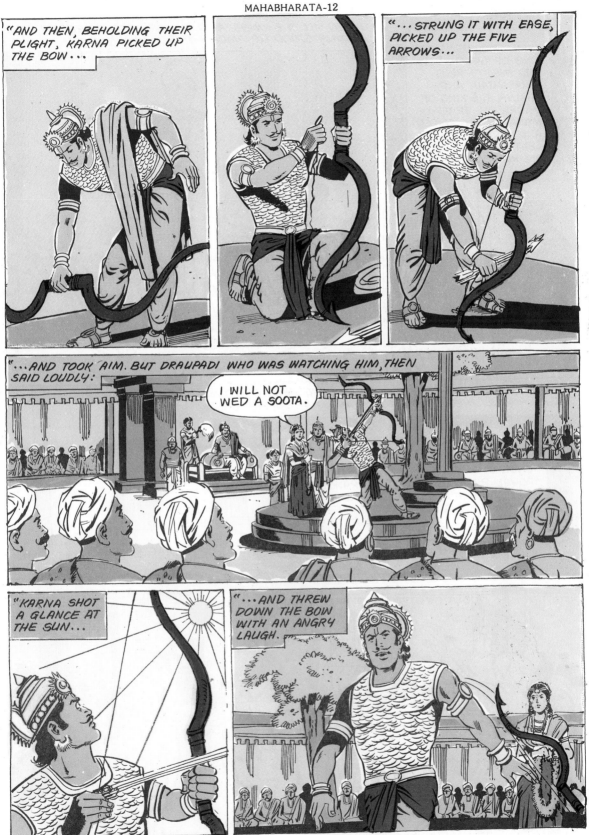

"AND THEN, BEHOLDING THEIR PLIGHT, KARNA PICKED UP THE BOW...

"... STRUNG IT WITH EASE, PICKED UP THE FIVE ARROWS...

"...AND TOOK AIM. BUT DRAUPADI WHO WAS WATCHING HIM, THEN SAID LOUDLY:

I WILL NOT WED A SOOTA.

"KARNA SHOT A GLANCE AT THE SUN...

"...AND THREW DOWN THE BOW WITH AN ANGRY LAUGH.

amar chitra katha

THEN SHISHUPALA THE KING OF THE CHEDIS, AND MIGHTY KING JARASANDHA AND SHALYA THE KING OF MADRA ALL TRIED, O MONARCH, BUT FAILED. AND JARASANDHA LEFT FORTHWITH FOR HIS KINGDOM.

"WHEN ALL THE KINGS AND THE PRINCES WITHDREW, ARJUNA STOOD UP AMONG THE BRAHMANAS...

"...AND STRODE TOWARDS THE BOW. BEHOLDING THIS THE ELDERS AMONG THE BRAHMANAS, RAISING A CLAMOUR, SAID:

STOP HIM! IF HIS TEMERITY ENDS IN FAILURE, ROYAL RIDICULE WILL BE THE LOT OF A BRAHMANA.

HOW CAN A BRAHMANA STRIPLING, A STRANGER TO ARMS, HANDLE THE BOW WHICH THE MIGHTY KSHATRIYAS FAILED TO STRING?

"...AND BROUGHT IT FALLING TO THE GROUND. THEN, O MONARCH, SOUNDS FROM THE SKIES AND THE EARTH RENT THE AIR. THE CELESTIALS SHOWERED FLOWERS ON ARJUNA. THE BRAHMANAS WAVED THEIR DEERSKINS IN JOY. THE KINGS AND PRINCES UTTERED CRIES OF WOE. AS THE DIN SWELLED UP, YUDHISHTHIRA AND THE TWINS LEFT THE SCENE AND DRAUPADI TURNED HER STEPS TOWARDS ARJUNA.

"THEN THE SHOCK OF THE KINGS AND PRINCES GRADUALLY TURNED INTO ANGER AND THEY SAID:

IT IS ORDAINED THAT THE SWAYAMVARA IS FOR KSHATRIYAS. BRAHMANAS ARE NOT ELIGIBLE AT ALL!

YET, SLIGHTING US, DRUPADA WOULD GIVE AWAY THIS GEM OF A WOMAN TO A BRAHMANA.

WE MUST ENSURE THAT NO SUCH HUMILIATING SWAYAMVARA WILL BE HELD HENCEFORTH!

WE CANNOT SLAY A BRAHMANA. SO LET US SLAY THIS TREACHEROUS KING AND HIS SON AND CAST HIS DAUGHTER INTO THE FIRE BEFORE WE RETURN TO OUR KINGDOM.

AS THOSE MIGHTY WARRIORS TOOK UP THEIR WEAPONS AND RUSHED AT DRUPADA, O MONARCH...

amar chitra katha

"...ARJUNA STOOD READY WITH HIS BOW AND THE RUGGED BHEEMA, UPROOTING A BIG TREE, STOOD BESIDE HIM LIKE A MACE-WIELDING YAMA.

"AND THE BRAHMANAS BRANDISHING THEIR SACRED VESSELS SAID:

BE NOT AFRAID! WE SHALL FIGHT THE KINGS.

"ARJUNA SMILED AND SAID TO THEM:

YOU BE HERE AS SPECTATORS. MY SHARP ARROWS SHALL CONTAIN THE VICIOUS KINGS AS DO MANTRAS, THE SNAKES.

"THEN THE FEARLESS BROTHERS BROKE INTO THE RANKS OF THE RAGING KINGS. AND THEY, LED BY KARNA, SAID:

THE SLAUGHTER OF BRAHMANAS WHO COME TO FIGHT IS DEEMED FAIR.

"AND, AS THEY CHARGED, DURYODHANA AND OTHERS EFFORTLESSLY CONTAINED THE BRAHMANAS WHILE SHALYA TOOK ON BHEEMA, AND KARNA, ARJUNA.

"THE SWIFT SHARP ARROWS DISCHARGED BY ARJUNA THREW KARNA INTO A DAZE.

amar chitra katha

THEREFORE LET US GIVE UP THIS BRAHMANA-INFESTED BATTLE. BESIDES BRAHMANAS, EVEN IF GUILTY, DESERVE PROTECTION.

LET US FIRST ASCERTAIN THEIR LINEAGE AND THEN WE SHALL FIGHT THEM FAIR.

" AT THAT JUNCTURE KNOWING THE TWO TO BE THE SONS OF KUNTI, KRISHNA RESTRAINED THE KINGS SAYING:

DRAUPADI HAS BEEN WON IN A PROPER MANNER.

" DEXTROUS WARRIORS THOUGH THEY WERE, THE KINGS WITHDREW FROM FURTHUR FIGHTING...

"...AND RETURNED TO THEIR DWELLINGS AMAZED AT THE TURN OF EVENTS.

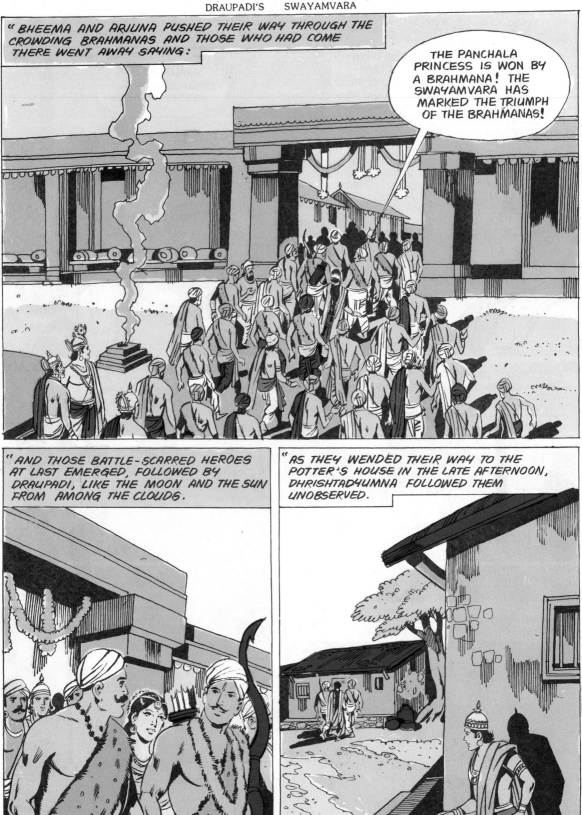

"BHEEMA AND ARJUNA PUSHED THEIR WAY THROUGH THE CROWDING BRAHMANAS AND THOSE WHO HAD COME THERE WENT AWAY SAYING:

THE PANCHALA PRINCESS IS WON BY A BRAHMANA! THE SWAYAMVARA HAS MARKED THE TRIUMPH OF THE BRAHMANAS!

"AND THOSE BATTLE-SCARRED HEROES AT LAST EMERGED, FOLLOWED BY DRAUPADI, LIKE THE MOON AND THE SUN FROM AMONG THE CLOUDS.

"AS THEY WENDED THEIR WAY TO THE POTTER'S HOUSE IN THE LATE AFTERNOON, DHRISHTADYUMNA FOLLOWED THEM UNOBSERVED.

"MEANWHILE KUNTI, WORRIED OVER THE DELAY IN THE RETURN OF HER SONS FROM THEIR ROUNDS, THOUGHT OF ALL THE ACCIDENTS THAT COULD HAVE BE-FALLEN THEM. THE THOUGHT OF HER SONS BEING SLAIN BY THE SONS OF DHRITARASHTRA STRUCK HER.

"NEXT IT WAS THE THOUGHT OF A RAKSHASA GETTING AT HER SONS BY SORCERY.

"AND SHE ASKED HERSELF:

COULD IT BE THAT THE GREAT VYASA HIMSELF HAS BEEN PROVED WRONG?

"AT THIS JUNCTURE THE SONS ENTERED AND ANNOUNCED THAT THEY HAD RETURNED WITH ALMS.

"KUNTI WHO WAS INSIDE AND COULD NOT SEE THEM ADVISED:

ENJOY IT, ALL OF YOU TOGETHER.

"AND THEN WHEN SHE SAW DRAUPADI SHE EXCLAIMED:

OH! WHAT HAVE I SAID!

"FEARFUL OF TRANSGRESSING PROPRIETY...

"...KUNTI ADDRESSING YUDHISHTHIRA SAID:

YOUR BROTHERS ANNOUNCED DRAUPADI AS "THE ALMS" AND HEEDLESSLY I SAID, ENJOY IT, ALL OF YOU TOGETHER.

TELL ME HOW MY WORDS CAN BE KEPT TRUE EVEN AS DRAUPADI IS SAVED FROM DILEMMA AND DAMNATION.

"THUS ADDRESSED BY HIS MOTHER, YUDHISHTHIRA REFLECTED FOR A WHILE AND THEN SAID TO ARJUNA:

DRAUPADI WAS WON BY YOU. THEREFORE LIGHT THE FIRE, TAKE HER HAND AND WED HER RIGHTFULLY.

"ARJUNA REPLIED:

WHAT YOU SAY DOES NOT CONFORM TO OUR CODE OF CONDUCT. YOU THE ELDEST MUST WED FIRST, THEN BHEEMA, THEN I, THEN NAKULA AND LAST OF ALL SAHADEVA.

CONSIDER ALL THIS AND DO WHAT WOULD BE RIGHTEOUS, WELL SPOKEN OF, AND BENEFICIAL TO KING DRUPADA. WE ARE HERE TO DO YOUR BIDDING.

"HEARING THE WORDS OF ARJUNA SO FULL OF RESPECT AND AFFECTION AND ALSO BEHOLDING THE EYES OF HIS YOUNGER BROTHERS IMPLANTED IN THE RECIPROCATING GLANCES OF DRAUPADI...

"...YUDHISHTHIRA KNEW WHAT TROUBLED THEIR MINDS. THEN REMEMBERING MY GURU VYASA'S WORDS AND FEARFUL OF A SPLIT AMONG THE BROTHERS, HE SAID:

THE GRACIOUS DRAUPADI SHALL BE THE WIFE OF US ALL.

"AS THE HEROES JOYFULLY RUMINATED OVER THE WORDS OF THE ELDER BROTHER, KRISHNA AND BALARAMA CAME THERE.

"THEN KRISHNA, FOLLOWED BY BALARAMA, APPROACHED YUDHISHTHIRA AND BENT DOWN AND TOUCHED HIS FEET SAYING:

I AM KRISHNA.

"THEN THOSE TWO YADAVA HEROES TOUCHED THE FEET OF KUNTI, THEIR FATHER'S SISTER.

"AFTER THE PANDAVAS HAD EXCHANGED PLEASANTRIES WITH KRISHNA, YUDHISHTHIRA ASKED HIM:

HOW DID YOU TRACE US HERE? WE HAVE BEEN LIVING IN SECRECY.

"KRISHNA REPLIED WITH A SMILE:

FIRE THOUGH SHROUDED WILL STILL SHOW. WHO AMONG MEN BUT THE PANDAVAS COULD SHOW SUCH MIGHT!

IT IS FORTUNATE THAT THE SONS OF DHRITARASHTRA AND THEIR COUNSELLORS FAILED IN THEIR PURPOSE. FARE YOU WELL.

AND LEST ANY OF THE KINGS SHOULD RECOGNIZE YOU IF THEY SEE US HERE, WE SHALL RETURN TO OUR CAMP.

"THEN TAKING LEAVE OF YUDHISHTHIRA, KRISHNA AND BALARAMA HASTILY WITHDREW FROM THE SCENE.

"AND BHEEMA AND ARJUNA AND THE TWINS WENT OUT AS USUAL COLLECTING ALMS...

"...AND RETURNING AT DUSK GAVE ALL THAT THEY HAD COLLECTED TO YUDHISHTHIRA.

amar chitra katha

" KUNTI ASKED DRAUPADI TO SET ASIDE A PORTION AS OFFERINGS TO THE GODS, TO BE GIVEN AWAY, AND TO DIVIDE THE REST INTO TWO HALVES.

" THEN SHE SAID:

GIVE ONE HALF TO BHEEMA BECAUSE HE ALWAYS CONSUMES MORE.

DIVIDE THE OTHER INTO SIX SHARES — FOUR FOR EACH OF THE BROTHERS, ONE FOR ME AND ONE FOR YOU.

" DRAUPADI OBEYED THE INSTRUCTIONS OF KUNTI AND ALL ATE THE FOOD.

"THEN SAHADEVA MADE A BED OF KUSHA GRASS AND THE VALIANT ONES SPREADING THEIR DEERSKINS ON IT...

"...LAID THEMSELVES DOWN TO SLEEP WITH KUNTI AT THEIR HEADS AND DRAUPADI AT THEIR FEET.

"THEN THESE BRAVE MEN STARTED TALKING AMONG THEMSELVES.

"AND THEY, IN THEIR MARTIAL AUTHORITY, TALKED OF SWORDS, MACES, BATTLE-AXES, ELEPHANTS, CHARIOTS AND CELESTIAL MISSILES.

"THE SON OF THE PANCHALA KING OVERHEARD ALL THAT THEY HAD SAID, AND HASTENED...

"... TO REPORT IT TO DRUPADA. DRUPADA ASKED DHRISHTADYUMNA:

O WHERE IS KRISHNAA? WHO HAS LED HER AWAY? GIVE ME THE DETAILS OF THE ONE WHO HAS OBTAINED MY DAUGHTER.

"AND DHRISHTADYUMNA RECOUNTED ALL THAT HE HAD WITNESSED. THEN HE SAID:

THE TALK OF THOSE VALIANT ONES UNDOUBTEDLY PROVED THEM TO BE KSHATRIYAS OF A HIGH ORDER. OUR HOPES SEEM FULFILLED. HAD WE NOT HEARD OF THE ESCAPE OF THE PANDAVAS FROM THE BURNING HOUSE OF LACQUER?

"DRUPADA EXCLAIMED:

ARE THE SONS OF PANDU ALIVE? WAS IT ARJUNA WHO LIFTED THE BOW AND BROUGHT DOWN THE TARGET?

"DHRISHTADYUMNA REPLIED:

ALL THAT HAS BEEN SEEN AND HEARD MAKE THEM OUT TO BE THE PANDAVAS WANDERING IN DISGUISE.

"THEN, KEEN ON TESTING THE IDENTITY OF THE VALIANT MEN, DRUPADA KEPT READY A LARGE COLLECTION OF FRUITS, GARLANDS, CARPETS; AND SEEDS, ROPES AND FARMING IMPLEMENTS; AND DIVERSE MARTIAL EQUIPMENT AND CHARIOTS AND STEEDS.

"AND A MESSENGER CAME TO YUDHISHTHIRA IN HASTE AND SAID:

THE PANCHALA KING HAS PREPARED A FEAST FOR THE BRIDEGROOM AND HIS KINSFOLK. THESE ROYAL CHARIOTS WILL TAKE YOU TO THE KING'S RESIDENCE WHERE THE WEDDING WILL BE PERFORMED.

"THE PANDAVAS AND KUNTI AND DRAUPADI PROCEEDED TO DRUPADA'S PALACE IN THESE MAGNIFICENT CHARIOTS.

"BEHOLDING, O MONARCH, THOSE HEROES STRIDING IN, THEIR TORSOS CLAD IN DEER-SKIN, THE KING AND HIS SON AND THEIR RETINUE BECAME EXCEEDINGLY GLAD.

"THEN THOSE VALIANT ONES WENT UP TO THEIR SEATS AND OCCUPIED THEM WITHOUT DIFFIDENCE OR SURPRISE WHILE KUNTI AND DRAUPADI WENT INTO THE INNER APPARTMENTS.

"AND WELL-DRESSED ATTENDANTS AND SERVANTS BROUGHT EXCELLENT FOOD IN PLATES OF GOLD AND SILVER WHICH THE HEROES ENJOYED TO THE FULL AND FELT PLEASED.

"THEN THE PANDAVAS WENT TO THE SPOT WHERE THE MARTIAL EQUIPMENT WAS DISPLAYED, PAYING LITTLE HEED TO THE REST OF THE ARTICLES. DRUPADA, HIS SON AND THE COUNSELLORS OBSERVED ALL THIS AND DECIDED THAT THESE WERE THE PANDAVAS.

"THEN DRUPADA SAID TO YUDHISHTHIRA:

ARE WE TO TAKE YOU FOR BRAHMANAS OR KSHATRIYAS OR CELESTIALS COME DOWN SEEKING THE HAND OF KRISHNAA?

IN KEEPING WITH YOUR REPLY, I SHALL MAKE THE REQUISITE PREPARATIONS FOR MY DAUGHTER'S WEDDING.

"YUDHISHTHIRA REPLIED:

WE ARE KSHATRIYAS AND THE SONS OF PANDU. I AM THE ELDEST OF KUNTI'S SONS.

AND THOSE ARE BHEEMA AND ARJUNA WHO WON YOUR DAUGHTER.

THESE ARE NAKULA AND SAHADEVA. KUNTI IS IN WITH KRISHNAA.

I HAVE TOLD YOU THE TRUTH. YOU ARE AN ELDER TO US AND OUR REFUGE.

OVERCOME BY THE UTMOST JOY, DRUPADA COULD HARDLY SPEAK AND THEN, CONTROLLING HIS EMOTIONS, HE ASKED THE PANDAVAS HOW THEY ESCAPED FROM VARANAVATA.

WHEN HE HEARD ALL THE DETAILS, HE CENSURED DHRITARASHTRA AND ASSURED YUDHISHTHIRA THAT THIS KINGDOM WOULD BE RESTORED TO HIM.

" THEN HE SAID TO YUDHISHTHIRA:

LET ARJUNA WED MY DAUGHTER ACCORDING TO RITES ON THIS AUSPICIOUS DAY.

" YUDHISHTHIRA REPLIED:

O KING, I SHALL ALSO HAVE TO WED.

" DRUPADA SAID:

THEN TAKE THE HAND OF MY DAUGHTER YOURSELF ACCORDING TO RITES OR GIVE HER IN MARRIAGE TO THE BROTHER YOU CHOOSE.

" YUDHISHTHIRA SAID:

YOUR DAUGHTER, O KING, SHALL BE WIFE TO US ALL. THIS IS ALREADY COMMANDED BY MY MOTHER AND IT IS A RULE WITH US THAT WE SHARE EQUALLY WHAT WE OBTAIN.

" DRUPADA SAID:

MANY HUSBANDS TO ONE WOMAN HAS NEVER BEEN HEARD OF. YOU KNOW THE WAYS OF VIRTUE. HOW CAN YOU DEVIATE THUS AND GO AGAINST THE CANNONS OF VIRTUE AND PRACTICE?

" YUDHISHTHIRA REPLIED:

VIRTUE IS COMPLEX. I UTTER NO LIE NOR DO I THINK EVIL. THIS IS WHAT MY MOTHER HAS ORDERED AND I APPROVE IT.

"JUST THEN MY GURU VYASA ARRIVED THERE AND, ACCEPTING THE RESPECTFUL SALUTATIONS OF ALL, SAT DOWN. THEN DRUPADA ASKED HIM:

O GREAT SAGE, HOW CAN ONE WOMAN BE THE VIRTUOUS WIFE OF MANY MEN WITHOUT BEING DEFILED?

"HE REPLIED:

THIS PRACTICE HAS BECOME OBSOLETE BUT THE VIRTUOUS KRISHNAA...

...HAS BEEN ORDAINED BY SHIVA TO BECOME THE WIFE OF FIVE HUSBANDS. NOW, YOU DO AS YOU WISH.

"THEN DRUPADA SAID:

WHEN IT IS THE WILL OF SHIVA— BE IT RIGHT OR WRONG—NO BLAME WILL COME TO ME.

AS DESTINED, LET THESE HEROES WED KRISHNAA ACCORDING TO THE RITES.

"THEN MY GURU SAID TO YUDHISHTHIRA:

O SON OF PANDU, ON THIS AUSPICIOUS DAY, YOU TAKE THE HAND OF KRISHNAA FIRST.

"WHEN VYASA SAID SO, DRUPADA MADE PREPARATIONS FOR THE WEDDING AND INVITED HIS RELATIVES, HIS COUNSELLORS, THE BRAHMANAS AND THE CITIZENS. THEN HE LED THE BEDECKED KRISHNAA INTO THE ASSEMBLY. THE PANDAVAS IN ALL THEIR FINERY CAME ACCOMPANIED BY THEIR PRIEST DHOUMYA.

"THEN DHOUMYA LIT AND SANCTIFIED THE SACRED FIRE WITH LIBATIONS AND MANTRAS AND YUDHISHTHIRA AND KRISHNAA CIRCUMAMBULATED THE FIRE.

"WHEN THE WEDDING OF YUDHISHTHIRA AND DRAUPADI WAS PERFORMED, DHOUMYA LEFT THE PLACE AND RETURNED THE NEXT DAY TO PERFORM THE WEDDING OF THE SECOND PANDAVA. IN THIS MANNER THE FIVE PANDAVAS TOOK THE HAND OF DRAUPADI ON SUCCEEDING DAYS.

THEN DRUPADA, WITH FIRE AS WITNESS, PRESENTED TO EACH OF THOSE PRINCES A HUNDRED CHARIOTS, FOUR HUNDRED STEEDS, A HUNDRED ELEPHANTS, A HUNDRED MAIDS AND ROBES AND ORNAMENTS AND GOLD.

AND THE SONS OF PANDU NOW IN POSSESSION OF WEALTH AND POWER PASSED THEIR DAYS IN THE CITY OF THE PANCHALAS, HAPPY IN THE COMPANY OF VIRTUOUS DRAUPADI.

THUS ENDS THE TWELFTH SESSION OF OUR RENDERING OF VAISHAMPAYANA'S RECITAL OF VYASA'S IMMORTAL ITIHASA, THE MAHABHARATA.

Mahabharata – 13
The Pandavas recalled to Hastinapura

THEN, O MONARCH, THE NEWS THAT DRAUPADI WAS WEDDED TO THE PANDAVAS WAS CARRIED TO THE KINGS BY THEIR LOYAL SPIES.

THEY WHO HAD HEARD OF THE DEATH OF KUNTI AND HER SONS IN THE HOUSE OF LACQUER NOW CONSIDERED THEM AS BORN ANEW.

"WHEN VIDURA LEARNT THAT THE PANDAVAS HAD WON DRAUPADI, HE WENT TO DHRITARASHTRA AND ANNOUNCED IN ALL JOY:

GOOD FORTUNE BRINGS PROSPERITY TO THE KURUS!

" THE BLIND KING MISUNDERSTOOD AND THOUGHT THAT HIS ELDEST SON, DURYODHANA, WAS CHOSEN BY DRAUPADI. IMMENSELY PLEASED, HE SAID:

VIDURA, THIS IS INDEED GOOD LUCK!

AND THE KING ORDERED THAT AMPLE ORNAMENTS BE MADE FOR DRAUPADI AND THAT SHE BE CEREMONIALLY BROUGHT OVER BY DURYODHANA.

IT WAS THEN THAT VIDURA EXPLAINED HOW THE PANDAVAS WERE THE CHOSEN ONES AND HOW THEY WERE BEING FELICITATED BY DRUPADA AND THE MANY POWERFUL KINSMEN WHO HAD GATHERED FOR THE SWAYAMVARA.

"THEN DHRITARASHTRA SAID:

THOSE CHILDREN ARE AS DEAR TO ME AS TO PANDU. NAY, MORE! THEY HAVE ACQUIRED MANY FRIENDS AND STRONG ALLIES.

WHICH KING WOULD NOT REJOICE AT GETTING DRUPADA WITH HIS KINSMEN AS AN ALLY?

"HEARING THESE WORDS, VIDURA SAID:

MAY THIS WISDOM BE WITH YOU FOR A HUNDRED YEARS!

"AND HAVING SAID THIS VIDURA LEFT FOR HIS ABODE.

"THEN, O MONARCH, DURYODHANA AND KARNA SAID TO DHRITARASHTRA:

O FATHER, WE COULD NOT SPEAK OUT IN VIDURA'S PRESENCE.

O KING, NOW YOU ARE ALONE. WE SHALL SPEAK OUR MINDS.

O FATHER, YOU MISTAKE THE PROSPERITY OF YOUR FOES AS YOUR OWN AND THEN PRAISE THEM IN FRONT OF VIDURA.

amar chitra katha

OR WITH AMPLE WEALTH, LET US LURE DRUPADA, HIS SON AND HIS MINISTERS AWAY FROM YUDHISHTHIRA.

OR LET OUR SPIES INDUCE THE PANDAVAS TO STAY ON IN THE LAND OF THE PANCHALAS BY DETAILING THE PERILS OF STAYING HERE...

...OR TURN DRAUPADI AGAINST THEM BY ENTICING THEM WITH BEAUTIFUL WOMEN.

OR LET BHEEMA BE KILLED SECRETLY. WITHOUT HIM — THE STRONGEST OF THE PANDAVAS — THEY WILL NOT ATTEMPT TO REGAIN THE DOMINION.

YES, WITHOUT HIM, ARJUNA WILL NOT MEASURE UP EVEN TO A FOURTH OF KARNA IN COMBAT. ARJUNA IS INVINCIBLE ONLY WITH THE SUPPORT OF BHEEMA.

TIME IS RUNNING OUT. WE MUST STRIKE BEFORE THEIR FAITH IN DRUPADA BECOMES FIRM. AFTERWARDS IT WILL BE IMPOSSIBLE.

WHAT DO YOU THINK, O KARNA?

"KARNA REPLIED: WHAT YOU SAY DOES NOT SEEM TO BE VIABLE.

IT IS IMPOSSIBLE TO SPLIT THOSE WHO ARE HAPPY WITH A COMMON WIFE.

THE KING OF PANCHALA IS SCRUPULOUS AND HE IS NOT GREEDY. HE WILL NOT SACRIFICE THE PANDAVAS FOR ALL YOUR KINGDOM.

NOR CAN DRAUPADI BE SEPARATED FROM THE PANDAVAS. SHE CHOSE THEM WHEN THEY WERE HAPLESS.

WILL SHE SPURN THEM NOW THAT THEY ARE PROSPEROUS?

amar chitra katha

TACT, BRIBES AND SCHEMES WILL NOT WORK WITH THE PANDAVAS.

ONLY AGGRESSION WILL. AND IT WILL HAVE TO BE BEFORE KRISHNA AND HIS YADAVA ARMY REACH THE LAND OF THE PANCHALAS TO RESTORE THE PATERNAL KINGDOM TO THE PANDAVAS.

ATTACK THEM. TRIUMPH OVER THEM AND MAKE THE WHOLE WORLD YOURS. I SEE NO OTHER WAY.

THE GREAT BHARATA CONQUERED THE WORLD BY FORCE. FORCE IS THE PRIME VIRTUE OF THE BRAVE. LET US USE FORCE, VANQUISH DRUPADA AND IMPRISON THE PANDAVAS.

"DHRITARASHTRA APPLAUDED THE WORDS OF KARNA AND SAID:

O KARNA, YOU ARE WISE AND YOU ARE A GREAT WARRIOR. IT IS ONLY MEET THAT YOU EXTOL THE VIRTUES OF FORCE. BUT...

O DURYODHANA, YOU ARE ALREADY BLAMED, MUCH MORE THAN PUROCHANA, FOR THE CALAMITY IN THE HOUSE OF LACQUER. FORTUNATELY THE REAPPEARANCE OF THE PANDAVAS, ALIVE, CLEANSES YOUR REPUTATION.

IN DEFERENCE TO DUTY, MY WISHES, AND THE WELFARE OF ALL, GIVE HALF THE KINGDOM TO THEM.

"AFTER BHEESHMA, DRONA SAID:

O KING, IT IS ENJOINED THAT THOSE SUMMONED FOR ADVICE SHOULD SPEAK WHAT IS RIGHT, USEFUL AND FRUITFUL.

I CONCUR WITH BHEESHMA. LET THE SONS OF KUNTI BE GIVEN AN EQUAL DIVISION. THIS IS IN ACCORDANCE WITH TRADITIONAL MORALITY.

SEND A COURTEOUS MESSENGER TO DRUPADA WITH PRECIOUS GIFTS FOR THE PANDAVAS, AND THEIR BRIDE. HE MUST AVER HOW ELATED YOU ARE AT THIS ALLIANCE WITH DRUPADA AND HIS SON, AND HOW YOU REJOICE AT THE TURN OF EVENTS.

LET THE MESSENGER THEN SPEAK OF THE RETURN OF THE PANDAVAS. AND WHEN THEY COME HERE YOU MUST WELCOME THEM, AND INSTALL THEM ON THEIR ANCESTRAL THRONE, IN KEEPING WITH THE WISHES OF THE PEOPLE.

THIS, I BELIEVE, SHOULD BE YOUR ATTITUDE TO YOUR CHILDREN AND TO THE PANDAVAS.

"THEN KARNA SAID:

O KING, YOU HAVE ALWAYS HONOURED BHEESHMA AND DRONA WITH RESPECT AND WITH GIFTS, AND YOU LOOK UP TO THEM AS YOUR TRUSTED COUNSELLORS.

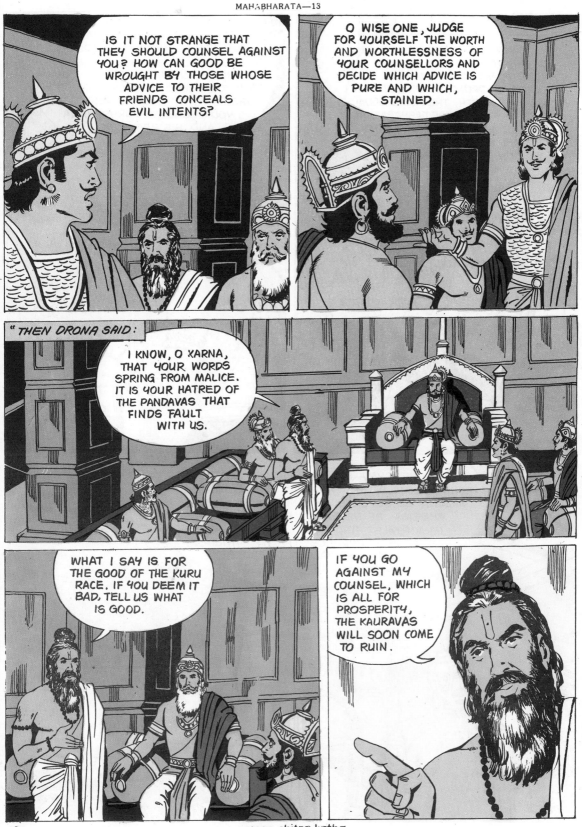

amar chitra katha

" THEN VIDURA SPOKE:

I CANNOT THINK, O KING, OF ANYONE WHO IS A BETTER FRIEND TO YOU THAN EITHER BHEESHMA OR DRONA, OR ONE WHO IS WISER. IN TRUTH, THEY ARE EQUAL TO RAMA, THE SON OF DASHARATHA. INDEED WHAT THESE MEN, RIPE IN AGE, EXPERIENCE AND WISDOM, SAY IS FOR YOUR GOOD.

THOSE WHO WOULD EXPOSE YOUR LATENT PARTIALITY IF ANY, FOR YOUR CHILDREN, DO YOU NO GOOD. THOSE WHOSE ADVICE IS MALICIOUS TO THE PANDAVAS, ARE NOT YOUR WELL-WISHERS. INDEED THE PANDAVAS ARE AS MUCH YOUR SONS AS DURYODHANA AND HIS BROTHERS.

WHAT BHEESHMA HAS SAID REGARDING THE INVINCIBILITY OF THE PANDAVAS TOO IS TRUE. CAN ARJUNA BE DEFEATED BY INDRA HIMSELF? CAN BHEEMA BE DEFEATED EVEN BY THE IMMORTALS? AND HOW CAN YUDHISHTHIRA, IN WHOM ENDURANCE, CHARITY, PATIENCE, HONESTY AND VALOUR DWELL, BE OVERCOME IN BATTLE?

THEY WHO HAVE BALARAMA ON THEIR SIDE, KRISHNA AS THEIR COUNSELLOR, DRUPADA AS FATHER-IN-LAW AND DHRISHTADYUMNA AS BROTHER-IN-LAW ARE INDEED INVINCIBLE. WE HAD OUR CLASH WITH DRUPADA EARLIER. HIS ALLIANCE NOW WILL BE TO OUR ADVANTAGE.

THE MIGHTY LEGION OF THE YADAVAS IS THERE WHERE KRISHNA IS; AND VICTORY IS WHERE KRISHNA IS. AWARE OF THIS, AS WELL AS OF THEIR SUPERIOR CLAIM OF INHERITANCE TO THE KINGDOM, BEHAVE DECENTLY WITH THE PANDAVAS.

WASH AWAY THE STAIN BROUGHT ON YOU BY PUROCHANA'S DEED, O KING, WHO BUT ONE CURSED BY THE GODS WILL CHOOSE DISCORD WHEN ACCORD CAN ACHIEVE HIS GOAL?

amar chitra katha

DURYODHANA, KARNA AND SHAKUNI ARE YOUNG, MISCHIEVOUS MISCREANTS. DO NOT LISTEN TO THEM. I HAD TOLD YOU LONG AGO THAT THE SINS OF DURYODHANA WILL DRAG THE PEOPLE TO RUIN.

THESE OMENS PORTEND THAT YOUR ELDEST SON SHALL BE THE RUIN OF YOUR RACE AND THIS LAND.

YEO-O-OO EE-E GR-R-R-

"THEN DHRITARASHTRA SAID:

THE WISE BHEESHMA, RISHI DRONA AND YOU SPEAK THE TRUTH AND SPEAK FOR MY GOOD. THE VALOROUS SONS OF PANDU ARE MORALLY MINE ALSO. AND SO ARE THEY ENTITLED TO THIS KINGDOM— JUST AS MY SONS ARE.

GO THEREFORE, O VIDURA, AND BRING THE PANDAVAS AND THEIR MOTHER AND DRAUPADI HERE WITH ALL DUE HONOURS.

THEN AS COMMANDED, O MONARCH, VIDURA WENT TO DRUPADA AND THE PANDAVAS CARRYING WITH HIM GREAT WEALTH FOR THEM AND FOR DRAUPADI.

"DRUPADA WELCOMED HIM IN ALL PROPRIETY...

"...AND VIDURA MET KRISHNA AND THE PANDAVAS THERE.

"AS SOON AS HE SAW THEM HE EMBRACED THEM, O MONARCH, AND THEY IN TURN PAID THEIR RESPECTS TO HIM.

"HE THEN FORMALLY GAVE THE PANDAVAS AND KUNTI AND DRAUPADI AND DRUPADA AND HIS SONS, THE WEALTH THE KAURAVAS HAD SENT THROUGH HIM.

"THEN HE SAID TO DRUPADA:

I BRING YOU THE GOOD WISHES OF DHRITARASHTRA AND BHEESHMA AND ALL THE KURUS AND DRONA. THEY ARE PLEASED WITH THIS ALLIANCE AND ARE ELATED MUCH MORE THAN AT THE ACQUISITION OF DOMINIONS.

THE KURU LADIES AND THE CITIZENS AND OUR SUBJECTS—ALL, ALL ARE EAGER TO BEHOLD THE SONS OF PANDU AND THE PANCHALA PRINCESS.

THESE VALIANT MEN AND KUNTI, AWAY FROM THEIR LAND FOR A LONG TIME, ARE EAGER TO BE THERE AGAIN. THEREFORE LET THEM PROCEED TO THEIR CITY. INSTRUCT THE PANDAVAS AND THEIR WIFE, O KING, TO SET OUT WITHOUT DELAY.

"THEN KRISHNA SAID:

I THINK THAT THEY SHOULD. BUT LET THE WILL OF DRUPADA, WHO KNOWS WHAT IS PROPER, BE DONE.

"THEN YUDHISHTHIRA SAID:

O KING, WE SUBMIT TO YOUR WILL.

"DRUPADA SAID:

I ABIDE BY WHAT KRISHNA DECIDES BECAUSE THE PANDAVAS ARE AS DEAR TO HIM AS TO ME. HIS CONCERN FOR THE WELFARE OF THE SONS OF PANDU EXCELS THAT OF EVEN YUDHISHTHIRA.

O MONARCH, HAVING THEN OBTAINED THE PERMISSION OF DRUPADA, THE PANDAVAS, KRISHNA AND VIDURA, ACCOMPANIED BY KUNTI AND DRAUPADI, SET OUT FOR HASTINAPURA.

AND DHRITARASHTRA, INFORMED OF THEIR ARRIVAL, ASSIGNED VIKARNA AND CHITRASENA AND DRONA AND KRIPA TO RECEIVE THEM.

"THEN THE PANDAVAS MADE THEIR WAY TO DHRITARASHTRA AND BHEESHMA AND PAID OBEISANCE TO THEM.

THEN, AT THE BEHEST OF DHRITARASHTRA, THEY ENTERED THEIR APARTMENTS. AND AFTER THEY HAD RESTED FOR A WHILE THEY WERE SUMMONED BY DHRITARASHTRA AND BHEESHMA.

"AND DHRITARASHTRA SAID:

TAKE POSSESSION OF HALF THE KINGDOM AND RULE OVER IT FROM KHANDAVAPRASTHA, SO THAT THERE IS NO FURTHER DISSENSION. NO HARM WILL COME TO YOU THERE WITH ARJUNA TO PROTECT YOU.

"ACCEPTING THE PROPOSAL, THE PANDAVAS SET OUT FROM HASTINAPURA, AND LED BY KRISHNA...

"...THEY ARRIVED AT KHANDAVA-PRASTHA.

" THEN THOSE HEROES, UNDER THE GUIDANCE OF MY GURU VEDA VYASA, HAD A PLOT MEASURED AND CONSECRATED FOR BUILDING A CITY.

" AND THE CITY THAT WAS BUILT, HAD SKY-HIGH WALLS AND WAS SURROUNDED BY A MOAT. THE CITY-GATES WERE LIKE THE OUTSPREAD WINGS OF GARUDA. THERE WERE ARMED GUARDS ON THE TURRETS AND WARRIORS ALL ALONG THE WALL. SHARP HOOKS, HEAVY BARBED PILLARS, LARGE IRON WHEELS AND OTHER MACHINES WERE THERE ON THE RAMPARTS, TO MAKE THE CITY IMPREGNABLE.

amar chitra katha

" THE STREETS OF THE CITY WERE WIDE AND SAFE. IT WAS A CITY OF GARDENS AND ORCHARDS AND PLEASURE-HOUSES AND MAN-MADE HILLS, LAKES AND PONDS WITH LOTUSES AND LILIES AND SWANS AND DUCKS. AND THE HEAVENLY CITY CAME TO BE CALLED INDRAPRASTHA.

" THE PALACE OF THE PANDAVAS BUILT IN AN AUSPICIOUS AND BEAUTIFUL PART OF THE CITY WAS REPLETE WITH WEALTH AND RICH AS KUBERA'S ABODE.

AND THERE CAME TO STAY IN THAT CITY LEARNED BRAHMANAS AND MERCHANTS AND ARTISANS. AND THE PROSPERITY OF THE PANDAVAS LIVING IN THAT CITY PEOPLED BY GOOD MEN, O MONARCH, INCREASED DAY BY DAY.

" THEN, HAVING SETTLED THE PANDAVAS, KRISHNA ALONG WITH BALARAMA TOOK LEAVE OF THEM AND LEFT FOR DWARAKA.

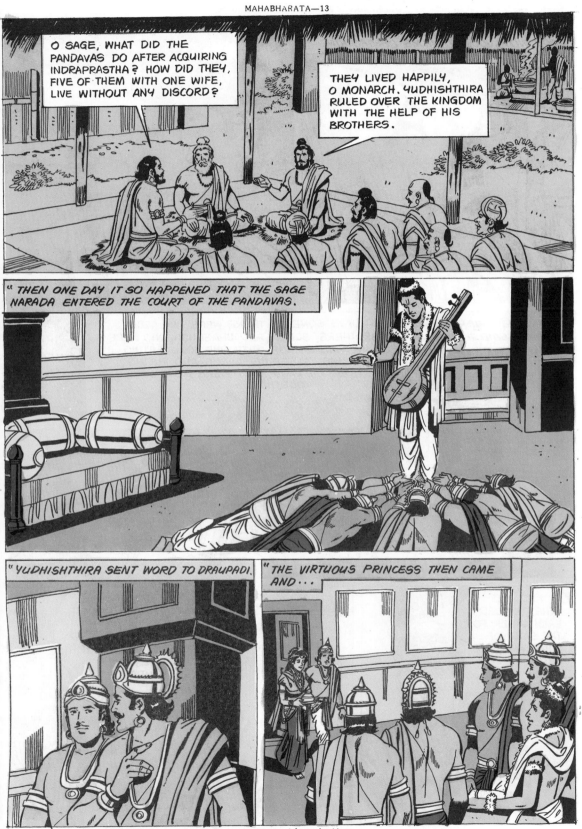

O SAGE, WHAT DID THE PANDAVAS DO AFTER ACQUIRING INDRAPRASTHA? HOW DID THEY, FIVE OF THEM WITH ONE WIFE, LIVE WITHOUT ANY DISCORD?

THEY LIVED HAPPILY, O MONARCH. YUDHISHTHIRA RULED OVER THE KINGDOM WITH THE HELP OF HIS BROTHERS.

"THEN ONE DAY IT SO HAPPENED THAT THE SAGE NARADA ENTERED THE COURT OF THE PANDAVAS.

"YUDHISHTHIRA SENT WORD TO DRAUPADI.

"THE VIRTUOUS PRINCESS THEN CAME AND...

"...PAID OBEISANCE TO THE RISHI AND STOOD WITH JOINED PALMS BEFORE HIM WHILE HE BLESSED HER.

"WHEN THEY WERE ALONE, THE RISHI SAID TO THE PANDAVAS:

IN DAYS GONE BY THERE WERE TWO ASURA BROTHERS, SUNDA AND UPASUNDA, WHO WERE LIKE TWO BEINGS WITH ONE SOUL. EATING, DRINKING, SLEEPING, LIVING AND RULING OVER THE LAND, THEY WERE ALWAYS TOGETHER.

AND YET THEY KILLED EACH OTHER FOR THE SAKE OF TILOTTAMA, THE APSARA.

THEREFORE, IN MY AFFECTION, I TELL YOU TO DEVISE SOME ORDER LEST YOU SHOULD QUARREL AMONG YOURSELVES OVER DRAUPADI.

THE AFFECTIONATE BROTHERS THEN LAID DOWN A RULE IN THE RISHI'S PRESENCE. THE RULE WAS THAT WHEN ONE OF THEM WAS WITH DRAUPADI SHOULD ANY OF THE OTHER FOUR SEE THEM, HE MUST RETIRE TO THE FOREST FOR TWELVE YEARS AND LIVE IN CELIBACY.

"PLEASED WITH THE DECISION OF THE PANDAVAS, NARADA WENT HIS WAY.

"DAYS AFTERWARDS, O MONARCH SOME THIEVES DROVE AWAY THE COWS OF A BRAHMANA.

"THE BRAHMANA, BESIDE HIMSELF WITH ANGER, HASTENED TO THE PALACE OF THE PANDAVAS AND RAISED AN ALARM. HE SAID:

O PANDAVAS, IN OUR LAND, SOME WICKED WRETCHES ARE STEALING OUR CATTLE-WEALTH. GO AFTER THEM.

THE WHOLE WORLD REVILES A KING WHO LEVIES ONE-SIXTH OF THE PRODUCE OF THE LAND AND YET FAILS TO PROTECT HIS SUBJECTS.

TAKE UP ARMS, O PANDAVAS, FOR ONE WHO CRIES IN GRIEF.

"ARJUNA HEARD THE WORDS OF THE WEEPING BRAHMANA AND SAID:

FEAR NOT.

BUT, O MONARCH, YUDHISHTHIRA AND DRAUPADI WERE TOGETHER WHERE THE WEAPONS OF THE PANDAVAS WERE AND THEREFORE ARJUNA COULD NOT GO IN. NOR COULD HE GO OUT UNARMED.

"... HE CHEERFULLY TOLD THE BRAHMANA:

LET US HASTEN LEST THE WRETCHED THIEVES SHOULD GO FAR AHEAD.

WE SHALL GO TOGETHER AND I SHALL HAVE YOUR WEALTH RELEASED FROM THE CLUTCHES OF THE THIEVES.

"AND ARJUNA, MOUNTING THE CHARIOT WITH ITS FLAG ALOFT...

"... WENT AFTER THE THIEVES...

"... AND PIERCING THEM WITH ARROWS...

"...FORCED THEM TO GIVE UP THE BOOTY.

"THEN ARJUNA RETURNED TO THE CAPITAL AND PAID OBEISANCE TO HIS ELDERS...

"...WHO IN TURN CONGRATULATED HIM.

"AND THEN ARJUNA SAID TO YUDHISHTHIRA:

I HAVE BROKEN THE RULE BY BEHOLDING YOU WITH DRAUPADI. I SHALL THEREFORE GO INTO THE FOREST AS AGREED AMONG US.

GIVE ME LEAVE TO FULFIL THE VOW.

amar chitra katha

"STUNG BY GRIEF, YUDHISHTHIRA SAID IN AN UNSTEADY VOICE:

WHY?

O INNOCENT ONE, IF I AM THE AUTHORITY THEN LISTEN TO ME.

I KNOW VERY WELL THE REASON FOR YOUR ENTRY INTO MY CHAMBER, WHICH YOU THINK DISPLEASED ME.

BUT I BEAR NO ILL WILL IN MY MIND. THEREFORE TURN AWAY.

DO AS I SAY. YOU HAVE COMMITTED NO TRANSGRESSION. NEITHER HAVE YOU SLIGHTED ME.

A YOUNGER BROTHER MAY, WITHOUT BLEMISH, GO IN WHERE THE ELDER BROTHER SITS WITH HIS WIFE.

IT IS THE ELDER BROTHER WHO HAS NO SANCTION TO GO IN WHERE THE YOUNGER ONE IS WITH HIS WIFE.

" ARJUNA REPLIED :

I HAVE HEARD YOU SAY THAT DHARMA IS NOT TO BE OBSERVED WITH PREVARICATION. I CANNOT WAVER FROM TRUTH. I SAY THIS UNDER THE OATH OF MY WEAPONS.

" AND ARJUNA PROCEEDED TO THE FOREST ACCOMPANIED BY BRAHMANAS WHO HAD MASTERED THE VEDAS, MUSICIANS, ASCETICS AND BARDS SINGING OF ANCIENT TALES.

THEY JOURNEYED ON ACROSS THE LAKES AND INTO THE FORESTS TILL THEY REACHED THE SOURCE OF THE GANGA. AND THERE, O MONARCH, THE MIGHTY HERO DECIDED TO DWELL.

THUS ENDS THE THIRTEENTH SESSION OF OUR RENDERING OF VAISHAMPAYANA'S RECITAL OF VYASA'S IMMORTAL ITIHASA THE MAHABHARATA.

Mahabharata – 14
ARJUNA'S 12-YEAR EXILE

ARJUNA AND THE BRAHMANAS WHO ACCOMPANIED HIM DECIDED, O MONARCH, TO CAMP NEAR THE SOURCE OF GANGA. THE BRAHMANAS PROPITIATED AGNI WITH SACRIFICIAL OFFERINGS.

"...AND THEIR BLAZING SACRIFICIAL FIRES AND CHANTS AND OFFERINGS OF FLOWERS MADE THE REGION EXCEEDINGLY BEAUTIFUL.

"ONE DAY IN PREPARATION FOR THE SACRIFICIAL RITUAL, ARJUNA BATHED IN THE GANGA.

" AS HE WAS ABOUT TO FINISH BATHING...

"...HE WAS PULLED BY ULOOPI, THE DAUGHTER OF THE KING OF THE NAGAS...

"...DOWN TO THE BED OF THE RIVER...

"...AND INTO THE BEAUTIFUL MANSION OF HER FATHER.

"THERE HE SAW A SACRIFICIAL FIRE ALREADY ABLAZE. BEHOLDING THAT FIRE...

"...ARJUNA COMPLETED HIS SACRIFICE TO AGNI.

" AND AGNI WAS PLEASED BY HIS DEVOTION. THEN BEHOLDING ULOOPI...

"...ARJUNA SMILED AND SAID TO HER:

O IMPETUOUS GIRL, YOUR ACTION WAS RASH. WHICH IS THIS LAND AND WHOSE DAUGHTER ARE YOU?

"ULOOPI TOLD HIM WHO SHE WAS AND THEN SAID:

O PRINCE, WHEN I SAW YOU, I CAME UNDER THE SPELL OF KAMADEVA. I AM STILL UNWED. GIVE YOURSELF UP TO ME.

"ARJUNA REPLIED:

COMMANDED BY YUDHISHTHIRA, I AM UNDERGOING THE VOW OF BRAHMACHARYA* FOR TWELVE YEARS. I AM NOT FREE TO ACT AS I LIKE.

"ULOOPI SAID:

I KNOW OF YOUR BROTHER'S COMMAND AND OF YOUR EXILE. BUT THE ORDER OF EXILE HAS REFERENCE TO DRAUPADI AND THERE- FORE HERE THERE IS NO MORAL LAPSE.

* CELIBACY

amar chitra katha

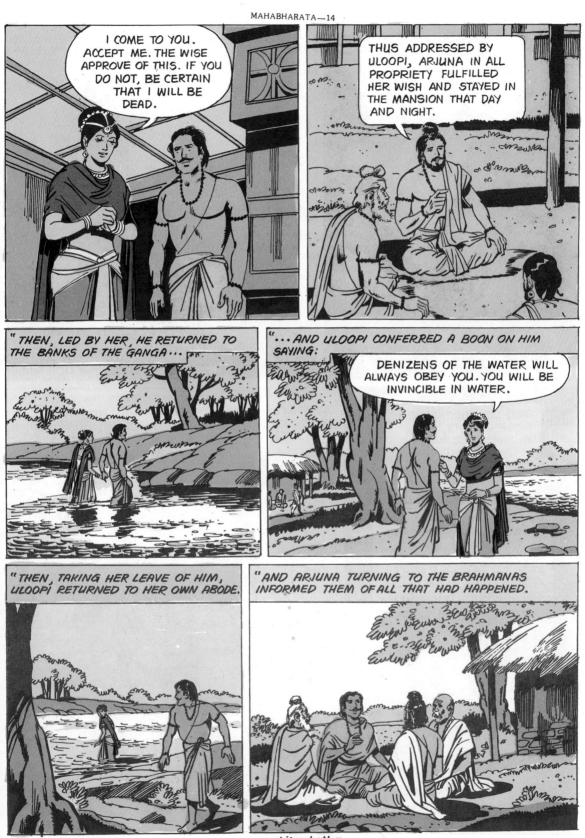

amar chitra katha

"THEN ACCOMPANIED BY THEM HE SET OUT FOR THE HIMALAYAS.

"HE VISITED THE SITES CONSECRATED BY AGASTYA, BY VASISHTHA AND BY BHRIGU.

THEN DESCENDING FROM THOSE HEIGHTS, HE JOURNEYED TOWARDS THE EAST TO BEHOLD THE REGIONS THAT LAY IN THAT DIRECTION.

HE VISITED ALL THE SACRED SPOTS OF ANGA, VANGA AND KALINGA. THE BRAHMANAS ACCOMPANYING HIM, BADE HIM FAREWELL AND ARJUNA CAME TO THE MAHENDRA MOUNTAINS...

"...AND THEN WENT TO MANIPURA, WALKING LEISURELY ALONG THE SEASHORE.

"AND VISITING ALL THE SACRED PLACES IN THAT LAND, HE CALLED ON ITS RULER.

"THERE, ACCIDENTALLY HE SAW CHITRANGADA, THE RULER'S DAUGHTER AND HE WAS FILLED WITH DESIRE FOR HER.

"AND HE SAID TO THE RULER:

GIVE AWAY YOUR DAUGHTER TO ME, O KING. I AM A NOBLE KSHATRIYA.

I AM ARJUNA, THE SON OF PANDU AND KUNTI.

amar chitra katha

"THE KING REPLIED:

O ARJUNA, I HAVE ONLY THIS MAIDEN TO PERPETUATE MY LINE. I LOOK UPON HER AS MY SON. THEREFORE THE SON BEGOTTEN OF YOU ON HER SHALL BE THE PROGENY OF MY LINE.

THAT SON SHALL BE THE BRIDE-PRICE YOU PAY. ON THIS CONDITION, O PANDAVA, YOU MAY WED HER.

"ARJUNA ACCEPTED, SAYING:

SO BE IT.

"AND HE SPENT THE NEXT THREE YEARS WITH CHITRANGADA IN THAT CITY. AND AFTER A SON WAS BORN TO HER HE SET OUT ON HIS WANDERINGS AGAIN.

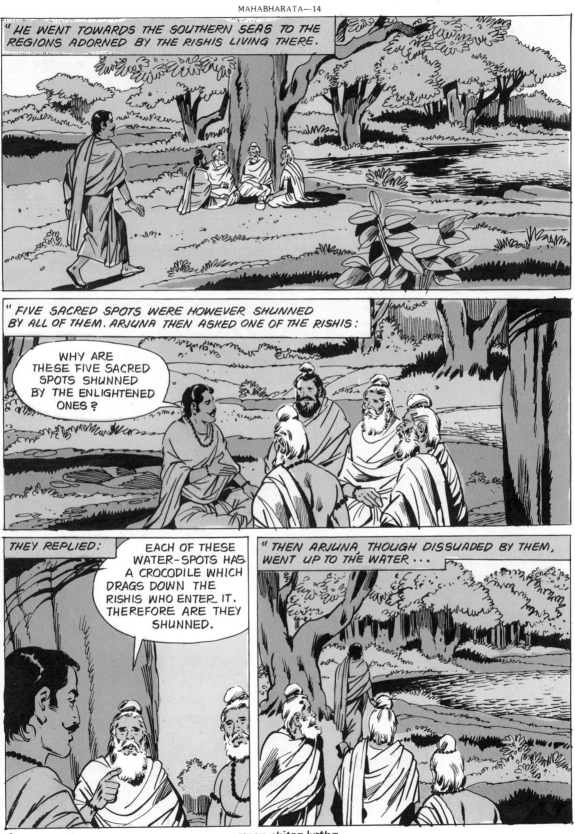

"HE WENT TOWARDS THE SOUTHERN SEAS TO THE REGIONS ADORNED BY THE RISHIS LIVING THERE.

"FIVE SACRED SPOTS WERE HOWEVER SHUNNED BY ALL OF THEM. ARJUNA THEN ASKED ONE OF THE RISHIS:

WHY ARE THESE FIVE SACRED SPOTS SHUNNED BY THE ENLIGHTENED ONES?

THEY REPLIED:

EACH OF THESE WATER-SPOTS HAS A CROCODILE WHICH DRAGS DOWN THE RISHIS WHO ENTER IT. THEREFORE ARE THEY SHUNNED.

"THEN ARJUNA, THOUGH DISSUADED BY THEM, WENT UP TO THE WATER...

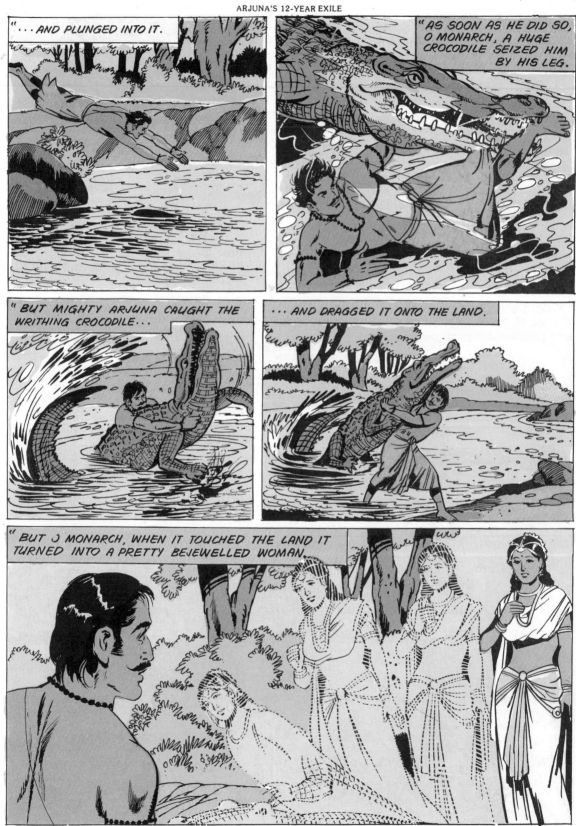

"...AND PLUNGED INTO IT.

"AS SOON AS HE DID SO, O MONARCH, A HUGE CROCODILE SEIZED HIM BY HIS LEG.

"BUT MIGHTY ARJUNA CAUGHT THE WRITHING CROCODILE...

...AND DRAGGED IT ONTO THE LAND.

"BUT O MONARCH, WHEN IT TOUCHED THE LAND IT TURNED INTO A PRETTY BEJEWELLED WOMAN.

"AND, AMAZED, ARJUNA ASKED HER:

WHO ARE YOU, O PRETTY WOMAN?

" SHE REPLIED:

I AM AN APSARAS. MY FOUR COMPANIONS AND I WERE CURSED BY A BRIGHT BRAHMANA WHEN WE TRIED IN VAIN TO DIVERT HIM FROM HIS STEADFAST MEDITATION.

" IN ANGER HE SAID:

YOU SHALL BE TURNED INTO CROCODILES AND LIVE THUS FOR THE NEXT ONE HUNDRED YEARS.

AT THE END OF THAT PERIOD A GREAT MAN WILL LIFT YOU UP FROM THE WATER AND THEN YOU WILL REGAIN YOUR EARLIER FORMS.

YOU HAVE BEEN MY DELIVERANCE. MY FOUR COMPANIONS ARE STILL IN THOSE OTHER WATER SPOTS. LIBERATE THEM ALSO.

ARJUNA, O MONARCH, DELIVERED ALL OF THEM FROM THEIR CURSE AND LET THEM GO WHEREVER THEY CHOSE. THEN, INTENT ON MEETING CHITRANGADA...

"... HE PROCEEDED TO MANIPURA. THERE HE BEHELD BABHRUVAHANA, THE SON HE HAD BEGOTTEN WITH CHITRANGADA AND...

... WHOM HE CEREMONIALLY PRESENTED TO THE KING SAYING:

ACCEPT THE SON, BEGOTTEN OF ME ON CHITRANGADA, AND FREE ME OF MY DEBT.

TAKING LEAVE OF CHITRANGADA, O MONARCH, ARJUNA PROCEEDED TOWARDS GOKARNA. THEN VISITING, ONE AFTER ANOTHER, THE SACRED SPOTS ON THE SHORES OF THE WESTERN OCEAN, HE REACHED PRABHASA.

Himalayas

Indraprastha

Pushkara

Ganga

Anga

Vanga

Dwaraka

Prabhasa

Kalinga

Mahendra Mountains

Manipura

Gokarna

KEY TO ARJUNA'S JOURNEY

Journey completed:

Journey to be undertaken:

Outline of the map reproduced from the Survey of India Map No. 2498 HD' 70-1000-500' 72-1500' 74

"KRISHNA HEARD OF HIS ARRIVAL AND WENT TO GREET HIS FRIEND.

"AND AFTER ARJUNA NARRATED IN DETAIL THE EVENTS OF HIS TRAVEL...

"...THEY SET OUT IN A GOLDEN CHARIOT FOR DWARAKA, THE CAPITAL OF THE YADAVAS.

"AND, O JANAMEJAYA, THE CITY OF DWARAKA, WITH ITS HOUSES AND GARDENS, WAS GAILY DECORATED IN HONOUR OF ARJUNA'S VISIT. AND THE CITIZENS OF DWARAKA THRONGED THE ROYAL PATH TO SEE THE SON OF KUNTI. ARJUNA WHO WAS RECEIVED BY THE YADAVAS...

"...ARRIVED AT THE PALACE OF KRISHNA WHICH WAS ENCRUSTED WITH GEMS.

AND HE STAYED THERE WITH KRISHNA FOR MANY DAYS. NOW WAS HELD THE FESTIVAL OF THE YADAVAS ON THE RAIVATAKA MOUNTAIN ADORNED WITH BEJEWELLED DWELLINGS AMONG ABUNDANT TREES.

MUSICIANS, SINGERS AND DANCERS PERFORMED THERE. THE CITIZENS SOME ON FOOT, SOME IN CARRIAGES, WITH THEIR WIVES AND THEIR ATTENDANTS WERE THERE IN THEIR THOUSANDS.

"AND WHILE KRISHNA AND ARJUNA STROLLED TOGETHER AMONG THE WONDROUS SIGHTS THERE..."

"...THEY SAW SUBHADRA, THE DAUGHTER OF VASUDEVA, AMIDST HER FRIENDS. AND ARJUNA WAS SMITTEN BY KAMADEVA.

amar chitra katha

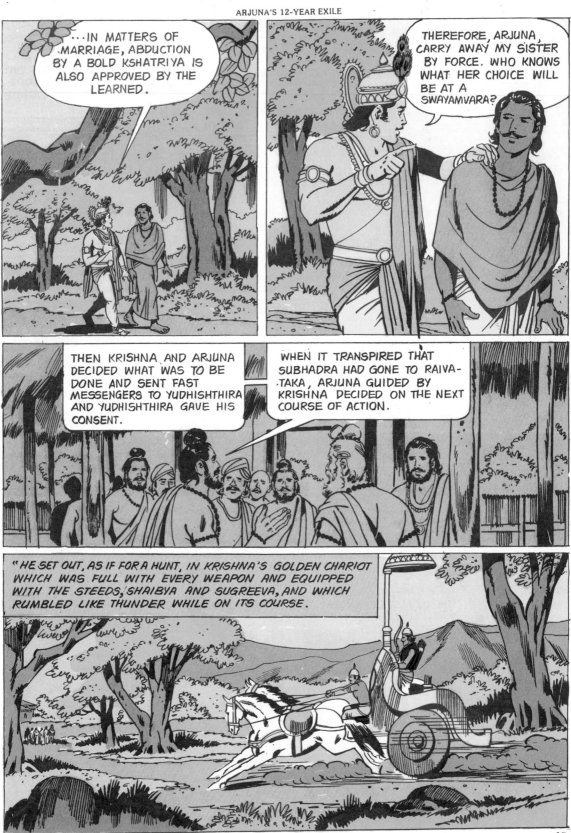

...IN MATTERS OF MARRIAGE, ABDUCTION BY A BOLD KSHATRIYA IS ALSO APPROVED BY THE LEARNED.

THEREFORE, ARJUNA, CARRY AWAY MY SISTER BY FORCE. WHO KNOWS WHAT HER CHOICE WILL BE AT A SWAYAMVARA?

THEN KRISHNA AND ARJUNA DECIDED WHAT WAS TO BE DONE AND SENT FAST MESSENGERS TO YUDHISHTHIRA AND YUDHISHTHIRA GAVE HIS CONSENT.

WHEN IT TRANSPIRED THAT SUBHADRA HAD GONE TO RAIVA-TAKA, ARJUNA GUIDED BY KRISHNA DECIDED ON THE NEXT COURSE OF ACTION.

"HE SET OUT, AS IF FOR A HUNT, IN KRISHNA'S GOLDEN CHARIOT WHICH WAS FULL WITH EVERY WEAPON AND EQUIPPED WITH THE STEEDS, SHAIBYA AND SUGREEVA, AND WHICH RUMBLED LIKE THUNDER WHILE ON ITS COURSE.

"MEANWHILE, SUBHADRA, HAVING WORSHIPPED THE RAIVATAKA MOUNTAIN AND THE DEITIES THERE, WAS RETURNING TO DWARAKA.

"ARJUNA THEN RUSHED TOWARDS THAT MAIDEN OF PERFECT FEATURES...

"...FORCIBLY CARRIED HER INTO HIS CHARIOT...

"...AND PROCEEDED TOWARDS HIS OWN CITY, INDRAPRASTHA. THE WARRIORS AS THEY SAW SUBHADRA BEING CARRIED AWAY...

" ...RAN TOWARDS DWARAKA, SHRIEKING AND SHOUTING.

" THEY REACHED THE YADAVA COURT AND INFORMED THEIR CHIEF OF ARJUNA'S BOLD- NESS. HE LISTENED TO THEIR TALE...

"...AND BLEW HIS GOLDEN TRUMPET OF IMMENSE BLARE, SUMMONING ALL TO ARMS.

"AGITATED BY THAT SOUND...

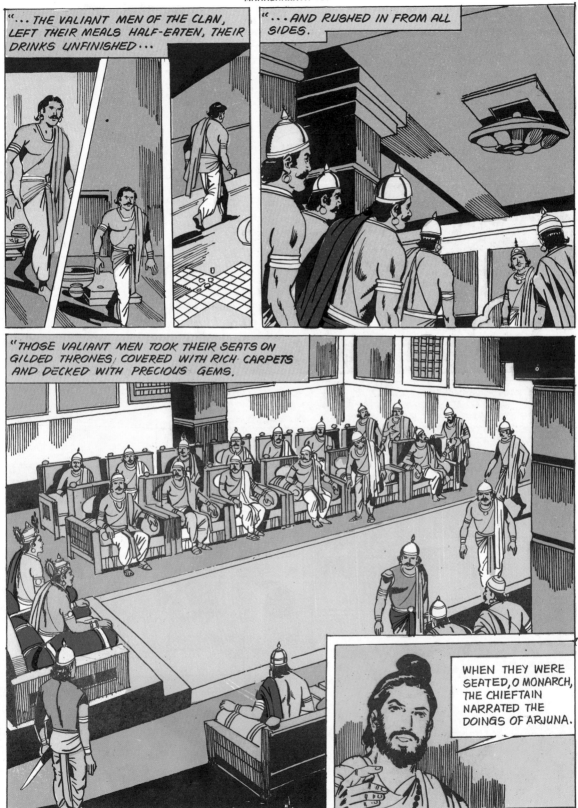

"...THE VALIANT MEN OF THE CLAN, LEFT THEIR MEALS HALF-EATEN, THEIR DRINKS UNFINISHED...

"...AND RUSHED IN FROM ALL SIDES.

"THOSE VALIANT MEN TOOK THEIR SEATS ON GILDED THRONES, COVERED WITH RICH CARPETS AND DECKED WITH PRECIOUS GEMS.

WHEN THEY WERE SEATED, O MONARCH, THE CHIEFTAIN NARRATED THE DOINGS OF ARJUNA.

amar chitra katha

"AND THE VALIANT YADAVA MEN, THEIR EYES RED FROM DRINKING WINE, SPRANG UP FROM THEIR SEATS RAGING AGAINST ARJUNA:

YOKE OUR CHARIOTS!

WHERE ARE THE BOWS?

BRING FORTH OUR WEAPONS!

" THERE WAS A VERITABLE TUMULT AS THEY BROUGHT THEIR CHARIOTS, AND SOME, IMPATIENT, YOKED THEIR HORSES THEMSELVES TO THEIR CHARIOTS. THEN BALARAMA, CLAD IN BLUE ROBES AND ADORNED WITH GARLANDS OF FLOWERS, INTOXICATED AND YET ERECT LIKE THE GREAT KAILASA, SAID:

WHAT ARE YOU WITLESS MEN DOING WHEN KRISHNA SITS SILENT?

WITHOUT KNOWING HIS MIND, THIS OUTBURST OF ANGER IS TO NO PURPOSE. LET WISE KRISHNA EXPRESS HIS OPINION. THEN LET HIS WILL BE DONE PROMPTLY.

"ALL OF THEM LISTENED TO THE WORTHY WORDS OF BALARAMA AND BECAME SILENT AND WENT BACK TO THEIR SEATS.

" BALARAMA THEN SPOKE TO KRISHNA

YOU HAVE WITNESSED ALL THIS AND ARE YET SILENT. KUNTI'S SON WAS WELCOMED BY US BECAUSE OF YOU. BUT...

ARJUNA KNOWS WE ARE NOT MERCENARY. HE KNOWS ALSO THE UNCERTAINTIES OF A SWAYAMVARA. I THINK HE HAS CONSIDERED ALL THESE QUESTIONS BEFORE HE TOOK AWAY THE MAIDEN BY FORCE, WHICH IS IN KEEPING WITH PROPRIETY.

AND I DO NOT SEE ANYONE IN ALL THE WORLDS SAVE SHIVA WHO CAN CONQUER ARJUNA.

IF ARJUNA GOES BACK TO HIS CITY AFTER DEFEATING YOU BY FORCE THEN YOU WILL ALL LOSE YOUR REPUTATION.

THERE IS NO DISGRACE, HOWEVER, IN PEACEFUL ACCORD.

GO AFTER HIM AND BRING HIM BACK IN PEACEFUL ACCORD.

"THE YADAVAS, O MONARCH, LISTENED TO THE WORDS OF KRISHNA AND ACTED ACCORDINGLY.

"HALTED BY THEM...

"...ARJUNA RETURNED TO DWARAKA...

"...AND WAS UNITED IN MARRIAGE WITH SUBHADRA.

CHERISHED BY THE YADAVAS, ARJUNA SPENT A YEAR IN DWARAKA AND THEN, IN THE LAST YEAR OF HIS EXILE, HE STAYED IN THE SACRED SPOT OF PUSHKARA.*

"AND AFTER THE TWELVE YEARS WERE COMPLETED HE CAME BACK TO INDRAPRASTHA.

"HE PAID HIS RESPECTS TO THE KING FIRST AND THEN...

"...WENT TO DRAUPADI WHO IN JEALOUSY SAID TO HIM:

GO BACK TO WHERE SUBHADRA IS.

* NEAR MODERN AJMER

amar chitra katha

A SECOND KNOT IS BOUND TO LOOSEN THE FIRST ONE, HOWSOEVER CLOSE IT MIGHT HAVE BEEN.

AND DRAUPADI WAILED MUCH IN THIS MANNER, WHILE ARJUNA CONSOLED HER AND SOUGHT PARDON REPEATEDLY.

"THEN ARJUNA RETURNED HASTILY TO SUBHADRA WHO WAS DRAPED IN RED SILK...

"...AND SENT HER INTO THE WOMEN'S APARTMENTS. SHE WAS DRESSED NOT AS A QUEEN BUT AS ONE OF THE COWHERDESSES.

"THE NOBLE SUBHADRA HOWEVER LOOKED MORE ATTRACTIVE IN THAT DRESS.

"SHE FIRST PAID OBEISANCE TO KUNTI...

"...WHO BROUGHT DOWN HER FACE TO SUBHADRA'S HEAD IN DEEP AFFECTION.

"WHEN KRISHNA HEARD THAT ARJUNA HAD REACHED INDRAPRASTHA, HE WENT THERE WITH BALARAMA AND OTHER YADAVA NOBLEMEN. HE ALSO BROUGHT WEDDING GIFTS IN PLENTY. YUDHISHTHIRA, WHEN HE HEARD OF KRISHNA'S VISIT, SENT THE TWINS OUT TO RECEIVE HIM.

"AND THE YADAVA PROCESSION ENTERED INDRAPRASTHA WHICH WAS BRIGHT WITH FLAGS AND FESTOONS. THEY CAME INTO THE CITY...

"...AND THEN ENTERED YUDHISHTHIRA'S PALACE.

KRISHNA GAVE MUCH WEALTH TO THEM AND THE WEDDING GIFTS SENT BY HER KINSMEN TO SUBHADRA.

"THE VALIANT MEN OF THE KURU AND YADAVA RACES PASSED MANY DAYS TOGETHER IN PLEASURABLE PURSUITS.

"THEN THE YADAVAS, LED BY BALARAMA, RETURNED TO THE CITY OF DWARAKA CARRYING WITH THEM THE DAZZLING, PRECIOUS JEWELS PRESENTED TO THEM BY THE GREAT KURUS.

"KRISHNA REMAINED IN INDRAPRASTHA WITH ARJUNA AND ROAMED THE BANKS OF THE YAMUNA HUNTING DEER AND WILD BOAR.

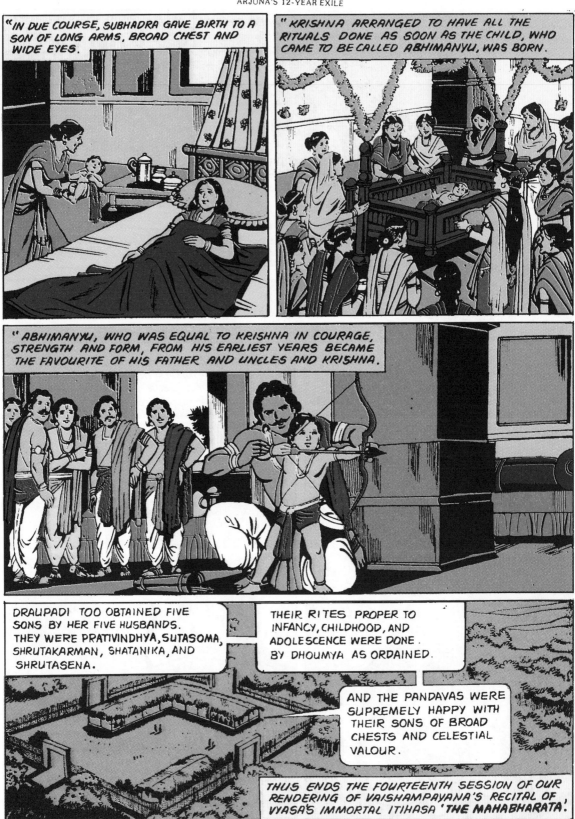

"IN DUE COURSE, SUBHADRA GAVE BIRTH TO A SON OF LONG ARMS, BROAD CHEST AND WIDE EYES.

"KRISHNA ARRANGED TO HAVE ALL THE RITUALS DONE AS SOON AS THE CHILD, WHO CAME TO BE CALLED ABHIMANYU, WAS BORN.

"ABHIMANYU, WHO WAS EQUAL TO KRISHNA IN COURAGE, STRENGTH AND FORM, FROM HIS EARLIEST YEARS BECAME THE FAVOURITE OF HIS FATHER AND UNCLES AND KRISHNA.

DRAUPADI TOO OBTAINED FIVE SONS BY HER FIVE HUSBANDS. THEY WERE PRATIVINDHYA, SUTASOMA, SHRUTAKARMAN, SHATANIKA, AND SHRUTASENA.

THEIR RITES PROPER TO INFANCY, CHILDHOOD, AND ADOLESCENCE WERE DONE. BY DHOUMYA AS ORDAINED.

AND THE PANDAVAS WERE SUPREMELY HAPPY WITH THEIR SONS OF BROAD CHESTS AND CELESTIAL VALOUR.

THUS ENDS THE FOURTEENTH SESSION OF OUR RENDERING OF VAISHAMPAYANA'S RECITAL OF VYASA'S IMMORTAL ITIHASA 'THE MAHABHARATA.'

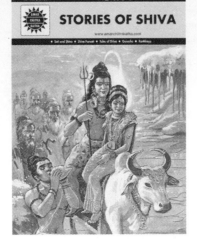
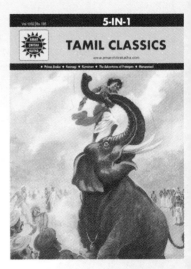
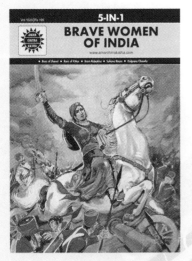
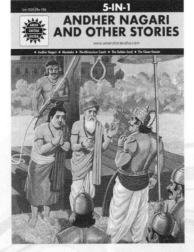